FIRST

OR

GRENADIER GUARDS

IN SOUTH AFRICA

1899—1902.

RECORDS OF THE SECOND BATTALION

COMPILED BY

BRIGADIER-GENERAL F. LLOYD, C.B., D.S.O.

RECORDS OF THE THIRD BATTALION

COMPILED BY

BREVET-MAJOR HON. A. RUSSELL.

The Naval & Military Press Ltd

❖

Reproduced by kind permission of the Central Library,
Royal Military Academy, Sandhurst

Published by

The Naval & Military Press Ltd

Unit 10, Ridgewood Industrial Park,

Uckfield, East Sussex,

TN22 5QE England

Tel: +44 (0) 1825 749494

Fax: +44 (0) 1825 765701

www.naval-military-press.com

© The Naval & Military Press Ltd 2005

The 2nd Battalion Grenadier Guards in South Africa, 1900-1902.

—=⟨⟩=—

CHAPTER I.

MOBILISATION AND DEPARTURE.

WHEN the Guards were first sent to Gibraltar, in 1897, it was decided that the old roster for active service should be superseded, and that the Battalion or Battalions actually at that station should be the first for service. On the breaking out of war with the Boer Republics in 1899 the new arrangement did not, in point of fact, make any difference to the priority of service of the 2nd Battalion of the Grenadiers over the other Battalions of the Regiment, the 3rd having served at Suakim in 1885, and the 1st at Khartum in 1898.

In 1899 the 2nd Battalion of the Grenadiers and the 1st Battalion of the Coldstream—the two Battalions of the Guards' Brigade then stationed at Gibraltar—were officially warned for service in South Africa to form, in combination with two other battalions to be sent from England, a Guards' Brigade at the seat of war.

The first intimation was a telegram from the Lieutenant-Colonel of the Regiment (Colonel The Hon. Herbert Eaton*), dated 21st August, 1899 :—

> " London, 5.15 p.m. If troops sent Transvaal, Second Battalion forms part. 1112 all ranks. Reserves from June, 1898, will be called out. Letter follows. Confidential. 'Guardroom.'†"

On 31st August a further telegram was received from the Lieutenant-Colonel saying that the Reservists would be equipped in England.

On 13th September Lieutenant-Colonel Lloyd telegraphed to the Lieutenant-Colonel asking if the Battalion would be kept at Gibraltar over the Transvaal crisis. The answer by telegram was that the 3rd Battalion would relieve the 2nd Battalion at Gibraltar immediately.

Although the 3rd Battalion had originally been ordered to hold itself in readiness to embark for Gibraltar as early as 13th September, it was deemed advisable to postpone the embarkation till 23rd September, in order to enable the 2nd Battalion to quit Gibraltar without delay on the arrival of the relief from England.

On 23rd September the 3rd Battalion, under the command of Lieutenant-Colonel Crabbe, embarked on board the P. & O. ss. "Nubia" at the Albert Docks, the relief being carried out at Gibraltar on the 28th. The 2nd Battalion embarked the same day, but the ship was detained by the receipt of an ambiguous order by telegraph from the War Office directing " Battalion " to " hold itself in readiness for service in South Africa." For some hours the issue was in suspense which Battalion was the one intended. Finally a telegram was received from the War Office directing the 2nd Battalion to sail

---

* Afterwards Lord Cheylesmore.
† The telegraphic address of the regimental orderly room.

for England, and the 3rd Battalion to be held in readiness to proceed to South Africa.

The 2nd Battalion accordingly returned to England.

The following sailed from Gibraltar on 28th September in the " Nubia " :—

Lieutenant-Colonel Lloyd, D.S.O. (Commanding).

Major R. Gordon-Gilmour (Second-in-Command).

Major The Hon. G. Legh.

Major R. Scott-Kerr.

Captain E. G. Verschoyle.

Captain The Lord Ardee.

Captain A. St. L. Glyn.

Lieutenant G. L. Bonham.

Lieutenant I. A. Broadwood.

Lieutenant W. S. Blackett.

Lieutenant F. L. Swaine.

Lieutenant J. A. Morrison.

Lieutenant G. D. Jeffreys.

Lieutenant J. A. C. Quilter.

Lieutenant E. Seymour.

Lieutenant H. St. L. Stucley.

Lieutenant The Hon. G. H. Douglas-Pennant.

2nd Lieutenant The Hon. A. Weld-Forester.

2nd Lieutenant The Hon. B. Gordon-Lennox.

2nd Lieutenant The Lord O'Hagan.

2nd Lieutenant S. D. Shafto.

2nd Lieutenant The Hon. M. B. Parker.

2nd Lieutenant G. R. Houstoun-Boswall.

Captain and Adjutant M. Earle.

Honorary Lieutenant and Quartermaster W. G. A. Garton.

Surgeon-Major Sheldrake (Grenadier Guards).

Captain R. M. Cooper, R.A.M.C.

Sergt.-Major W. Fletcher.

Capt. Nugent, Grenadier Guards, A.D.C. to Major-General Sir H. E. Colvile, was also on board as an "indulgence" passenger. The strength of other ranks leaving Gibraltar was 763, the total strength of the Battalion being 790 of all ranks. The remaining 170 had been transferred to the 3rd Battalion and were left behind at Gibraltar.

The "Nubia" arrived at Southampton on 3rd October, and the Battalion disembarked the same day, proceeded to London, and took up its quarters at Wellington Barracks.

On 7th October, the Regiment received the order for the mobilisation of a certain number of Reservists, and on Saturday, 21st October, the 412 Reservists of the Regiment who had been called up sailed under Major Kinloch to join the 3rd Battalion at Gibraltar. They were accompanied by fifty Non-commissioned Officers and men of the 2nd Battalion, among whom were No. 8498 Drill-Sergt. J. Rolinson,*§ No. 1200 Assistant Drill-Sergt. A. Thomas,†§ and No. 3070 Colour-Sergt. W. Acraman,‡— Lt.-Colonel Lloyd having selected the best men that he had for the purpose required.

On 22nd October, Capt. Earle, the Adjutant, sailed for South Africa on special service, Lt. Swaine taking over the Acting Adjutancy till Lt. C. E. Corkran was appointed to fill that position on 18th November.

---

* Drill-Sergt. Rolinson afterwards rejoined in South Africa from the 3rd Battalion, to which he had been lent, becoming Sergt.-Major of the 2nd Battalion and subsequently Quartermaster of the 1st Battalion.

† Drill-Sergt. Thomas was afterwards Sergt.-Major of the 1st Battalion.

‡ Colour-Sergt. Acraman was afterwards Sergt.-Major of the 2nd Battalion.

§ These two Non-commissioned Officers were the only two men of any rank who were present at both the battles of Belmont and Biddulphsberg.

On 3rd November, about 250 men of the 3rd Battalion, who were unfit for active service, arrived from Gibraltar under Major Fox-Pitt, Lt. Lethbridge, and Lt. P. A. Clive, and joined the 2nd Battalion.

On 16th December, Lts. The Hon. B. Gordon-Lennox and Sir Robert Filmer left the 2nd Battalion to join the 3rd Battalion in South Africa.

On 19th January, 1900, the official order was received that an Eighth Division was to be sent out to South Africa under the command of Major-General Sir H. M. Leslie Rundle, K.C.B., C.M.G., D.S.O., and that the 2nd Battalion of the Grenadier Guards, together with the 2nd Battalion of the Scots Guards, was to form part of it. Sir Leslie Rundle* was a young Major-General who had seen much service, especially in the Sudan, where he had served both in peace and in war almost continuously since the battle of Tel-el-Kebir—in which engagement he had been a subaltern of Artillery—till the battle of Khartum, where as a Major-General he was Chief-of-the-Staff to Sir Herbert (afterwards Lord) Kitchener.

The division was to be sub-divided into brigades, the 16th Brigade being composed as follows :—

> 2nd Batt. Grenadier Guards, under Lieutenant-Colonel Lloyd, D.S.O.
>
> 2nd Batt. Scots Guards, under Colonel Inigo Jones.
>
> 1st Batt. East Yorkshire Regiment, under Lieutenant-Colonel Ward.
>
> 1st Batt. Leinster Regiment, under Lieutenant-Colonel Martin.

---

* Sir Leslie Rundle served in the Zulu campaign, 1879, including battle of Ulundi; Transvaal campaign, 1881; Egyptian campaign, 1882, including battle of Tel-el-Kebir; Sudan Expedition (Nile) 1884-85; Sudan, 1885-6-7-9-91; Dongola, 1896; Nile, 1897; Nile, 1898, including battle of Khartum; eight times mentioned in despatches; once received the thanks of both Houses of Parliament; a K.C.B., C.M.G., and D.S.O.; once slightly wounded.

The Brigade was placed under the command of Major-General B. B. D. Campbell,* M.V.O., who had formerly commanded the Scots Guards, Captain Gascoigne,† D.S.O. Grenadier Guards, being appointed Brigade-Major.

On 20th January, Lieutenant-Colonel Lloyd received the order to hold the Battalion in readiness for active service.

On the 22nd the Battalion was medically examined for active service in the field.

On the 27th, Sergt.-Major Fletcher,‡ who had been appointed on 18th February, 1891—when the Battalion went to Bermuda—and who had done much for it, was relieved of his duties, being absolutely unfit, on account of ill-health, to proceed on active service. Both Drill-Sergeants being with the 3rd Battalion in South Africa, the senior Acting Drill-Sergeant, Pay and Colour-Sergt. Parry-Jones, took over the duties temporarily.

On 31st January, Capt. Earle, who had virtually resigned the Adjutancy in October, 1899, in order to proceed on special service to South Africa, sent in his official resignation, and Capt. Corkran was gazetted as his successor, he having held the appointment only temporarily since the 18th November, 1899, when he took up the duties of Acting-Adjutant.

The Reservists were called up as follows :—

1st, under Army Order of 7th October, 1899—first day of mobilisation, 9th October, 1899 — " All   men

---

* Major-General Campbell served as a Captain and Lieutenant-Colonel in command of a company in the Egyptian expedition of 1882, including the battle of Tel-el-Kebir.

† Capt. Gascoigne served as Adjutant of the 1st Batt. Grenadier Guards in the Nile expedition of 1898, including the battle of Khartum ; mentioned in despatches ; D.S.O.

‡ Sergt.-Major Fletcher sailed for Bermuda 24th November, 1890, and joined the 2nd Battalion there in December. His discharge was dated 28th February, 1900.

transferred to Sections A, B, and C of Army Reserve since 30th June, 1898."

These numbered 412, and formed the main portion of the draft under Major Kinloch, which, with Major Count Gleichen and Capt. F. Hervey Bathurst, and 469 N.C.O.'s and men, sailed 21st October, 1899, to join the 3rd Battalion.

2nd, under Army Order of 11th November, 1899—first day of mobilisation, 13th November, 1899—" Such men of Section A, B, C, as may receive notices to join."

These numbered 115, and, completed to a strength of 120, sailed as a draft for the 3rd Battalion on 2nd January, 1900, under Major R. J. Cooper.

3rd, under Army Order of 20th December, 1899—first day of mobilisation, 26th December, 1899—" All Reservists of Sections A, B, and C, not yet called out."

These were mobilised at Wellington Barracks, when 1,375 were passed by the surgeon as fit for service, the first 900 of them being posted to the 2nd Battalion, fitted out, and sent on furlough at their option. Reservists found unfit were sent back temporarily to the Reserve. The men on furlough rejoined the colours as follows :—

In January	38	} presumably at their option ;
In February	48	
In March	541	on receipt of telegrams.
Total	627	

The remainder, some 235, were transferred to the 1st Battalion without being re-called.

There were practically no absentees on mobilisation.

The regimental mobilisation was really completed, and the men clothed, a few days before sailing ; but the

fact was not officially so considered till 17th March.
Each man took out the following :—

    1 red serge jacket.

    2 pairs of blue trousers (Reservists only one).

    2 khaki jackets.

    2 pairs of khaki trousers.

    1 great-coat.

    1 helmet and pugaree, with a patch of Guards' ribbon
        on each side as a distinguishing badge.

    1 worsted cap.

    1 field-service cap.

    2 pairs of boots.

    1 pair of canvas shoes.

    2 flannel shirts.

    2 pairs of socks.

    2 flannel body-belts (or kamarbands).

    1 clasp knife with lanyard.

    1 field-dressing, sewn in the coat.*

    2 pairs of puttees.

    1 towel.

    1 haversack.

    1 pair of braces.

    1 cloth brush.

    1 shaving brush.

    1 comb.

    1 hold-all, with table-knife, fork, and spoon.

    1 tin of grease.

    1 housewife.

    1 razor.

    1 mess tin.

    1 black infantry kit-bag.

    1 pipeclay sponge.

---

* The field-dressing was sewn under the flap of the coat skirt on the
right side, the man's name and number being under the left flap.

In addition, each man was given a cardigan jersey out of the canteen funds.

It is worthy of notice that when the Reservists joined the colours in Wellington Barracks—which they did with, it is believed, only two absentees—it seemed as if they had lost all the appearance of soldiers, and as if the sense of discipline had also totally disappeared ; but that, from the moment they found themselves once more in uniform, they took their places in the ranks as if they had never been absent from duty. In order to test their steadiness as soldiers, and to see how much they had remembered in the way of drill and work, the Commanding Officer had a battalion-drill on the Horse Guards parade. Much to his astonishment, it was found that they were quite as good as they had been on the day that they had passed to the Reserve. They stood as still and drilled as well as it was possible for men to do. This shows that, after a thorough grounding in drill—which, after all, means discipline—and two or three years' service with the colours, a private soldier has learnt as much as he can assimilate ; and it proves also that he does not, by going into civil life, lose what he has once learnt, or, at any rate, until after the lapse of some considerable time.

On Friday, 9th March, The Colonel, Field-Marshal H.R.H. The Duke of Cambridge, K.G., inspected the Battalion in Wellington Barracks. Numbering 1,035 of all ranks, it was certainly as magnificent a battalion as has ever stood on parade. The average age must have been about 28 years, and height about 5 ft. 9½ ins.

The Officers having been presented to their Colonel by Lieutenant-Colonel Lloyd, H.R.H. addressed the Battalion, and, after wishing all ranks " God speed!" and saying how certain he was that they would do their duty

by their Queen and country, the Duke bade them an
affectionate farewell, observing finally that, being now
over eighty years of age, he could never hope to see them
again.   At the conclusion of his speech, H.R.H. was
heartily cheered.

On the afternoon of Saturday, 10th March, Her
Majesty the Queen inspected the two Battalions—*i.e.*, the
2nd Battalion Grenadiers and the 2nd Battalion Scots
Guards—in the gardens of Buckingham-palace.   The
Battalions were drawn up in line of quarter-columns facing
the Palace.   The N.C.O.'s and men were dressed, as they
had been for H.R.H. the Colonel's inspection the day
before, in khaki and helmets, as for active service; the
officers in blue frock-coats and forage caps.   Having been
received with a royal salute, Her Majesty drove round the
Battalion, after which Lieutenant-Colonel Lloyd and
Colonel Inigo Jones presented the officers of their respec-
tive Battalions by name to Her Majesty.   The Queen
then ordered both Commanding Officers to bring up a
man for Her Majesty to see, which was done, each trying
to outvie the other in producing the taller and finer man.
The Battalion finally defiled past Her Majesty in fours,
reformed line, and gave the Queen three cheers.   Her
Majesty said, "I rejoice to be able to see you before you
leave for South Africa.   My thoughts will always accompany you, wherever you go, and I know you will always
do your duty as you have ever done."

The Queen having left the ground, the troops returned
to barracks through an immense crowd which had
assembled in Buckingham-palace-road.   Before dis-
missing his Battalion, Lieutenant-Colonel Lloyd, by Her
Majesty's desire, conveyed Her Majesty's gracious message
to all ranks, wishing them God-speed, victory, and a

speedy termination to the war. The colours were handed over to the 1st Battalion for safe custody.

On Sunday, 18th March, réveille was sounded at 3 a.m. and 5 a.m. for the two half-battalions respectively, and "the general" was played. The first half-battalion, consisting of Nos. 1, 2, 3, and 6 companies, paraded at 5 a.m. under Major Gordon-Gilmour. Having marched to Nine Elms station, they entrained for Southampton. Lieutenant-Colonel Lloyd, D.S.O., having ridden back to Wellington Barracks, the remaining half-battalion paraded under his command at 7 a.m., and having marched to Nine Elms, entrained at 9 and went down to Southampton. A very large, orderly, and well-behaved crowd accompanied them to the station, only two of the men being drunk. The morning was very fine, but the weather became very cold as Southampton was approached.

A furious gale was blowing when the Battalion— which the *Times* pronounced to be emphatically the finest and best-disciplined that had left Southampton for the front—embarked on the British India ss. "Dunera," which sailed at 2.10 p.m. She carried 29 officers and warrant officers, and 1,082 Grenadiers of other ranks; total, 1,111.

The following is a list by companies :—

1. Major R. Scott-Kerr, Lieutenant J. A. C. Quilter, 2nd Lieutenant The Hon. M. B. Parker.

2. Captain W. Murray-Threipland, Lieutenant F. L. Swaine, Transport Officer (joined at the Cape), 2nd Lieutenant L. R. V. Colby.

3. Captain E. G. Verschoyle, Lieutenant M. R. A. Cholmeley, 2nd Lieutenant The Lord Francis Scott.

4. Captain The Lord Ardee, Lieutenant H. St. L. Stucley, 2nd Lieutenant G. R. Houston-Boswall.

5.   Captain G. L. Bonham, Lieutenant The Hon. G. H. Douglas-Pennant, 2nd Lieutenant G. T. Tryon.

6.   Captain The Hon. W. Cavendish, Lieutenant E. Seymour, 2nd Lieutenant A. H. Murray.

7.   Captain The Viscount Kilcoursie, Lieutenant The Hon. A. Weld-Forester, 2nd Lieutenant The Hon. Lucius Cary (Master of Falkland), Lieutenant W. S. Blackett, Assistant-Adjutant (machine-gun).

8.   Major W. Marshall, Lieutenant G. D. Jeffreys, 2nd Lieutenant E. B. Loraine.,

Lieutenant-Colonel F. Lloyd, D.S.O. (Commanding), Major R. Gordon-Gilmour (Second-in-Command), Adjutant Captain C. E. Corkran, Honorary Lieutenant and Quarter-master W. G. A. Garton, Surgeon-Captain J. H. Austin R.A.M.C., Surgeon attached.

There were no other troops on board with the exception of Major Agar, R.E., Captain Mellish, Scottish Rifles, The Rev. C. Tobias, and Civil Surgeon Copland.

CHAPTER II.

FROM THE EMBARKATION TO BIDDULPHSBERG.

(Extract from the Diary of Lieutenant-Colonel F. Lloyd, D.S.O., Commanding the Battalion.)

March 19th—22nd. On the night of March 18th—19th we anchored off the Needles and did not finally sail until early morning. Owing to the rough weather of the next few days it was the 22nd before the Battalion shook down. On parade I read two congratulatory telegrams—one from the Major-General commanding the Home District, and the other from the Lieutenant-Colonel of the Regiment.

March 26th.—St. Vincent was reached, where we found several transports—on board one of them being Sir Frederick Carrington, formerly our Brigadier at Gibraltar. We heard with great grief of the death of Lygon, and of Crabbe, Codrington and G. Trotter being severely wounded.

March 28th.—We coaled and sailed again at 5.15 a.m. I was inoculated for enteric, as were several of the officers. It made me feel very ill all day on the 29th, but on the 30th I was better. I talked to all the men about it, and persuaded a great many to be operated upon. There seems to have been an extraordinary prejudice against it, some stupid man having put about reports as to its ill effects. We never heard throughout the campaign what was the result of these particular inoculations, but I have been assured that inoculation rendered the cases less severe than they otherwise might have been. The men inoculated suffered very much for a day, but in forty-eight hours, with very few exceptions, they were as well as if they had never undergone the operation. The following is a return of the inoculations made:—28 officers, 107 N.C.O.'s, 367 men, 14 casuals; total, 516.

March 29th.—No. 3212, Private T. Baines, of No. 6 Company, died of enteric, and was buried at sea.

April 4th.—No. 2176, Private Bennet, of No. 4 Company, died of pneumonia. He was buried at sea next day.

April 9th.—I had up all the valises and packed them for disembarkation according to regulation. They were never used, however, but were stored at Cape Town, the men carrying all necessary articles as best they could in their great-coats.

April 11th.—We arrived at Cape Town, where a telegram was received as follows:—" Ship proceed Port

Elizabeth. Battalion for Bloemfontein viâ Norvals Pont."
We coaled and sailed on the 13th for Port Elizabeth.

April 15th, 16th.—We arrived at Port Elizabeth on the
15th, but did not disembark until the 16th at 7.45 a.m. By
2.45 p.m. we had all started for the front in three trains—
No. 1 train contained baggage; No. 2, Head-quarters and
Companies 1 to 4; No. 3, Companies 5 to 8. I sent
Gilmour in command of the second train, and came myself
with the third.

April 17th, 18th.—We breakfasted at 6 a.m. on the
17th at Craddock, and on the morning of the 18th we
arrived at Springfontein. Here Sergt.-Major Rolinson
and Drill-Sergt. Thomas re-joined us from the 3rd Battalion.
After some delay we went on to Edenburg, passing the
C.I.V.'s on the way. It was raining heavily and the men
in the open trucks suffered considerably. The last train
got in about 1.30 p.m. Private Crane of No. 7 Company
selected this moment to cut his throat in the van. He was
attended to and sent back, but died soon after. At about
4 p.m. I marched for Reddesburg, leaving the transport,
including seven ox-waggons, to follow. I was prevented
from marching earlier because no sooner had the oxen
been handed over than I was informed that they had to be
outspanned for two hours and fed. This enabled me only
to march the men for about an hour-and-a-half before dark,
as I had neither guides nor cavalry, and no one to show
me the road. All I could do was to bivouac, throwing out
such outposts as I could. The transport passed us by my
order, and stopped at the Riet River. At 11.30 p.m. I
marched again and at about 12.45 a.m. on the 19th reached
the river, where I again bivouacked.

April 19th.—At 6 a.m. I started, and having been told
that the Riet was half way to our destination, I decided

not to breakfast until I got in. Bitterly did I repent it, for we had not really completed a third of the way. Not knowing whether the water on the road was good I dared not risk drinking it. We forded the river and went on, the men marching capitally. But the journey was trying, and it was not till nearly one o'clock p.m. that we struggled, after a waterless march, into Reddesburg. Yet, in spite of all, only nine men out of the whole 1,100 had fallen out of the ranks. We were bitterly disappointed on arrival to find that our transport was not in, the ox-waggons having stuck. Luckily Garton got hold of some fresh meat, and we dined. Dr. Polson, who lived in the town, was most kind and helped us considerably. Part of the transport arrived in time for us to have tea at 9.30, the rest of it remaining out all night. I did not much relish the outlook, for I knew nothing either of the country or of the situation ; but I made the best dispositions I could, and luckily the Boers made no attempt to attack us. This was fortunate, as with us there was a large convoy of ammunition, supplies, etc. The night was bitterly cold, especially towards dawn, and everything was wet through.

April 20th.—I was glad when we stood to our arms at dawn. At 9 a.m. some more of the transport came in, but a good deal was still out. Having been ordered to convoy the ammunition I marched, leaving Swaine and a section to bring on the transport. I sent No. 8 Company under Marshall and No. 7 under Kilcoursie as escort, I myself following with the Battalion. We marched through a magnificent country of veldt and kopjes, and at noon reached Rosendal, where we stopped for dinner. I then moved on and halted again for tea about 4. As I was doing so, a large convoy of ammunition came up under an artillery officer, who asked me to escort him. I said I

B

would do so, though I had no orders, and though it was undertaking a somewhat heavy responsibility with the little knowledge I had of what was going on. Soon after this we had a false alarm of an attack, as I saw what appeared to be a large force of Boers, who, however, either did not see us, or else did not think us worth troubling about. As I was in a good position, I believe I should have been able to give an account of them. I bivouacked that night some six or seven miles further on.

April 21st.—We marched at 5 a.m., and, seeing from a Nek that there were troops ahead, I rode forward and found the 2nd Battalion Scots Guards, who were the tail of the Division. They moved on before, and the Battalion got in about 8.30 and bivouacked. Having been told that we were likely to be wanted, since the Boers were entrenched some 10 miles ahead and guns could be heard from time to time, I determined to push on. At 3 p.m., after a little food—we were on less than half-rations—I marched again. Though we had done a considerable distance in the morning, the men went off admirably. When I arrived within a couple of miles of the Division, Gascoigne, the Brigade Major, came up, saying that we were required to line a kopje which was about four miles ahead. It proved, however, to be a much greater distance before we had climbed on the plateau. We met no staff officer and wandered about, till at last I found General Campbell's head-quarters, and was told I might bivouac where I was. This I did, everyone being dead-beat. We had, however, done what was wanted. It was a heavy march, about 45 miles having been covered between 4 p.m. on Wednesday and 7 p.m. on Saturday, after two days and two nights spent in the train, with little sleep, and following upon a month at sea. We also carried a heavy load, and were, besides, on half-rations.

April 22nd.—At day-break I moved down to the water, and was afterwards placed in position by General Campbell. General Rundle, our Divisional General, came up and told me to withdraw. He complimented us on our march, saying that he wanted us badly, and that now we were to rest all day in reserve. Towards evening we moved up nearer to the enemy's position, and No. 5 went on picket. I also had four companies forming a line of outposts from the Battalion to a kopje about a mile off.

April 23rd.—At Wakkerstroom I stood to arms at 5 a.m. Soon after daylight the East Yorkshire fell back from the advanced position they had held, and it was then occupied by the Berkshire. The Boers at once began to shell both them and us, and continued to do so for about an hour. We had nobody hit. The men were much amused at the shells and the "pom-poms," and many of their remarks were very funny, the first shot being received with "Halt, who comes there?"—"Why are you trying to hurt us, Mr. Kruger, we have done you no harm?" and so on. Later, the Scots Guards fell back, and the Brigade was relieved by the Highland Light Infantry and the Scottish Rifles. We bivouacked. General Rundle came round and desired me to convey to the Battalion his appreciation of the march, and the way in which the men had responded when he really wanted them. The men had all grown beards, but the officers shaved. The nights were cold and the days hot.

April 24th.—Réveille at 4 a.m. I marched at 6, carrying one day's half-rations on the men, besides the emergency ration and two days' half-rations in the carts. The men's waterproof sheets were also carried in the carts. After marching about three miles, we were ordered to halt, and remained where we were till General Rundle came up and explained the situation—that Lord Roberts was marching south, and so were Generals French and Pole-Carew; that in fact we were trying to hem the Boers in. We were also told that General Brabant had relieved Wepener, thus preventing reinforcements being sent to the Boer force in our front, said to be about 4,000 strong.

April 25th.—Marched at 5 a.m. eastwards without the cavalry which should have covered our front, as they were late. At about 7 I was ordered to attack to the east-ward, extending 10 paces, though the General told me that he was afraid the enemy had gone. He explained clearly and concisely what he required me to do. As the whole of No. 1 was already extended as an advance guard, I did not attempt in any way to alter the formation, but simply changed direction a quarter-circle and increased the extension, ordering No. 2 to support Scott-Kerr's Company (No. 1). The remainder of the Battalion, with the Scots Guards, came on as a support in the same formation, and the extension covered about 1,200 yards of front. It worked well, though I preferred having half-companies or sections in front, supported by the remainder of their own companies. Many miles of country were traversed in this formation, we pivoting on our left. The Boers, it was found, had evacuated their positions at 2 a.m., which was a pity. It is probable that, had Brabazon's Cavalry been a little quicker, we might have got them. We joined hands with General French, and General Pole-Carew's Division was no great distance away. We reached Dewetsdorp at about 2 o'clock and then marched on about four miles to our bivouac on the Modder River, where we arrived pretty well tired out.

April 26th.—Everything wringing wet. We stood to arms at 5 a.m. and marched about 11. We were to have been the advance guard, but, owing to some transport difficulties, the 17th Brigade marched first. We formed the rearguard, the left of the half-battalion under Gordon-Gilmour being the rear portion. During the march we saw the dust of General Pole-Carew's Division, which contained the Guards' Brigade. We had great hopes of meeting, but alas! our routes diverged, and we never afterwards met the 3rd Battalion during the whole campaign.* Our destination was reached at 5 p.m., the left half-battalion not getting in, as they were a long way in rear. An order came out that commanding officers could commandeer sheep or oxen, giving a receipt, but no money, for them. I got fifteen sheep which I caught, and the half-battalion had a good meal on half that quantity.

27th April.—I marched at 6.15 a.m., leaving word for the left half-battalion to follow me. We marched steadily till about 10.30, when we halted till 11.45. At 3 p.m. we arrived at the intended bivouac, but as the enemy were holding the hills, it was decided to be unsafe, and we accordingly struggled on and reached Thaba 'Nchu—22 miles— a fair march, considering that we carried heavy haversacks, waterproof sheets, blankets and 150 rounds. The left half-battalion under Gilmour, who started six miles behind us, came in about 8.30 or 9. Lieutenant-

---

* "April 27th, 1900.—Our 2nd Battalion was sighted some eight miles off. This was the only occasion on which the 2nd and 3rd Battalions were in the same part of the theatre of war."—Extract from the 3rd Battalion's "History."

General Rundle published the following order of the day :
" Lieutenant-General Sir Leslie Rundle has directed the
Commanding Officer to convey to the 2nd Battalion
Grenadier Guards his appreciation of the fine march they
made when called upon by him."

April 28th.—We were to have had two days' rest, but
in the afternoon General Rundle sent for me and showed
me the situation. He told me it was possible that the
Boers, being surrounded, would try to break out over a certain Nek which he pointed out to me, and which he wanted
held. It was now past 5 p.m., and I accordingly galloped
back, got out the Battalion and marched. It was just
dark, but I was able to take up a good position. This was
much facilitated by my Captains knowing their work
so well.

April 29th.—At dawn I received orders from General
Campbell to occupy the top of Thaba'Nchu Mountain and
to hold the ridge. After giving the men their breakfast, I
started, and reached the top—about 3,000 feet above the
plain—by 11 a.m. It was a plateau surrounded by
gigantic rocks, with good water. Near one end of it it
was connected with another mountain by a narrow ridge,
not more than 10 feet wide on the top—a veritable razor-
back! This kopje was about 1,600 yards east of me. I
relieved the West Kent by sending No. 1 into the advanced
position, No. 2 in connection, Nos. 3 and 4 in support, and
the remainder in reserve. I was only able to occupy the
advanced position by sending men in singly. Every man
was shot at, and the fire continued all day, but only one
man was slightly hit—in the head. We replied and hit
two or three men, whom we saw carried off. This kept
down the enemy's fire. Towards evening I went into the

advanced trench held by No. 2, under Murray-Threipland.
Bullets were dropping fairly thickly, when suddenly, to
our horror, the Boers began to shell with accuracy. They
burst time-shrapnel over our heads, and Gilmour had a
narrow escape. At dusk the fire ceased altogether.
General Rundle heliographed to ask if I required support.
I said I did not. It was a bitterly cold night, and the
officers' great-coats did not arrive till midnight. I wished
I had carried mine as the men did. The mules being
stampeded by the Boer shells, the officers got no food from
6 a.m. to 7 p.m.

April 30th.—I relieved some of the Companies before
daylight, but I could not relieve the advanced post until
after it was light, with the result that, coming away, they
were heavily fired at, though no one was hit. The enemy,
having got the range accurately, shelled us pretty heavily
at intervals during the day. I was asked by General
Rundle if I wished to be relieved. I told him in reply that
I should be glad to do whatever was required of me. The
Boers got more guns up, but although they shelled us
heavily they did no harm. A very cold night. I could
make out a considerable force of Boers on the ridge, and
also saw that they were bringing another gun up. About
midnight Lieutenant-Colonel Romilly appeared with a
message from General Rundle to say that if I and Colonel
Romilly thought that the Boer position could be assaulted
without great loss of life, I was to take it with my Battalion, supported by the half battalion of Scots Guards. I
decided at once against it, and Romilly agreed. As soon
as I had communicated with the General, he gave orders
that there was to be no forward movement for the present.
The Brigade-Major came up after this and arranged that,
as soon as half the Battalion of the Scots Guards arrived,

half of my Battalion was to go down, and to be followed by the other half next morning. I went
down myself and rode over to see General Rundle
and explained the situation. He quite approved all I
had done.

May 3rd.—The second half-battalion came down
and were heavily shelled in moving to their position—
luckily, without loss, though there were many close
shaves.

May 5th.—At 12.30 a.m. the Brigade-Major arrived
with orders to move to the other side of the valley
before dawn, so as to avoid being shelled, and to be
ready to march thence at 10 a.m., carrying one day's
rations on the men. I got over safely. The operations of the day were explained to me by an A.D.C.
sent by General Rundle. The cavalry were to make
a wide turning movement round the right flank of
the Boers, supported by the 17th Brigade, my Battalion
making a frontal demonstration to draw the enemy,
and, if the place should be unoccupied, to seize it;
but on no account to make a frontal attack. I was to be
supported by the East Yorkshire and a half-battalion of
Scots Guards, the other half-battalion to attack over the
"razor-back" from the top of Thaba' Nchu if possible.
This latter Romilly and I at once said was impossible if a
rock called Stonehenge were held by the Boers. After
dinner I formed for attack in column of double half-companies. The left half-companies of Nos. 3 and 4 were the
front line, supported by their right half-companies. The
firing line was extended to 15 paces, the supports to 10
paces. Between the first and the second lines the distance
was 300 paces, the intervals between the other lines being

50 paces.* After some time I went into the firing line, as I saw that General Campbell was there. Nothing was effected until we got to within 1,500 yards, when the advanced companies fired a few group volleys. This drew a considerable but harmless fire. I received, by an A.D.C., an order from General Campbell, who had retired, to say that I was to advance. I ordered No. 4 to do so, but only for 50 yards. The enemy now ceased firing. I was then ordered to advance a short distance further, which order I carried out. This drew a great deal of fire, and I was ordered to remain where I was till dusk. Soon after, Captain Verschoyle was shot, and at the same time I saw several Boers seizing a kopje about 500 yards

---

* There was 50 paces' distance between the lines, except between the first two, which were 300 paces apart ; 15 paces was the interval between the men in the first two lines ; in the remainder it was 10 paces :—

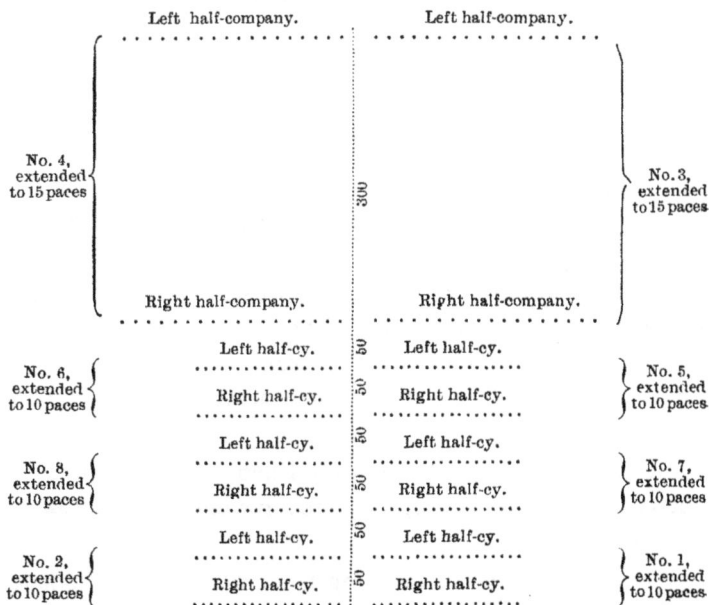

	Left half-company.		Left half-company.	
No. 4, extended to 15 paces	. . . .		. . . .	No. 3, extended to 15 paces
	Right half-company.	300	Right half-company.	
	. . . .		. . . .	
No. 6, extended to 10 paces	Left half-cy.	50	Left half-cy.	No. 5, extended to 10 paces
	Right half-cy.	50	Right half-cy.	
No. 8, extended to 10 paces	Left half-cy.	50	Left half-cy.	No. 7, extended to 10 paces
	Right half-cy.	50	Right half-cy.	
No. 2, extended to 10 paces	Left half-cy.	50	Left half-cy.	No. 1, extended to 10 paces
	Right half-cy.	50	Right half-cy.	

nearer than the one they had originally held.   As we were
under considerable fire, and the object was gained, I ordered
the Battalion to fall back, not waiting till it was dusk.
This was effected without further loss.   I understand that
General Rundle was quite satisfied with what was done,
and was particularly anxious that life should not be sacri-
ficed uselessly.

As soon as the Battalion was clear of fire, I went to see
Verschoyle, who was being carried to the rear.   He was
shot through the left breast while lying down.   He seemed
cheerful, and the doctors had good hopes of his life.   He
was kept in camp all night, and sent to hospital next
morning.   I arrived in camp with the last two companies
at 7 p.m.

May 6th.—Verschoyle died suddenly in hospital at
11.30 a.m.   A report came in by two Kaffirs that the Boers
had trekked, and an advance was accordingly made.   We
were in reserve.   We bivouacked beyond the plateau on a
Nek at Eden.

May 7th.—Kilcoursie, Bonham, Cholmeley and Francis
Scott went into Thaba 'Nchu to attend poor Verschoyle's
funeral.   I could not leave the Battalion, nor could more
officers be spared. General Rundle and staff attended. Bagot
and Kennard were among those present.   Wrapped only
in a blanket, as a soldier should be, he was buried in Thaba
'Nchu cemetery, and a wooden cross was soon after put
up over his grave until the wishes of his family could be
known.

May 10th.—We moved from Eden to Andrewsfontein,
nothing particular having occurred beyond several alarms
of attack.

May 11th.—In the morning General Campbell sent for
me and ordered me to take two guns and the Battalion to

where Lieutenant-Colonel Grenfell was with his colonial corps. I was to make a frontal demonstration, Grenfell turning the flank of the enemy's position, and General Brabant meanwhile acting on the other flank. This I did. It all came off, but, as might have been expected, the Boers trekked. I bivouacked near the spot for the night at Ruis Kop.

May 13th.—Having heard that a neighbouring farmhouse was a harbour for Boers, I determined to try and surround them. I accordingly marched at 1 a.m. with two companies under Threipland and Ardee, a Kaffir guide being tied to Colour-Sergeant Morgan, who spoke Dutch. We surrounded the house, but the Boers, who undoubtedly had been there, had fled.

May 14th.—We marched at 6 a.m. and bivouacked at Lieuwriver Drift.

May 15th.—Marched to Le Souvenir. We bivouacked low down in one of the coldest places I ever was in.

May 16th.—Paraded at 6.30 on a damp foggy morning, with a considerable amount of frost; but as we moved on to higher ground it became warmer. We arrived at Mequatling's Nek about 1 p.m.

May 17th.—Marched at 6.30. There were handed over to me, to guard, 44 Boer prisoners, who were removed after my arrival at the next camp.

May 18th.—Marched at 6 a.m., halted at 10.30 for two hours, and reached Trommel at 3 p.m.

May 19th.—A day of rest, which was a good thing, as both men and horses required it badly. This was principally to allow the convoy to come up, as we had not had any biscuit for some days, and had been living on commandeered flour which the men made into a sort of dough cake without yeast. It rather amused them at first, but the want of biscuit was distinctly felt. There was now plenty of meat. There was also a lack of fuel, dried dung being the only substitute obtainable. There were Boers about in small parties. One Yeoman was wounded, but otherwise there was no fighting.

May 21st.—At Trommel heard of the relief of Mafeking.

May 23rd.—Parker sent to Port Elizabeth to fetch up baggage, etc.

May 24th.—Marched at 6 a.m. I carried some bully beef, which I broke into, and so gave the men a meal on the road. We were all on quarter-rations, so my Battalion came off better than the rest of the force. This being the Queen's birthday, a double ration of rum was served out.

CHAPTER III.

BIDDULPHSBERG.

May 25th, 1900.—The Battalion marched at 7 a.m., having stood to arms at 5. The route lay over a great level plain, with the East Yorkshire as advanced guard. On arriving at a plateau overlooking Senekal, the Artillery had their guns unlimbered, the East Yorkshire advancing in attack formation. The Commanding Officer soon after received the order to support the guns, which had opened fire on either flank. The left battery, protected by half-a-battalion under Major Gordon-Gilmour, advanced; the other battery remained stationary, protected by the other half-battalion. At about 3 p.m. the Commanding Officer,

who was with the latter, received the order, " The Grenadiers will take the town." He at once galloped to the
advanced half-battalion, took command, and ordered
Major Gilmour to bring on the other as soon as possible in
support. An A.D.C. now rode up with the information
that the town was held in front, and that the Battalion was
to push on as quickly as possible. To do this, the extension, which had been at ten paces, was lessened, and a
donga rushed which the enemy was believed to occupy,
but which they were found to have evacuated. Soon after
some Yeomen, looking very much like Boers, appeared,
and brought the news that Major Dalbiac had rashly tried
to storm a kopje with a few men, and that he had been
killed with one sergeant and one trooper. Kennard, late
of the Grenadiers, and three men had been severely
wounded. Lieutenant-Colonel Lloyd then occupied the
town with the Battalion. Soon afterwards General Rundle
came in, and the British Flag was run up, all ranks presenting arms to it. General Rundle placed Lieutenant-
Colonel Lloyd in command of the town, telling him to
make the best dispositions he could against attack. He
then left, making his head-quarters some little way out.
As it was nearly dark, picquets had to be quickly thrown
out and arrangements made for picquetting the water-
supply, the bank, the post-office, etc. A proclamation
was issued confining the inhabitants to their houses, and
the Landrost was sent for and ordered to produce food, etc.,
for the Battalion. This man was a double traitor, and it
was found that marching him about in escort, with fixed
bayonets, greatly promoted civility and punctuality. A
large fire, kindled in the centre of the town, gave much-
needed light and warmth.

May 26th.—General Rundle came in and made his
head-quarters in the town, Lieutenant-Colonel Lloyd

remaining as Commandant. In the afternoon Major Dalbiac and the Yeomen who had been killed the day before were buried in the cemetery. A Boer Field Cornet, who had been killed at the same time, was also buried. The Grenadiers found the funeral party.

May 27th.—Before church parade General Rundle inspected the Battalion, and expressed himself much pleased with everything, saying how proud he was to have it under his command, and that he hoped soon to let the Grenadiers have a real turn at the enemy as a reward for their hard work. A service then followed in the Dutch Church, the Presbyterian minister of the Scots Guards officiating, and amalgamating the Church of England and Presbyterian services as best he could.

May 28th.—The Commandant instituted a house-to-house search of the town, but, while it was in progress, an order was received that the force would march at once. After dinner, the Battalion moved out about four miles, Major Gordon-Gilmour, with half a battalion, protecting some guns on the left ; while Lieutenant-Colonel Lloyd, with the other half-battalion, supported some Yeomanry said to be heavily engaged. The Boers were very active during this march, the Yeomen on our right losing some horses from artillery fire, while our left was shelled freely. Both half-battalions bivouacked where they were, about half-a-mile apart. Capt. Cavendish went on the staff temporarily, to assist the Intelligence Officer, on the understanding that he was to return to the Battalion whenever any fighting took place.

29th May, 1900.—BATTLE OF BIDDULPHSBERG.— Réveille at 4 a.m. The Battalion was ready to march before daylight, as it was expected that the bivouac would

be shelled. It actually moved off at 7. Lieutenant-Colonel
Lloyd had determined in future not to attack with a single
company in firing line supported by other single companies, as he considered the extension to be too great for
one Captain to look after. He, therefore, formed up his
half-battalion in column of sections so that each Captain
should command in depth rather than in breadth. Major
Gilmour knew this; but, not having bivouacked in column
of sections, and being obliged to hurry off in the morning,
he advanced in single companies supported by the other
companies, as had been done hitherto. When the Commanding Officer came up in support, he conformed to this
arrangement, as it would have been difficult then to alter
the formation, though there is little doubt that the attack
on a smaller front with a greater depth is more convenient.

General Rundle gave the point of direction himself,
ordering the right of the Battalion, which was leading, to
keep well clear of a kopje on the right, from which he
expected to draw fire. He also directed the Commanding
Officer to seize the ridge in front, and then change
direction to the right. This was done, but the " ridge " was
found to be a long, level plain. Some distance ahead a
party of Yeomanry were seen. A new point to march on
was given after the change of direction, and a halt
ordered as soon as the Battalion had wheeled round—a
somewhat difficult operation, it being in extended
order, with 15 paces interval, and also because a
heavy veldt fire was raging. It remained thus for
perhaps a quarter of an hour, the guns coming up and
opening fire, which drew a Boer gun in response.

The Commanding Officer then received the order: "The
Grenadiers will take the gun." Everything being ready,
there was nothing to do but to order the advance, which

was in the following order of companies: 5, 6, 7, 8, 1,
2, 3, 4. The route lay at first through a field of mealies, very
high and thick. General Rundle now sent for the Commanding Officer, who got on his horse and went to him.
The ground was explained, Lieutenant-Colonel Lloyd
agreeing that the attack was feasible, as it appeared to
both that cover could be gained by getting under the
kopje, about 2,500 yards on the right front, and moving
along it. It did not appear at that time that the enemy
were holding it strongly. Some Yeomanry came in and
reported that "four" Boers had been seen on the kopje:
otherwise, "all clear"! General Rundle's directions to
the Commanding Officer were as follows: "You will get
under the kopje, move up it, leaving a containing Company,
and proceed along it. I think you will be able to do this."
Lieutenant-Colonel Lloyd agreed, and having got on
his horse rode away to carry out the order. The Boers
were at this time bursting shell over the Battalion, but
there was no rifle fire from them. The Commanding Officer
quickly saw that the only means of moving the Battalion
in the new direction—so widely extended as it was, it
being in eight lines, at 15 paces extension, with from 100
to 150 yards between lines—was to ride to the second line
and move it half-right, trusting that those in rear would
conform, and then to alter the direction of the firing line.

Be it remembered that at this time there was absolutely
no rifle fire from the enemy, and that it was not supposed
that the kopje was held in any strength. The Commanding Officer at once galloped to the second line and
ordered it to move half-right, and then rode towards the
firing line. Before he had got half way, the Boers opened
a heavy fire, slightly wounding him as he jumped from his
horse. He then ran into the firing line, striking No. 5,

which he prolonged to the right with the half-company of No. 6, under Lieutenant E. Seymour. It was most difficult to see, as the grass was very long, and the fire from the enemy was so heavy that it was impossible to hear or make the voice heard. He realised that the only chance of carrying out the orders of the Lieutenant-General was to advance half-right by alternate rushes, trusting to the remainder of the Battalion to follow. These rushes were gallantly led by Lieutenant Seymour and 2nd Lieutenant A. H. Murray, who were seconded with equal bravery by N.C.O.'s and men. The advance must have continued for some 300 yards or more when Murray was hit, his last words being, " Go on, Grenadiers, follow your Commanding Officer." At the next halt, Lieutenant-Colonel Lloyd was shot through the body, and practically the whole of the advancing line was wiped out, for on Lieutenant Seymour calling upon them to fire a volley, only three men responded. The whole of the initiative of the advance was now ended, and all lay still under a murderous fire of big guns, " pom-poms," and small arms. Lieutenant-Colonel Lloyd was again hit on the stomach, but his life was saved by Drummer Haines, who was at that moment endeavouring to pull him behind an ant heap, and whose forearm was shattered by the bullet. The range was about 1,200 yards, but there were a party of Boers in a donga on the left front some 300 yards away who brought a heavy cross-fire to bear.

At about 12.30 p.m., the veldt, which had been on fire some time, having been lit by accident previously to the Battalion forming for attack, now began to burn towards the kopje. The fire came steadily down, but the wind changing, it turned and went in the opposite direction. Later on the wind again changed, the fire resumed its

C

original course, and burnt towards where the wounded men were lying. It has been stated that the fire was lit by the Boers, but there is no question that this was not the case ; it was undoubtedly lit accidentally by someone throwing a match into the dry grass on the veldt.

The whole of the attack was at a standstill, the men lying down now by order, and returning the fire, which was very heavy, with—as was afterwards learnt—considerable effect.

At about 3 p.m. the order was given to retire, which was done by the companies in front passing through the others, and so gradually withdrawing.

It was about this time that the fire burnt down on the firing line where the wounded were lying. Several of the men who had been lying there until then were ordered by the Commanding Officer to get up and try to save themselves, it being hopeless for them to remain there any longer, as they would have been burnt to death. Several of them made their way through the fire to the dressing station. The Commanding Officer was assisted to rise by Drummer Haines and Private Fruin, and, stumbling through the fire, was able to crawl away until he was picked up and taken to the dressing station. There were, however, a certain number of men who, being unable to move, were burnt—some to death.

During the retirement, and after it had been seen that nothing more was to be done in the way of attack, Lieutenant Quilter, who was in the 5th line, obtained leave from General Rundle to take a dozen men, unarmed, and remove as many of the wounded as possible from the fire. This work was most gallantly carried out by them, many lives being undoubtedly saved by their gallantry under a heavy and persistent fire.

Lieutenant Quilter was subsequently recommended for the Victoria Cross for this, and the names of the men of his party were sent in for reward. Nothing, however, was given them—on the purely technical ground of a regulation under which this distinction is not bestowed on men who lay down their arms.

The retirement was carried out steadily, without hurry, and in perfect order. After the action the Battalion returned to the camp it had occupied in the morning. The wounded were left on the field, and the Boers who came down did their best, in conjunction with the British surgeons and stretcher-bearers, to alleviate their sufferings.

The casualties for the day were :—

Officers wounded (including the C.O.), 2nd Lieutenant Alesdair Murray subsequently dying of his wounds ..	5
N.C.O.'s and men killed	33
Died of wounds and burns	7
Wounded dangerously, severely, slightly, or burnt	95
Missing, prisoners :—	
Unwounded	6
Wounded	2
Total casualties	148

Lieutenant-Colonel Lloyd's Account.

29th May. Battle of Biddulphsberg.

Réveille at 4. Ready to march off before daylight, *i.e.*, 5.30, as Rundle expected us to be shelled. I tried to eat something, but could not, and was very

sick, luckily for me. We moved at 7. I had always
determined never to form for attack again with a
single Company in firing line supported by other single
Companies, as the extension is too great for one Captain
to look after, and I had my half-Battalion formed up in
column of sections, so that each Captain should command
in depth rather than in breadth. Gilmour knew this, but
not having bivouacked in column of sections as I had done
—I had formed for attack on the night before—he had
not time to adopt my plan, though of course he was in
more or less close formation during the night. He
therefore quite correctly launched a company intact,
followed by other companies. When I came up I conformed. We went on, so far as I could judge, due North,
with a very high kopje on our right front, said to be
occupied (and it proved to be so).

General Rundle now sent for me, gave me a point
of direction, told me to keep my right well clear of the
kopje as he expected me to draw fire from it, and to seize
the ridge in front and then change direction right. This
latter order was later changed to half-right. When I
reached the ridge, I found it to be not one in reality, but a
long level plain. Some distance ahead I saw some
Yeomanry. As I was not nearly abreast of the kopje,
I had to clear it before I could change front. I reported to
Sir Leslie, who sent for me and ordered me to do so, gave
me a point of direction, and after getting square, to await
development. This I did with some difficulty, as there
was a heavy veldt fire, and I had to dodge it.

I now halted for some little time, perhaps fifteen
minutes. Our guns came up and opened. A Boer gun also
opened on our guns. I now received the order, "The
Grenadiers will take the gun." The Battalion being

in extended order, I had nothing to do but order it to advance, get off my horse and go on with the support. The order of companies was as follows :—5, 6, 7, 8 ; 1, 2, 3, 4. We advanced at first through a mealie field, very high and thick. As I was going along, an A.D.C. galloped to me with the order to go and see General Rundle. I ran back, got on my chestnut horse (some hundred yards, I dare say) and went to him. He then explained the ground, and I agreed that it was feasible, following his plan, thinking as we both did that I could gain cover and that the kopje was not very strongly held. Having got his directions, my only course was to gallop to the support, give them the new orders, which was to take ground to the right continuously till the cover of the kopje I wanted was gained. I then galloped as hard as I could to the firing line.

When I was about midway I came under such a hail of bullets that I jumped off my horse and let him go. As I did so I was hit on the thumb and rifle, and my wallets were shot through. I then ran to No. 5 and led them. I prolonged the line to the right with a half-company of No. 6 under Seymour. It may not have been more than a section. What with the long veldt grass and the fire, it was difficult to see and impossible to make oneself heard. I, however, advanced with two half-companies or sections half-right by rushes in the endeavour to gain cover (as a first parallel, as the drill book says). The rushes were led with the utmost gallantry by Seymour and Murray, and followed with equal bravery by the N. C. O.'s and men. Just before the last rush I called upon Murray to go on, but the answer was that he was down. I then rushed the lot with the poor boy calling " Go on Grenadiers, follow your Commanding Officer."

At the next halt my right-hand man was hit, my left-hand man was hit, I was hit, and there was no more initiative because nearly all the men were down, and there was no one to go on and it was no use doing more. I therefore told everyone to lie still as the best chance. There were a few ant-heaps, but they were rotten and useless. I was behind one on my back with Drummer Haines and Fruin of No. 6. I tried to keep all the men separate as much as possible as the best chance of life. Only two went back, as they said, "to get dressed;" I told them to lie still or they would be shot. Whether they were or not I don't know.

There we lay under a hail of bullets. Every time one moved to get a bandage it produced a bullet within a foot or two. I guess the range to have been about 1,700 yards, unless, as I afterwards heard, there were men in a donga within 300 yards. *This I do not believe, as the bullets mostly descended. A considerable proportion of them apparently burst with a sharp crack. We must have been easy marks for the Boers, as naturally we showed up lying on the ground. I for one was absolutely on my back. I was doing all I could to keep them from moving, and gallantly they behaved, for not a man funked. Drummer Haines had got his arm over me, drawing me to him for protection, I suppose (I was a bit silly, but not very), when bang came a bullet that hit me on the stomach, but it was covered by his arm, which it broke, and I was only bruised fearfully. This, no doubt, saved my life. I tied him up with a handkerchief, and he put some stuff on my wounds, and there we lay. Seymour crawled up soon after this and said that something must be done, as the fire was rather more than less. I said, "Try a volley," so he gave the word of command, but there were only two men unhit in

---

* This was afterwards proved to have been true.

his section, so that was no good. He then said " I will try and go back, as I can do no good here, and get the artillery to fire on this particular spot where the fire is coming from." I said he would be killed, but he said it was no use staying here and off he crawled, to be shot in the foot before he got in ; he never got to the artillery.

Soon after this an ammunition-carrier, belonging to No. 8, came up as if nothing were happening—in fact, had it been in Hyde Park, I should have taken his name for moving in slow time. He was bringing up ammunition, he said, and did not seem to care a straw. I made him lie down, but he was twice hit immediately; his name was No. 1511 Private Bevan. I have sent it in.

Once or twice before, the veldt fire looked as if it were coming down upon us, but it had always moved off. So we lay on for three hours in all. I had intended remaining till dark, but there was no possibility of that, for the fire now came straight at us. I would not let anyone move till it was quite close, but when it was within two yards I gave the order for everyone to go who could. I did not think I could move, but they pulled me to my feet, and I stumbled through the flames, mercifully getting nothing more than a singeing. All moved, as I thought, except the dead and Murray, and his lot were too far off, he having fallen some way back. I had tried to communicate with him, but, getting no response, thought he was dead. As I stumbled along the Boers opened on us an appalling fire, which they kept up. I think only one man was hit, prin-cipally owing to the smoke. I looked back and saw wounded men helping one another, in fact everyone doing his best. I managed to struggle for 300 yards or so, when Colour-Sergeant Morgan came up and helped me. He was one of the few unhit. Bullets were falling thick, but I

reached a wire fence where I lay down behind a stone post
for a minute or two.   Colour-Sergeant Morgan and another
man then came and insisted on pulling me along, while
others received like aid, those who could walk helping those
who could not.   Some 200 yards further on I was put on to a
Scots Guards stretcher.   I was very silly by now, and was
carried past Rundle, who gave me some whisky and told
me we had done all that was possible.   At the collecting
station we were all quickly dressed, and then I was taken
to the dressing station, where I asked if I was mortally
hit; the surgeon answering he could not say.   I found Green-
wood and Moss there, both showing great sympathy.   The
thing that upset me most was finding Seymour on a stretcher,
but he quickly reassured me, saying it was in the foot.   As
soon as they could they put us into ambulances, and then
began the long weary jolt to camp.   I went with Seymour
and two men.   Arrived at the field hospital I was put in
a tent with the former, and dressed by Robinson, whose
investigations were satisfactory.

The above, of course, is purely my own personal
experience, but I understand from all sides that the whole
Battalion behaved as Grenadiers should, and that where
they fell back, they did so as if in the Park !   As Gilmour
took them out of action and was able to see, I asked him
to do all necessary reporting, except as to those who came
under my own eye and whose names I gave him.   I
cannot speak sufficiently of the kindness I received from
all the medical officers without exception, and the same
applies to the men.

When the fight was over the Boers came down, and
although they took Murray's watch and belt, and what
ammunition and rifles they could find, they covered the
wounded up and treated them kindly.   A good many were

sadly burnt. They were mostly brought in in ambulances that night, including Murray, who was very dangerously wounded, his thigh being broken.

I asked Gilmour to mention the following who came under my notice :—

Lieutenant E. Seymour, 2nd Lieutenant A. Murray, Colour-Sergeant Morgan.

Officers :—

Killed	—
Died of wounds	I
(2nd Lieutenant Alesdair Murray.)	
Wounded	4

(Lieutenant-Colonel Lloyd, Capt. Corkran, Capt. Bonham, Lieutenant E. Seymour.)

N.C.O.'s and Men :—

Total killed	33
Died of wounds (one of burns)	7
Wounded dangerously, severely, or slightly	95
(Seven of these were burnt.)	
Missing (prisoners)	8
(Two of these were wounded.)	
Total casualties..	148

The casualties reported on the spot show a total of 143, but the remainder were found afterwards.

LORD CAVAN'S* ACCOUNT.

My recollections of the action at Biddulphsberg are as follows :—

We regimental officers knew nothing of the tactical or strategical situation either before, or for some time

---

* Lord Cavan was at the time Captain The Viscount Kilcoursie.

after, the 29th May, 1900. I can, therefore, only say what happened on the day itself from my own point of view, leaving out everything I have heard since.

The Battalion had been divided on the 27th or 28th of May, and I believe the right half only joined the left half as we marched out of camp near Senekal early on the 29th. We started in eight lines of companies extended to 8 or 10 paces in the direction of Lindley. The order of companies was Nos. 5, 6, 7, 8, 1, 2, 3, 4.

We marched in this direction for three or four miles, with our right flank some 1,500 to 2,000 yards from the base of the big Biddulphsberg kopje. Nothing happened until the whole eight companies were exposed to view of the reverse side of the kopje, when a Boer gun close to a farm opened fire. We then got the order to change direction right, and so face the gun instead of presenting our right flank to it. We halted for a short time in rear of a mealie field. During this halt one of our batteries came into action on our left and fired at the Boer gun.

I could not see any sign of the enemy except the smoke from their gun. Very shortly after this I remember getting the stirring order, " The Grenadiers will take the gun."

We at once advanced through the mealies, and, on our coming out into the open, the enemy—still marvellously concealed—opened a heavy fire, but fortunately aimed rather high, as at first the bullets passed over our heads. I saw one man in No. 6 fall, but the lines pressed on through the high grass straight for the gun. After we had been going for about half-a-mile, the order suddenly came to halt and lie down. Personally, I was on tenterhooks lest No. 6 should advance and my company, No. 7, should not see them ; so for some two hours I bobbed up and down to see if anybody in my front moved. During this time I, with my glasses, spotted one Boer on the extreme top of the pinnacle at the nearest end of the kopje. He wore a straw hat. This was the only Boer I saw all day. While we lay in the grass the enemy's bullets kept on striking the ground all round, and I told the men near me to scrape up a bit of cover with their bayonets, which they did. As far as I was concerned, nothing further happened of interest until about 4 p.m., when the Adjutant came up to me and said, " The Battalion will retire by companies from the front, each company covering the retirement of the one next in front of it." I passed this order to my left and right down the ranks of my company, and waited for Nos. 5 and 6 to come back. After a short while, I saw about six men coming back toward me in slow time, and I conjectured that these were No. 5, and that the remainder must be further to a flank. I then got ready to cover the retirement of No. 6, but nobody came. After waiting some time, I went up to where I had seen No. 6, and found three or four men lying in the grass, and said, " Have you got the order to retire ?" They said they " hadn't heard it," so I told them to pass the order down their company, and then I went back to my old place. Still nobody came. Corkran then came up and said to me, " Why don't No. 6 retire ?" and I told him what had happened. He at once went up to them and in a few minutes returned to me. Again nobody came. I said, " It's my turn now," and went once more to No. 6 and told the men I saw to take the order from me to retire, as I guessed that probably their officers had been hit, though I knew nothing of what had really happened.

Some six or seven men came back then through my centre, and as I got back to where I had left Corkran, I found him wounded in the thigh. After firing a very few rounds at the kopje, I passed the order to No. 7 to retire, and waited some three or four minutes to let the order get to right and left of my company (Forester and Cary). I then started back, helping Corkran, and I saw, as I thought, the whole of my company retiring slowly in one good line. A man (McCormick) was hit in the calf, and was helped out by his neighbours, and the retirement was good, steady, and worthy of the Regiment. We passed through successive companies for some time, and I really forget exactly what happened then, except that a "pom-pom" shelled us on the way home, and we marched over miles of burnt ground.

The roll of the company was called on return, and we found 7 men missing. These men were all on the extreme left of the company; they did not receive the order to retire, and were captured by the Boers. I expect that, like many others in the rear lines during the long wait, they were overcome by the sun and fell fast asleep. Still I was responsible, and felt this incident very keenly. I ought to have found out sooner that they were missing, and either have gone back for them or else have asked No. 8 to help me: a valuable lesson in the extraordinary difficulty of keeping control of an extended line in action!

The above are the actual facts, which I saw for myself, relating to the small part that I played in the battle. I have put in nothing of what I merely heard, nor any points that were made obvious at a later date.

LIEUTENANT LORAINE'S ACCOUNT.

Tuesday, May 29th, 1900.—The previous evening we had camped six miles from Senekal. This morning the

Battalion advanced about six miles in attack formation, working round the right of the Boer position, which was on a steep kopje with a spur running out on the western face. We had to dodge a large grass fire which had started on our right, and we halted about 10 a.m. while our guns came into action on our left. A Boer gun opened from low down on a spur to our left front. After we had been shelling it for fifteen minutes, the order came, "The Grenadiers will advance and take the gun." The Battalion at once advanced in column, extending to five paces, with 200 paces distance between companies, in the following order—5, 6, 7, 8, 1, 2, 3, 4—first through a tall mealie field, and then across grass, till within about 2,000 yards (?) of the kopje, when the Battalion was ordered to lie down. The Boers started firing at us as soon as we entered the open.

No. 5 began firing volleys, and No. 6 went forward, prolonging the firing-line to the right, led by the Commanding Officer. At this point Murray was hit in the thigh by an expanding bullet. No 4 section of No. 6 did not get the order to join the firing-line, but remained in rear of No. 5 ; we got into position about 12. Our battery several times silenced the Boer gun for a short time, but it always opened fire again. The Boers were occupying a kopje on our left, and had another gun there. They enfiladed our lines with rifle fire. The C.O. was severely wounded in the front line, Bonham was shot through the shoulder, and Seymour was hit in the foot. About 3 p.m. the order was passed up to fall back. Corkran, while passing up this order with No. 7, was slightly wounded in the leg, but managed to ride back with No. 8. Directly Nos. 5 and 6 got up to fall back, a very heavy fire indeed was opened on them, and it lasted some time till the artillery partially got it under by vigorously shelling the hill. The Battalion fell back in very good order, company by company from the front. All this time the veldt fire had been raging on the right, and several wounded men were burnt to death. No. 8's ammunition-carriers behaved very well, and, together with two others, were the only men to reach the firing-line. Bevan was badly wounded, but Smart and Riley returned untouched. Just as No. 8 fell back, a "pom-pom" opened from Biddulphsberg, but the Battalion was screened by the smoke of the fire, and it caused only one casualty among the gunners.

Quilter went back with volunteers from No. 1 and rescued a number of wounded men from the fire.

Afterwards, when the R.A.M.C. and the Boers arrived on the field, he fell back. The Battalion returned to Monday night's camp and bivouacked.

Casualties :—

    1 officer killed (died of wounds, 3rd June).

    4 wounded.

    39 men killed.

    12 captured.

    92 wounded.

Nos. 5 and 6 each lost about a half-company.

The Boer General, de Villiers, is wounded in our hospital at Senekal. He is reported to have said that our retirement was the finest thing he had ever seen.

DETAILS OF THE BATTLE LEARNT AFTERWARDS BY LIEUTENANT LORAINE.

In front of Nos. 5 and 6—the firing line—the ground sloped gently down to a water course 400 yards away, with little natural grouse-butts hollowed out in the bank.

From one of these 270 empty cartridge cases were picked up. On our left front was a small dam, about 50 yards long, which had been occupied by the enemy, and from which most of our casualties were caused. In rear of these natural entrenchments the ground was clear for 500 or 600 yards to the foot of the hill. If our left or right had been extended by the length of a half-company, it would have been possible completely to enfilade and turn out these Boers ; they would have had no cover for their retreat, and all would have been killed before they reached the rocks on the hill-side. The gun on the hill was in a sheep kraal near a farm, and the ground all round was absolutely covered with shrapnel bullets.

ANOTHER OFFICER'S ACCOUNT.

The following is an account of the action written by a subaltern officer, who was present with one of the centre lines :—The early part of the day I will not touch on except to say that the advance through the mealie fields— the whole company in line with an extension of eight paces—was one of the stiffest jobs we had to do. That was before the Battalion changed direction to the right to attack the kopje. The company to which I belonged was somewhat in the centre of the Battalion—by the mercy of Providence, though at the time we cursed our bad luck? As we were too far back to see actually what was going on in front, I can only speak exactly to what I saw. My company was conforming to the movements of the others in front. Where we eventually halted and lay down was on the crest of a hardly perceptible ridge from which the ground sloped very gently down to the foot of Biddulphs-berg to the front and away to the dressing-station in the rear. The fall was more noticeable to the rear, and I remember the feeling of thankfulness with which I was able when we retired over this little ridge for the last time that day, to look back and see no more than the top half of the kopje. It gave one the mild feeling of security which cover from view does, but, as a matter of fact, the very fall of the ground was calculated to assist the fall of the bullets, and accounted for a good many of the casualties in rear.

The usual barbed wire fence ran rather diagonally across this ridge, and was a good landmark.

We lay there from about 12 noon to 4 p.m. when we retired. Of course, no one knew exactly what was going on in front, and the crest was too high for us to see. Ammunition-carriers and stretcher-bearers passed through to the firing line from time to time, but not many came back, and we could only gather that things were going pretty badly.

The men for a long time were anxious to get on, and then most of them went to sleep. The company had from 8 to 10 men hit, though none dangerously, which helped to maintain the interest.

A little time before we got the order from the second-in-command to retire, the veldt fire, which had been burning rather away from us most of the day, came round and bore down from the right-rear of the Battalion. The men lay where they were until compelled to move, and then lay down again in their old places.

I saw several of the men who had been some distance away from the N.C.O.'s, with their hair and their faces singed, having lain in their places rather than retire even a few paces without an order.

Soon afterwards, Major Gordon-Gilmour (second-in-command), who had, I believe, been up to the front with the Adjutant, passed through and gave the order for us to retire when the companies in front had passed through. It was only then that we learnt how bad things were, and that the Commanding Officer and Murray had been severely hit. Bonham we had seen from the distance going very short, and therefore knew he was wounded. When we got back to the dressing station, I heard that there were a number of wounded still left out and some burnt. It was at this time that Quilter—the fighting being practically over—obtained permission to take some men back and see what they could do to save the wounded. He called for volunteers, and I understand that the whole of his half-company urged him to take them back with him. As, however, time was pressing, he accepted the nearest twenty men, who took off their equipment, laid down their arms, and got what stretchers were available from the dressing station—I believe about four or five. Quilter then divided his men into couples, telling them they must work quite independently, and not look for orders or assistance from him or anybody else. He then extended each couple to 50 or 60 paces, and gave them the direction where they would probably find most of the wounded.

There was still a considerable amount of firing going on by the Boers, and on our side by the West Kents, who were covering our retirement; but the latter left off when told that the wounded were still lying on the field.

When Quilter's party had gone some distance towards the firing-line, the veldt fire had crossed diagonally to where the wounded were mostly lying, but they succeeded in rescuing several men who must otherwise have been burnt. It is difficult to estimate numbers, but it could easily be seen that the rescue party were working hard under a still heavy fire, and were picking up the men and

D

carrying them away. Quilter did his best to find the Commanding Officer and Murray, but it was impossible to do so, as no one knew exactly where they were lying. We afterwards heard that the former had been brought in.

By this time the firing was practically over, and the Boers were coming down to where our firing-line had been. I saw Austin and Corporal Thomas at work in the firingl ine and learnt that they had found poor Murray, and that he was dead. This, however, was not the case for he did not die until two days afterwards.

I had previously seen Austin go out, and I believe he came under a heavy fire. Curiously enough, neither Quilter nor any of his men were hit, although at times they were under a very considerable fire. They reached camp about 8.30 p.m., some time after my company and the remainder of the Battalion had got in.

CHAPTER IV.

MAJOR GORDON-GILMOUR'S COMMAND.

May 30th. The following wire was received from Lord Roberts:—"Boers reinforced from Heilbron. Clements' brigade will be in Senekal to-night. Rail open to Mafeking. I am across Vaal in several places." The Battalion marched to a fresh camp four miles S.W. of Senekal in consequence of a telegram from Brabant saying that he wished for help at Ficksburg. Clements was now at Senekal, and Lord Methuen marching to Lindley to relieve Colonel Sprague.

May 31st.—We marched six miles south to a fresh camp.

June 1st.—Marched 10 miles to Hibernia.

June 2nd.—Marched 10 miles to Hammonia, where Brabant and the Colonial Division were found in camp.

June 3rd.—A day of rest. We heard that the C.O. was doing well, and that Seymour and Bonham and 60 wounded had gone to Bloemfontein ; in fact, those who were well enough to move. Poor Murray died about 8 p.m. A telegram came in saying that Lord Roberts had seized the junction of the Natal and Orange Free State Railway, and that General French was in Johannesburg.

June 4th.—Nos. 3 and 4 went to occupy the hills E. and W. of camp. Bitterly cold nights, over ¼ in. of ice every morning.

June 5th.—The Battalion played a cricket match against the Scots Guards. At 5.45 p.m. a telegram came saying that Pretoria had unconditionally surrendered to Lord Roberts after severe fighting.

June 6th.—Scots Guards left for Klip Nek. Our ox-waggon and Cape boy started alone for Winburg through many of the enemy. (See 15th June.)

June 7th.—The Battalion marched 7 miles to Klip Nek on the road to Senekal. Furious thunderstorms and floods of rain, soaking everybody.

June 8th.—The 1st Battalion Leinster Regiment joined the Brigade. 2nd Lieutenant Stephen joined the Battalion.

June 9th.—We remained in camp. The Boers occupied a hill 4,000 yards away, whence they shelled the Yeomanry.

June 10th.—Still in camp in front of the Boer position, which extended from General's Hill to Spitz Kop. Rooi-

kranz, a precipitous cliff opposite, was said to be the main
position. At midnight No. 3 company was sent out to
support No. 8, which, with No. 1—the whole under Major
Marshall—was holding a high hill 1½ miles to the east ot
camp. The purpose was to repel a Boer attack, which,
however, never came off.

June 12th.—Still in the same position.

June 13th.—Same position. Lord Roberts's proclamation that all Boers who had not surrendered by the
25th would be treated as rebels, be fined £100 each, and
forfeit all their property, reached us.

June 14th.—The East Yorkshire and guns left us
for Hammonia, and a half-battalion of the Leinster left
with a convoy. The Battalion was on outpost duty, guarding the Nek.

June 15th.—Cooks and transport-men were formed
into a reserve. The Leinster outposts were sniped. The
ox-waggon which had started on 6th June for Winburg
returned safely with stores—a good performance.

June 16th.—Marched back to Hammonia. Bivouacked
on high kopjes on Trommel road.

June 17th.—In camp.

June 18th.—East Yorkshire left us for Trommel.

June 20th.—In the same position. Every kopje on
Senekal-Hammonia line was being garrisoned by small
parties of troops.

June 21st.—Scots Guards marched at 3 a.m. to the
Nek, as Dalgety had located 400 Boers on a kopje; but
they had vacated their position, Dalgety having withdrawn his men too soon.

June 22nd.—Marched 15 miles to Five-Mile Bottom. The Battalion was to hold the hill above Senekal and Klip Nek, and Boyes' Brigade Ficksburg and Hammonia. Clements was to move by forced marches on Bethlehem from Senekal, to attack Boers in rear.

June 23rd.—Marched 11 miles to Senekal. Our right flank got heavily sniped. The left half-battalion entrenched themselves on the hill above the town.

June 24th.—Half-rations.

June 25th.—Marched six miles down the Trommel road. The Scots Guards went to Winburg with convoy.

June 26th.—Marched eight miles to Doornfontein.

June 27th.—Full rations again except biscuit and flour.

June 28th.—Clements started for Bethlehem, the Boer seat of Government, with a flying column. We learnt that our ultimate destination was Harrismith.

June 29th.—The Scots Guards arrived with a convoy bringing Corkran, Parker, Henry Seymour, and a draft of 100 men. The Battalion for the first time slept in tents; there were 40 of these; we also got second blankets.

July 3rd.—The left half-battalion started for Winburg with a convoy, Major Gordon-Gilmour in command. It marched 30 miles, leaving the right half-battalion at Doornberg.

THE LEFT HALF-BATTALION.

July 4th.—We marched 12 miles.

July 5th.—We marched nine miles into Winburg. Arrived at 11.15 a.m. Drill-Sergeant Thomas left us to go to the 1st Battalion in England as Sergeant-Major.

July 8th.—We marched off at 6.45 a.m. with convoy bound for Senekal. We did 13 miles and came on the site of Clements' camp when he was attacked on the Senekal road.

July 10th.—Marched at 3 a.m., arriving at Senekal at 8 a.m., and found that the right half-battalion had proceeded in the direction of Bethlehem.

June 11th.—Nos. 6 and 7 companies went on with half the convoy. We heard that Clements and Rundle were at Middleburg and moving on Lindley, also that the Boers were in an entrenched position at Fouriesburg.

July 14th.—We marched at noon and came up with Clements on the far side of Middleburg at a place called Zurin Kranz.

July 15th.—Marched at 7 a.m., arriving at Witkop at 10 a.m. and found Rundle's last waggon just leaving. An escaped Yeoman reported 2,000 Boers opposite us, with 35 British officers as prisoners. Marched again at 1 p.m. to a point 7 miles off Wit Nek, where the right half-battalion was, with two guns and two naval 12-prs. belonging to the Cape Mounted Rifles.

THE RIGHT HALF-BATTALION.

July 4th.—Left half-battalion moved two miles west to Spitkop, where with two guns and some I.Y. they were to protect the supply depôt formed at that place. No. 2, under Murray-Threipland, went on escort duty to Hammonia, rejoining the half-battalion at 1.30 a.m., after a march of 28 miles.

July 5th.—Receiving orders to move the depôt at once to Vlakspruit we loaded up and got off at 9 p.m., arriving at our destination at 2 a.m. on the 6th.

July 7th.—Escorted convoy towards Senekal.

July 9th.—Marched at 6 a.m. to Senekal, thence on about three miles north.

July 10th.—Marched at 6 a.m., and bivouacked about two miles north of Biddulphsberg.

July 11th.—Marched at 6.30 a.m. nearly south, passing the field of Biddulphsberg; came to Clements' camp about four miles on, then on another four miles where we were to bivouac. As soon as the outposts were posted, we were ordered on again, marching in a circle, as our guide had lost his way. We bivouacked eventually at 7 p.m., within a mile of where we had been at 4 p.m.

July 12th-15th.—The half-battalion, with two guns, was ordered to occupy a hill about five miles from Witkop, where our main camp lay. We very nearly got burned up here by a grass fire. We remained on this hill till the 15th, when the half-battalion marched to near Wittener, where we were found by the left half-battalion.

July 16th.—Turned out at breakfast time to fire on a party of Boers entering Wit Nek. We drove them behind a hill, but they got into the Brandwater Basin, passing in after dark.

July 17th.—Sniping all day, especially at our outposts going out.

July 18th.—De Wet and Olivier with 1,500 Boers slipped out of the Brandwater Basin.

July 19th.—We marched at 3 30 p.m. Clements having arrived and reached, Berzuindenhouts Kraal at 8.30 p.m. where we found General Rundle, the Scots Guards and

Brabant. As the wagons stuck in a drift, the rear-guard did not get into camp until 3.30 a.m.

July 20th.—Rundle and the Scots Guards left the Boers in position at Rooi Kranz, 3,500 yards from the right front.

July 23rd.—The Battalion made a general demonstration against Rooi Kranz, moving out at 5.30 a.m. It advanced in attack formation, lay down, and, after firing all day, fell back at dusk. Only one casualty in No. 1. It was reported that Hunter had captured Reteifs Nek, and that Clements was about to attack Slabberts Nek.

July 25th.—The Boers evacuated the position on Rooi Kranz. Hunter and Clements joined hands inside the Brandwater Basin.

July 26th.—General Campbell, with three companies and some Yeomanry, made a reconnaisance to Rooi Kranz, and found the place deserted. Four Boers surrendered in the morning. General Rundle passed through Commando Nek and occupied Ficksburg. The Battalion remained at Berzuindenhouts Kraal.

July 28th.—Marched at 9 a.m. towards Fouriesburg, the Battalion having been sent for by General Rundle on the 25th; but unfortunately the native runner got drunk and was therefore three days late. Camped that night two miles beyond Great Nek.

July 29th.—Marched at 7 30 a.m. Drifts very bad. Oxen absolutely exhausted. Reached Commando Nek at midnight. Halted two hours and then went on to Generals Nek, were the Manchester was encamped.

July 30th.—Marched at 6.15 a.m. and crossing Generals Nek moved into the Brandwater Basin. At 9.50 a.m. an orderly arrived saying, that 5,000 Boers had

surrendered to General Rundle.   Hunter is at Fouriesburg,
Rundle 15 miles in front.   The Leinster has had a little
fighting (40 casualties).   The Scots Guards had one officer
wounded, two men killed, and 20 wounded, in an engagement near Golden Gate.   The Battalion crossed the Brand
River Drift at 11 a.m. and reached Brindisi at mid-day.
Bivouacked for the night three miles beyond Brindisi
en route for little Caledon Poort, 13 miles further on.   The
Manchester moved to Fouriesburg.

July 31st.—Marched at 6.45 a.m.   Crossed the Little
Caledon river.   Up to this only the Ficksburg commando
(8,000 men and one gun) had surrendered.   The Wepener,
Thaba 'Nchu, and another commando still undecided.   At
mid-day, Hunter's, Rundle's, Clements', and Paget's camp
was reached, but only Paget was still there.   Boer
prisoners in batches of 200 were passed returning to
Fouriesburg.   Camped a mile further on—*i.e.*, 11 miles.
Found a Boer gun and 8 waggons of ammunition in our
camp.

August 1st.—Marched at 6 a.m. 3 miles to Rundle's
camp on Surrender Hill, Slaapkranz, arriving at 9.40 a.m.
2,500 burghers surrendered this morning, passing through
a double line of sentries along the road.   Steyn, De Wet,
and Olivier had escaped.   Scots Guards went to Naauerpoort to relieve troops sent after De Wet.

August 2nd.—Prinsloo came in with all his burghers,
about 4,000 men.   The Battalion marched at 11.50 a.m. to
Naauerpoort Nek, 8 miles, and bivouacked.

August 3rd.—Marched at 7 a.m. to Groendraai, 16
miles on the Harrismith road, where we arrived at 11 a.m.
A great number of No. 1 Company's kits were burnt by a
grass fire.

August 4th.—Marched at 7 a.m. 12 miles.

August 5th.—Marched at 5 a.m. Crossed De Klerks Drift and halted after seven hours marching at Elands River Drift, 8½ miles. Marched again at 3.30 p.m. 10 miles to Roger's Farm, arriving at 7.30 p.m.

August 6th.—Marched 6 miles to a camp five miles west of Harrismith.

August 7th.—Formal entry into Harrismith. All the troops marched past the Lieutenant-General in the square, and then camped on the race-course. No. 3 Company was escort to the General. We found a guard at the railway station over 82 Boer prisoners.

August 9th.—First train arrived from Ladysmith. The Battalion took up ordinary camp routine—guards, pickets, battalion parades, etc.

August 10th.—Right half-battalion went into camp on the north side of the town.

August 12th.—No. 8 Company went to headquarter camp on the north side of the town.

August 13th.—Lieutenant Jeffreys went down to Ladysmith in charge of prisoners.

August 20th.—Nos. 5, 6, and 7 Companies came into headquarters.

August 26th.—The Battalion marched at 8.40 a.m. in the direction of Reitz, and bivouacked 12 miles from Harrismith. With the column was also the 79th Battery and some Yeomanry—the Scots Guards and the Leinster were to join later—General Campbell in command of the force. It carried food for 21 days in the wagons.

August 27th.—Marched at 8.10 a.m., crossed Wilge River, and camped eight miles from starting-point. At

5 p.m. the Captain of No. 7 Company sent in to say: "Enemy in sight and attacking in force." The Battalion stood to arms, but found that the alarm had been caused by two officers shooting ducks! Certain officers were therefore able to return to their previous occupation of experimenting as to how much cordite was necessary to blow up an ant-hill.

August 28th.—Did not move.

August 29th.—Marched 11 miles in the direction of Bethlehem.

August 30th.—Marched 14 miles to within sight of Bethlehem. The oxen dying fast owing to the very wet weather.

August 31st.—Marched 9 miles into Bethlehem. Nos. 6 and 7 on outpost N.W. of town, 4 and 5 in the town, 1, 2, 3, and 8 on outpost south of the town.

September 1st.—No move.

September 2nd.—The Leinster arrived. We held a dinner in commemoration of the anniversary of the battle of Omdurman, several officers having been at it with the 1st Battalion.

September 3rd.—The 2nd Battalion Scots Guards arrived, bringing Colby and Houstoun-Boswall with them.

September 4th.—Marched at 2.30 p.m. *en route* for Ficksburg, to relieve two companies of the Worcester, held up there by Haarsbroek. The Battalion camped at Retiefs Nek. An issue of clothing was made to the men.

September 5th.—Marched at 8 a.m. to Wit Hoek on the Brandwater River. About 11 miles.

September 6th.—Marched 16 miles to within two miles of Generals Nek.

September 7th.—Crossed Generals Nek and camped on Commando Nek, where we found a company of the Worcester.

September 8th.—Entered Ficksburg at noon, halted until 4 p.m. and then marched to Ladybrand Poort, where the Battalion bivouacked. Distance, 11 miles.

September 9th.—Marched 12 miles to Spitz Kop, over a big dam, where there was some excellent duck shooting. 1,500 Boers reported at Naauerpoort Nek. De Wet was said to be at Wit Kop, and a force of Yeomanry was also said to be holding Mequatlings Nek.

September 15th.—We still found ourselves at Spitz Kop on Wilkins's Farm.

September 16th.—Marched at 2 p.m. to Trommel, 11 miles.

September 17th.—Marched 20 miles to a camp near the Winburg-Senekal Road. 2,800 Boers were said to be in the Doornburg. General Rundle between Senekal and Ventersburg, with a draft for the Battalion, and the 17th Brigade. Bruce Hamilton at Winburg. Rundle had an engagement at Senekal Hill, and wounded Haarsbroek.

September 18th.—Marched 11 miles to a camp twelve miles from Senekal.

September 19th.—The Worcester went to join Rundle in Senekal. We were ordered to form a flying column with Le Gallais and continue the pursuit of De Wet. The Battalion marched 11 miles to Sjan Boksfontein in the direction of Wit Nek, the Boers being said to be at Wit Kop. Capt. Cavendish left in hospital at Winburg.

September 20th.—Marched 11 miles, leaving Tafelburg on the left, to a camp on Nek, four miles south-east of Wit Kop. The Boers, 800 strong, had sacked Hiscock's Store, on the Senekal-Bethlehem road, in the direction of Lindley.

September 21st.—Marched 13 miles round west side of Wit Kop and then, pointing N.E., bivouacked at Hiscock's Store. Douglas-Pennant rejoined the Battalion, also Shafto and Foster with a draft of 200 men.

September 22nd.—Marched 12 miles towards Bethlehem.

September 23rd.—Marched 10 miles into camp, three miles beyond Bethlehem.

September 25th.—Marched 14 miles towards Reitz and camped.

September 26th.—Marched 10 miles and camped at Fanny's Hole, on the left of the Bethlehem-Reitz road.

September 27th.—Marched 9 miles in the direction of Heilbron and camped in order to gain touch with General Rundle.

September 28th.—Marched 9 miles to Fontein Reit, east of Elands Kop, where General Rundle had driven off the Boers.

September 29th.—The Battalion marched out 4½ miles to meet General Rundle and the "Cow Gun" (5 in.), and escorted them into camp.

September 30th.—Marched 19 miles (the point being only 10) owing to a mistake of the guiding Staff Officer.

October 1st.—Remained in camp. General Hunter arrived with Le Gallais.

October 2nd.—Marched off at 5.45 a.m. in south-easterly direction. At noon the Battalion was heading N.W. and had covered 17 miles. A halt was then made for an hour, after which the Battalion again marched another 3 miles into camp. General Boyes left the column for Reitz.

October 3rd.—Marched 11 miles to Tafel Kop. The Yeomanry had a skirmish with the Boers and lost three men wounded.

October 4th.—Marched 16 miles to Diepfontein on the Vrede road.

October 5th.—Arrived at Vrede, six miles, at 8 a.m.

October 6th.—A convoy started for Standerton, escorted by the Scots Guards and Leinster, under General Campbell.

October 7th.—No. 8 company occupied a hill on the west of the town. Seymour's outposts heavily sniped at 10.30 p.m. for about half-an-hour, when all was quiet. No casualties. Many bullets came into the camp, which was pitched on the enemy's side of the hill.

October 8th.—The Battalion busy entrenching. Slight sniping during the day.

October 9th.—No. 7 company and guns went out in the morning to the east, and had a skirmish with about 70 Boers. Heavy firing, but no casualties. Shatfo and his company were sniped during the night on Signallers' Hill.

October 10th.—Entrenchments finished.

October 11th.—Lord Ardee's company had a certain amount of firing on Signallers' Hill in the morning. A convoy was in sight and arrived in camp after a heavy fight, bringing Lieutenant-Colonel Lloyd, who rejoined the Battalion, having recovered from his wounds.

CHAPTER V.

Lieutenant-Colonel Lloyd's Resumed Command.

October 12th.—The Battalion moved out at 7.30 a.m. for the purpose of devastating the country. It was part of the following force : the 2nd Battalion Grenadier Guards, the 2nd Battalion Scots Guards, Yeomanry, one Battery, and one 4·7 gun drawn by 24 oxen. Two companies under Major Scott-Kerr were sent to the west of a kopje about 1,000 feet high with orders to hold a kraal below it. Two other companies under Major Gordon-Gilmour held two ridges, and two companies were escort to the guns. The remaining two companies were held as a reserve to the Scots Guards. Major Scott-Kerr was soon engaged, and kept up a heavy fire of volleys. The other companies on the left becoming engaged at the same time, the Boers delivering a heavy fire on all points. The guns shelled the kopjes, and Scott-Kerr, finding his position commanded, scaled the heights above it with fixed bayonets, leaving Cholmeley to hold the kraal below. A donga in front was cleared by Threipland, and the Boers decamped. A farm was then heavily shelled by the 4·7 gun. This ended the skirmish. The Battalion lost five men wounded, four slightly, and one seriously.

October 13th.—The Battalion, about 1,000 strong, was paraded by the Commanding Officer, who told them how glad he was to have returned, and still more to hear how highly General Rundle spoke of the work they had done. During the night a veritable storm of thunder, lightning, dust and rain rose; no one had much sleep.

October 14th.—The force marched at 10 a.m., three companies of Grenadiers as advance guard, four companies right flank-guard. The march continued for some 14 miles through a heavy dust storm and then bivouacked. The Boers sniped more or less all day but had no effect.

THE ENEMY

Squadron of I.Y.

A Company extended in sections
20 paces between sections
5 paces between men

$\frac{1}{4}$ Company
1,000 yds. away

$\frac{1}{4}$ Company
1,000 yds. away

$\frac{1}{4}$ Company
1,000 yds. away

$\frac{1}{4}$ Company
1,000 yds. away

........About 1,000 yards........

A Company in line

Two guns

A Company | in fours

Rear-guard ambulance

October 15th.—The column made a long march to a camp about 14 miles East of Reitz, getting in at 5 p.m. The rear-guard, under the command of Lieutenant-Colonel Lloyd, and consisting of four companies of Grenadiers, two guns, and a squadron of Yeomanry, was disposed as follows :—(1) The squadron in the rear; (2) next a company extended in sections, with twenty paces between the sections, and five paces between the men; (3) about 1,000 yards in front of this—nearer the column—one company, practically in line; (4) in front of this again the two guns; (5) and still further in front the rear-guard ambulance. The flanks of the rear-guard were protected by a half-company on either flank in column of sections.

The other four companies of Grenadiers formed the right flank-guard of the column, while four companies of the Scots Guards formed the left flank-guard of the column. The flank-guards throughout the whole length of the column were generally disposed in sub-sections about 1,000 yards away. A long tiring day. The Yeomanry flank-guard was sniped. The weather hot by day, but thick ice on the buckets in the morning.

October 16th.—At 6.30 a.m. the Lieutenant-General with half a battalion under Gordon-Gilmour, Yeomanry, 4'7 gun, and guns, went back on yesterday's route to burn a barn where a woman had shot at Major Cavendish.*

October 17th (Vlakfontein).—The Battalion marched at 7.30., Lieutenant-Colonel Lloyd in command of the rear-guard. He had with him four companies of the Battalion. The enemy made several attempts to attack the rear-guard, but were easily driven off.

---

* Major Cavendish was Intelligence Officer to General Rundle and must not be confused with Captain Cavendish.

E

October 18th (Vlakfontein).—General Rundle went out at 5.30 on a punitive expedition, taking with him some guns and three companies of Grenadiers under Major Marshall. A farm was burnt, the inhabitants collected, etc., etc. There was a good deal of desultory fire but no casualties. After the return of this party the force moved off and in the evening reached Reitz, near which it bivouacked. The Cavalry killed and wounded three Boers during the day.

October 19th.—The force, starting at 6 a.m., made a long uneventful march through Reitz to Tiger Kloof Spruit, being sniped at most of the way; Lieutenant-Colonel Lloyd again commanding the rear-guard.

October 20th.—The force remained at Tiger Kloof Spruit, being joined by Generals Rundle and Boyce, who came on from Reitz, with a battalion which was to occupy Bethlehem.

October 21st.—The march continued to Muhlers Rust, Lieutenant-Colonel Lloyd commanding the rear-guard.

October 22nd.—March to Witkop, Lieutenant-Colonel Lloyd in command of the advance-guard.

October 23rd.—Instead of marching to Harrismith as was expected, the force marched to Vogelsfontein, five miles from Bethlehem. Lieutenant-Colonel Lloyd commanded the rear-guard and shelled the Boers, who at one time were somewhat aggressive, following up and sniping. A lot of firing all the morning in the direction of Bethlehem. The Boers sent in to borrow an ambulance, which was refused, but some bandages, etc., were sent instead.

October 24th.—Troops rested all day, but at 7 p.m. Lieutenant-Colonel Lloyd received an order to move the three squadrons of Yeomanry. a half-battalion of Grenadiers—Nos. 1, 3, 4 and 7—and two days' supplies to Bethlehem. This was done, the force arriving outside the town at about 10 p.m. after a pitch dark march. Owing to defective staff arrangements on the part of a Brigade Major of the 17th Brigade, the Battalion did not reach its bivouac on the other side of the town until 1 a.m., and then had to lie down without blankets or waterproof sheets in pouring rain.

October 25th (Bethlehem).—At 2.45 a.m. the half-battalion paraded in drenching rain with orders to attack a farm house which was said to be loopholed and strongly held. The advance was covered by guns. By good fortune the farm had been evacuated, otherwise it would have been a most disagreeable business. The force got back to camp by 8 a.m., wet through.

October 26th (Bethlehem).—The force marched at 5 a.m., Lieutenant-Colonel Lloyd in command of the advance-guard. After crossing the drift near Vogels-fontein, General Rundle rode forward with a squadron and reconnoitred the Langberg. He was suddenly fired on heavily at about 500 yards range. Lieutenant-Colonel Lloyd at once pushed forward with his advance-guard, one company of Grenadiers, and brought two guns into action. The enemy retired on to the Langberg, an enormous kopje about 200 yards in front. It was evidently strongly held. The other half-battalion of Grenadiers, the Scots Guards and the 4.7 gun were now sent for. They came up gradually and the position of the force was as follows : one company Grenadiers under Lord Ardee relieving the Yeomanry in the advanced position, with orders to hold but not to advance, which orders were carried out to the end of the day : No. 6 on the right, under Jeffreys, holding a kraal; No. 3, under Blackett, on the right rear; No. 1, under

Quilter, on the left front; No. 7, under Lord Cavan, escort
to the guns.   The other three companies were relieved by
the Scots Guards, and brought up to the Commanding
Officer with the guns by Gilmour.   Eventually No. 3
joined this company.   A very heavy fire was now being delivered and returned.   An attempt was made by the Scots
Guards to turn the left of the kopje, making a wide movement round our right, but owing to the rugged and
precipitous nature of the ground this was impossible.
General Campbell then took them round the left and
attempted to take a farm by a donga.   This farm was
under the kopje to the left front.   General Rundle's orders
were to take the farm without loss, if possible; if not, to lie
still till night, when he would storm the kopje.   The three
companies of Scots Guards were launched and passed
through Lord Ardee's company contrary to General
Rundle's intention, there having been some misunderstanding.   Suddenly the three companies at about 4 p.m.
got up and seized the kopje without loss.   In the meantime
the three companies of Grenadiers, under Gilmour—Nos.
5, 7 and 2—moved up the donga on the left and seized the
farm.   They then joined hands with the Scots Guards and
scaled the kopje.   Earlier in the day No. 1 and some
Yeomanry took two kopjes on the extreme left.   The fire
now died away, and General Rundle, in leaving Lieutenant-
Colonel Lloyd in command of the position, withdrew to
where he intended to camp on the other side of a spruit near
Witkop.   At dusk Lieutenant-Colonel Lloyd evacuated his
position and moved into camp.   The casualties were:
Imperial Yeomanry, two men wounded; Grenadiers, four
men wounded; Scots Guards, one officer, Lord Gerald
Grosvenor, wounded severely, two men killed, and nine
wounded.   The Grenadier machine-gun fired 1,200 rounds
during the day.

October 27th.—A day of rest. The dead were buried on the veldt.

October 28th.—The Battalion moved off at 6.30 a.m., and bivouacked at Tweefontein, the place which became famous as Christmas Kop a year later. Lieutenant-Colonel Lloyd commanded the rear-guard, composed of Scots Guards and guns, and had a considerable amount of fighting in passing through Tiger Kloof. The half-battalion of Grenadiers, under Major Gordon-Gilmour, formed part of the advance-guard, which was commanded by Lieutenant-Colonel Pratt, R.F.A.

October 29th.—The force moved on to Elands River bridge and had some fighting. Lieutenant-Colonel Lloyd commanded the advance-guard, composed of Scots Guards and guns, the Grenadiers forming the rear-guard. The camp was formed some five miles beyond Elands River bridge.

October 30th.—The force moved in to Harrismith, and the Battalion took up part of the defensive line. On arrival it was found that all the kits left at the base had been brought up.

October 31st (Harrismith).—Lord Cavan with No. 7 company went by train to Bloemhoff.

November 7th.—Received orders to march at 6 as part of an escort to a convoy under General Campbell to re-victual Reitz.

CHAPTER VI.

Major Gordon-Gilmour again in Command.

November 8th.—At 5.30 a.m. Lieutenant-Colonel Lloyd received orders to take command of the convoy, as General Campbell was ill. He, therefore, handed the command of the Battalion over to Major Gordon-Gilmour. The force, composed as follows, marched at 6.30 a.m.: 2nd Battalion of the Grenadier Guards, a half-battalion East Yorkshire, one company, four squadrons of Imperial Yeomanry, four guns, 60 days' supplies on 84 waggons, 12 days' supplies for the force, in all about 200 vehicles of all sorts.   At 2.30 Majores Drift was reached.   The advance-guard, under Major Wyndham-Quin, reported that they were heavily fired upon from a kopje above the drift, which was strongly held.   The advance-guard guns opened fire at about 2,500 yards, the East Yorkshire were ordered to take the kopje, which was heavily shelled, the Boers waiting for the infantry to come up.   This was done without any casualties, with the exception of one horse being hit.   It being too late to cross the drift, which was heavy and deep, the force encamped.   Very heavy wet and wind came on.

November 9th, 1900.—At 6 a.m. the far kopje was occupied with cavalry and then by the East Yorkshire. Having done this, the convoy was passed over the Wilge River, which was very swollen, and parked on the other side.   This took five hours.   The march was commenced at 11 a.m.   The advance-guard cavalry was sniped by a few Boers, who, however, did no harm.

November 10th.—Marched at 6 a.m., Major Gordon-Gilmour commanding the advance guard, and Major Marshall the rear-guard.   On approaching the kopje on the left and a long ridge on the right, about two miles from camp, the column was heavily fired upon from both flanks.   The one advance-guard gun was brought into action from the right, and the other was placed on a kopje on the left, which had been quickly evacuated by the enemy.   The rear-guard gun was also brought up to the front.   With some little trouble the Boers were driven off. One man of the Derbyshire Yeomanry was killed on the left flank, and another seriously wounded in the front. The advance was now continued. About a mile further on, a most determined attack was made by the enemy on the front and both flanks. The guns were again brought into action with the exception of one which was left to cover the passage of the convoy. The machine-guns were also brought into action. The infantry of the advance-guard and right flank-guard became engaged. After continued firing, the Boers, who had persistently attacked, were driven off with loss. The advance-guard then entered a further defile. The passage was made with safety, although the flanks were dangerously sniped. More open country was now reached, and finally the camping ground.

As it was being occupied, Lieutenant-Colonel Lloyd received a message from the Officer Commanding rear-guard to say that some 30 Yeomen were cut off, and that he was trying to extricate them. Mounted men were at once sent back, and half-a-battalion got ready in support, if necessary. The Yeomanry, in the meantime, extricated themselves and the rear-guard came in safely, though it had some fighting on its way. Total casualties—one killed, two wounded, all Yeomen. Four horses killed, five wounded. 127 shells were fired and a total of 8,000 rounds of S.A.A.

November 11th.—A thick fog prevented the column starting until 7 a.m. The left flank was heavily sniped, and there was also slight opposition in front, which yielded to shell fire. The whole of the column reached Reitz by 2.30 p.m., when it was reported that the Boers had intended if possible to take the convoy.

November 13th.—The column marched at 6 a.m. on its return journey to Harrismith. Instead of going through the defile to Coevins Hoek by which it had come, the other road was taken, and at about ten miles from Reitz the column turned to the right and marched along the ordinary road over Elands River.   There was much sniping on both flanks.   The march of about 18 miles was a heavy one, as there was a difficulty about water.

November 14th.—Marched at 7 a.m.   Very few Boers about until towards the afternoon, when about 100 were reported moving along the left flank, evidently intending to occupy the kopje at Elands River bridge.   It was, however, cleared without opposition, but soon after a heavy fire was delivered on the column from a kopje about 1,800 yards from the left flank.   This caused some delay, and it was therefore late before the column crossed the iron bridge, and encamped on a ridge above the river.   A very long march.

November 15th.—The column did not march till 8 a.m. in order that everyone might have a rest.   The head of the column reached Harrismith about 4 p.m.   It had been a long march to make in three days, but no one was apparently the worse.   About 50 women with children were brought in from Reitz.   The column had marched 105 miles in six days.

November 17th.—Lord Kitchener visited Harrismith for a few hours.   The Battalion was split up into companies to relieve the Scots Guards on the town defences.

November 18th.—No. 5 Company, under Colby, went to Bloemhoff to relieve the Scots Guards coming from there.

CHAPTER VII.

LIEUTENANT-COLONEL LLOYD COMMANDING.

December 4th.—The Battalion was paraded, and the names mentioned by the Lieutenant-General for despatches were read out :—

Special Divisional Order.

Harrismith, 19, 11, 00.

The following names have been brought to the notice of the Lieutenant-General by their Commanding Officers :—

For Valour.

6903, Corporal W. Dickens,
3450, Drummer Douglas Haines.

For Good Service During the Campaign.

8498, Sergeant-Major J. C. Rolinson,
  82, Quarter-Master-Sergeant A. W. Carter,
9796, Sergeant-Major Cook W. Andrews,
9330, Colour-Sergeant J. Morgan,
1721, Pay-Sergeant H. Phipps,
5749, Orderly Room Sergeant F. Martin,
1192, Drill Sergeant F. P. Jones,
1200, Drill Sergeant A. A. S. Thomas,
1703, Drill Sergeant A. Hazlegrove,
1368, Sergeant G. Lloyd,
2947, Sergeant J. Coggins,
4126, Sergeant W. Napier,
4838, Sergeant C. Trim (since dead),
3825, Sergeant F. A. Cooke,
5630, Lance-Sergeant R. James, }Signallers.
1136, Corporal W. Harbourne,

At Biddulphsberg on 29th May, 1900, the following incident occurred :—Lieutenant Quilter, 2nd Battalion Grenadier Guards, and a party of men belonging to his regiment, who volunteered, rescued 12 wounded men under a heavy fire, from being burned to death, as they otherwise would have been by the grass fire. The names of the men are as follows :—

7193, Private D. Petty,
2244, Private W. W. Martin,
4284, Private B. Williams,
2700, Private J. Sherwin,
7331, Private E. Hickman,
6067, Private H. Cooper,
5253, Private M. Dempsey,
7150, Private H. Armitage,
4720, Private R. Seaman,
7096, Private T. Danby,
4258, Private M. Giblin,
5900, Private G. Guilfoyle,
3589, Private W. Jarvis,
2326, Private A. Stagg,
3517, Private H. Houghton,
7317, Private J. Ward,
4740, Private T. Colin,
4744, Private J. Richmond,
7139, Private W. Church,
5417, Private F. White,
6603, Private W. Gorham,
5946, Lance-Corporal H. Gray.

By Order,

(Signed) G. E. HARLEY,
Colonel,
C.S.O., 8th Division.

December 10th.—The Battalion moved out of Harrismith. Our force, commanded by General Campbell, consisting of 2nd Battalion Grenadier Guards, 4 squadrons Imperial Yeomanry, four guns, 79th Battery, one pom-

pom, R.E., Field Hospital Bearer Company, with 14 days'
rations in supply, and three in regimental waggons, started
at 5 a.m. Gilmour was in commanu of the advance-guard,
and Scott-Kerr of the rear-guard, marched on a rounding-
up expedition 11 miles along the Reitz Road. Collected
1,126 cattle, 6,070 sheep. Very hot; halted for the night
at Zout de Beers farm. Very bad water.

December 11th.—Marshall and Cavan with three
companies went rounding-up. Scott-Kerr commanded the
escort, taking Captain Stock to Harrismith.

December 12th.—Marcheu 12 miles S. E., round the
Platberg. Some opposition at starting, which ceased after
three Boers were knocked over. Camped at The Oaks.

December 13th.—Marched at 6 a.m. Were followed
by 40 Boers, who, however, did not venture within range.
Camped at Glen Paul.

December 14th.—Short march up Mooi Hoek. Cavendish had a fall and put his shoulder out, so was obliged to
return to Harrismith.

December 15th to 24th.—The column continued its
rounding-up work.

December 24th.—The Battalion at Bloomfield Bridge.

December 26th.—Major Scott-Kerr was removed to
hospital very ill at Van Reenans Pass. The Battalion
marched at 6 a.m. to Bughtie, only eight miles off, but a
hard trek, as the passage of the Wilge was difficult for the
waggons, which often had to be man-handled.

December 27th.—Major Marshall took out four companies of the Battalion on a foraging expedition.

December 28th.—The Battalion marched at 6 a.m. to
a camp five miles in the direction of Bezuidenhouts Pass.

December 29th.—Major Gordon-Gilmour went out in command of two companies on a collecting expedition under General Campbell.

December 30th.—A rounding-up expedition. Several women and children were collected and sent into Harrismith.

December 31st.—Major Gordon-Gilmour went out in command of four companies on a rounding-up expedition.

January 1st, 1901.—The Battalion marched out about four miles. Some sniping.

January 2nd.—A rounding-up expedition.

January 3rd.—A rounding-up expedition. The Boers came down and fired on the cattle-guards, but were quickly turned away by the gun.

January 4th.—The Battalion marched about seven miles. Some Boers were driven away from Elands River Drift.

January 5th.—A strong patrol of No. 8 Company, under Major Marshall, went out at 3 a.m. and occupied the ridge. Four companies and a half went out later to round-up. There was a strong force of Boers in the neighbourhood.

January 6th.—Two companies were sent to round-up Glen Lenie. A Grenadier was mysteriously shot in the foot in the middle of the night. He was afterwards convicted by court martial of shooting himself purposely, and sentenced to 18 months' hard labour.

January 7th.—Marched at 6 a.m. The Boers harassed the rear-guard under Major Marshall. The column encamped about five miles from Harrismith.

January 8th.—Marched at 6 a.m. to Bloomfield.

January 19th.—It having been said that the Boers were able to pick off officers owing to their distinguishing marks, a company was taken out under Major Marshall to experiment. Half the company in extended order was drawn up 1,800 yards from the point of attack, which was occupied by officers with glasses. The men were in marching order, with, here and there, a few in hats or field service caps, and some without equipment at all. Among them were scattered six officers dressed as follows:—(1) Wolseley helmet, Sam Brown belt, double braces, walking-stick; (2) ordinary helmet, new Sam Brown leggings, walking-stick; (3) as a private soldier with equipment and revolver; (4) trousers, knee boots, warm coat (British), no equipment, Dutch hat; (5) Wolseley helmet, leggings, Sam Brown belt, cross sling, stick; (6) as a hospital orderly, with red cross on his arm.

At 1,800 yards no difference could be distinguished through telescope or glasses. On diminishing the distance from 1,500 to 1,100 yards, the following became indistinctly visible from time to time through the glasses—Sam Brown belt, officer carrying revolver, leggings, red cross on hospital orderly. Between 800 and 300 yards, practically all differences could be seen through the glass, nothing by the naked eye. At 300 yards everything became more or less visible to the naked eye. At 120 yards medal-ribbons were barely visible to the naked eye. On retirement from 800 to 1,000 yards, the white haversacks were distinctly visible to the naked eye, and the dark rolled coats more or less so. On further retirement from 1,100 to 1,500 yards both were visible, in diminishing proportion, through the glasses— only the haversacks to the naked eye. At all distances khaki showed up black on the veldt, where the latter was green. At all distances up to 300 yards, with a glass, nothing could be distinguished when the men were lying down. The practical outcome of the experiment was that between 1,800 and 1,000 yards differences could only be distinguished with the greatest difficulty with the glass; beyond 300 yards nothing could be distinguished by the naked eye, and at that distance details were very indistinct. At 700 yards officers, when walking about, could be distinguished from men. What did catch the eye was an officer or man getting up and walking about, or making movement of any kind.

January 21st.—The Battalion paraded at 6 a.m. on a bitterly cold morning, and marched through Harrismith to Wilge River bridge, where it camped.

January 22nd.—A reconnaissance was made to Elands River bridge, but only a few Boers were seen.

January 23rd.—The force marched in two columns at 5 and 5.45 a.m. respectively. Four companies of the Battalion went with one column, under General Campbell, and the other four under Lieutenant-Colonel Lloyd. General Campbell went to Elands River, and Lieutenant-Colonel Lloyd to Ardtully.

January 24th.—The Battalion heard that Queen Victoria was dead. Two flags were run up, and a salute of 21 rounds with live shell was fired, in honour of the accession of the King, after which the flags were lowered to half-mast. The Battalion marched at 1 p.m. and encamped at Wilge River.

January 26th—The column marched at 8 a.m. with an immense convoy, the rear-guard leaving camp exactly three hours after the advance-guard.

January 27th.—Marched at 6 a.m. Exchanged a few shots with a small party of Boers.

January 28th.—Marched at 5.15 a.m. Four companies of the Battalion advance-guard, under Gordon-Gilmour, and four companies with the main body. Passed through Tiger Kloof. Considerable sniping. Column camped at Witkop.

January 30th.—A company went out to protect the signallers, who were endeavouring to get communication with Harrismith.

January 31st.—The Battalion moved out to Smalfontein, and was sniped by about 100 Boers on the left flank.

February 1st.—A good deal of rounding-up was done. No. 1 Company was heavily shot at, but, luckily, no one was hit. At 2 p.m. the Battalion marched on Bethlehem, arriving at 5 a.m. The flank guard was sniped, but no damage done.

February 2nd.—Marched at 2 p.m. and camped at Lieuwpoort. The advance-guard was heavily sniped.

February 3rd.—Marched to Tiger Kloof. Desultory firing all day.

February 4th.—Marched to Lieuw Kuil. A considerable number of Boers hanging about.

February 5th.—Marched at 9.45 a.m. for Coevins Hoek. After crossing the Reitz-Harrismith road, the column ascended some high ground following the Vrede road. The advance-guard came under a heavy fire at about 1,000 yards, losing one man killed and one wounded. The advance-guard infantry, under Gilmour, moved up and drove the enemy off. One Grenadier severely, and one slightly, wounded. The column then moved down a long valley to Holland, where it encamped. Continuous firing took place on both flanks, the Boers harassing all day. Their number was estimated at about 250.

February 6th.—Commenced with cannonade by all four guns and pom-pom, which drove the Boers from the ridge in front, and dispersed them for the day. The river was so swollen at Stale Drift, that the further bank, which was a very steep one, was very difficult to ascend. The Engineers improved it with the assistance of Nos. 4 and 7 Companies. A few shots were fired at the rear-guard. The whole of the regimental transport was over by dark, when work had to be knocked off.

February 7th.—The crossing of the drift was recommenced at 5 a.m., a few Boers sniping the outposts. The whole column had passed the drift by 4 p.m. Had the enemy tried to dispute the passage it would have been a heavy business, as it was a perfect place to defend. Sniping continued till dark.

February 8th.—Sniping commenced at 3.15 a.m., and continued intermittently for some time. The column moved off at 7.30 a.m. along the road which ran under the kopjes. About 300 Boers hung on the flanks and rear all day; but, although there was continuous firing, they could do no harm, as the column moved along the top of a table land. Camp was reached at Holspruit at about 7 p.m.

February 9th.—The column was to have marched at 6 a.m., but could not do so until 7.30 a.m. owing to a heavy fog, which did not clear before that hour. The Maj.-General opened the day by a bombardment with his four guns and a pom-pom. Four companies, two of Grenadiers, and two of the East Yorkshire, were extended across the valley and made a demonstration against the kopje, which had been bombarded, and which the Imperial Yeomanry, supported by the infantry, then took. The Boers now opened from Pram Kopje, on the right front, but the advance-guard soon cleared them with machine gun and rifle fire. Considerable delay was caused by the ammunition waggon breaking down in a spruit, two companies having to go back to cover it while it was being extricated. The column camped at Davids Vlei.

February 10th.—Marched at 6 a.m. and were not molested till under the Rotheberg, a long kopje 600 or 700 feet high, on the right flank, under which the road ran, at about 2,500 yards distance. From this point of vantage, the enemy opened a very heavy fire, the column returning it at the same time. The convoy was moved out of range across the veldt. We arrived and camped a mile-and-a-half from Vrede at about 1.30 p.m. Had the column followed the ordinary road, there would have been trouble, but as it was there were no losses. Orders were received that the town was to be evacuated, and every living soul removed. It had been a hot-bed of enteric, and was no longer required strategically. Two Leinster officers had died, as also two men, while of the Royal Scots M.I., of which a detachment had been stationed here, seven were ill—one very seriously. There were also about 100 of other ranks ill. It was said that the enteric was caused by a well of impure water.

February 11th.—A day of rest, well-earned by both man and beast. A telegram was received saying that Quartermaster May, of the 3rd Battalion, had died of apoplexy. He was much regretted by the whole regiment.

February 12th.—The column started at 8.30 a.m., taking some 250 sick and all the inhabitants to Vrede. The

Leinster remained behind to garrison the town until our return.   Instead of going by the ordinary road, we moved over the veldt well to the east.   On arrival near the Ponder Spruit, which ran under some cliffs, a number of Boers, who had been harassing the column all day, were seen riding out of a farm with an ox-waggon and Cape cart. They were shelled and the waggon captured, which contained a piano !   The Spruit proved to be impassable without preparation, so the column encamped on its eastern side. It was a long, hot, waterless march.

February 13th.—The column commenced crossing the drift at 5 a.m., the Spruit not having risen, notwithstanding the wet night.   We were clear of it by 11.30 a.m., when we marched, and reached De Langes drift on the Klip River, crossing into the Transvaal at 4 p.m. and camped. There was no opposition during the day, but continuous firing all night, and the rear-guard was much harassed.

February 14th.—Marched at 6 a.m. and arrived at Standerton after a long, hot, march.   The rear-guard was harassed to some extent.

March 2nd (Standerton).—The following telegram was read to the Battalion, re No. 712 Lance-Corporal D. White's defence of a train :—

To General Campbell, Standerton.

87 Harrismith, 1st March, 1901.

Delighted to read of successful action by corporal and 15 men, 2nd Battalion Grenadier Guards, escort to train. Please convey appreciation to Colonel Lloyd, and send me name of corporal for publication in Divisional Orders if you concur.

(Signed) GENERAL RUNDLE.

On the 27th February, a party of nearly 100 Boers had attempted to blow up a train north of Heidelberg, which was escorted by 15 men of the 2nd Battalion Grenadier Guards, under Lance-Corporal D. White. The explosions, three in number, failed. The escort at once opened fire and drove off the enemy before they could do anything further.

March 4th.—Marched at 6 a.m. Reached De Langes Drift at 1 p.m., but the waggons had not crossed till late in the evening. The column was thus composed:—Three squadrons Imperial Yeomanry, four companies Grenadiers, one company Leinsters, one squadron 13th Hussars, and pom-pom. The outposts were sniped in the afternoon.

March 5th.—The column marched at 5.30 a.m. and took the proper or direct road. All went well till the hilly country near Tweefontein was reached, when the enemy began harassing both flanks, principally the right. The General had intended camping on the road, but a heliogram was received from Vrede, saying the doctor was down with dysentery, and that there were 34 fresh cases of enteric, including four officers; also that there was no one who could make up any medicines. The column, therefore, marched into Vrede, 18 miles direct, but much longer for the flank guard. A long, heavy day. Three casualties among the Imperial Yeomanry.

March 10th.—The column started at 6 a.m. on a very cold, damp, drizzly morning, with a strong wind. At about 7.30 a.m. heavy wet set in, which continued throughout the day. The Boers appeared to think that we were marching in the direction of Reitz, and accordingly stopped that road. When they saw that the intention was to make for Standerton, they tried, in considerable numbers, to move round the left flank, but were prevented to some extent by shell fire.   They attacked the rear-guard and killed some of them and slightly wounded three men.   The camp near Gruisplats was reached about 2.30 p.m., two miles from the drift.

March 11th.—It began raining again at 4 a.m., and rained heavily all day.   The spruit was negotiable, but the ground was so soft that a move must be a heavy business. The column had supplies for only six days. At ordinary times it was only two days' march to Standerton, but in heavy wet it may take much longer.   Nothing could be done owing to the rain.

March 12th.—At 6 a.m. the cavalry, under fire of the guns, took the opposite heights.   Working parties went down to the drift, and began cutting it down and preparing the roadway.   At 1 p.m. it was declared ready, and the column moved off.   The morning had been cold, dull, and drizzly, with occasional storms.   At about 1.30 p.m. the passage began.   The first waggon got over well enough, but as the operation went on the drift became worse and worse, in addition to which the rain came down in torrents. Camp was pitched on the heights beyond, but comparatively few waggons were over by dark.   The work went on in pitch darkness and pouring rain till 2 a.m. next morning when it was knocked off.   The last waggon did not come in till 3 a.m.   The rear-guard under Gilmour, 1, 7, and 8 Companies, (i.e., Forrester's, Cavan's, and Marshall's) were out all night.   Some sniping, but not much.

March 13th.—At day-break the work began again. The last waggon was over by 10.30 a.m.   A lovely drying day, every one getting dry and rejoicing.   Lieutenant Leicester of the Leinsters, died of enteric at 3.30 a.m., and was buried at 5 p.m.   Sniping at the outposts went on most of the day. The column had only moved 10 miles from Vrede in four days.

March 14th.—Marched at 6 a.m., the column following the road to the left, where a bad drift was encountered over a donga about two miles from camp. After about 20 waggons had passed, the drift fell in and became impassable. The column gradually moved up the donga on both sides, and struck the old road, the convoy still having to get across, which took some time. The largest drift was reached, the rear-guard being heavily attacked on the road, and the 13th Hussars losing three men wounded, of whom one died. The advance-guard also had a considerable amount of fighting. On arrival at the drift the river was found to be impassable, being some 18 feet deep and rising. There was nothing for it, therefore, but to camp.

March 15th.—The river went down about two feet in the night. There was some sniping.

March 16th.—Jeffreys went to hospital with fever, with a very high temperature. The river had sunk about one foot. There were still five or six feet of water in the middle of the drift, and the waggons could not cross. A thunderstorm came on in the afternoon, making matters worse. Not many provisions being left, the column was on three-quarter rations.

March 17th.—A wet night with a consequent rising of the river of about three feet. No chance of crossing. The morning was spent in constructing a raft, but without much success, for want of materials. The column is on half-rations of biscuit.

March 18th.—Not much rain in the night. A rounding-up expedition went out. A good raft having been constructed, the ambulances were floated across the river, the

men crossing over.   At 10 a.m. the convoy that the General
had asked for arrived from Standerton.   The sick,
including Jeffreys, were sent in.

March 19th.—The river getting lower.   About 50
waggons were got over by unpacking and floating them
across, the loads being taken over on the raft and repacked
on the other side.   The animals swam across.

March 20th.—The work of crossing going on steadily
and the river falling.

March 21st.—The work of crossing still going on.
All over except the Grenadiers.

March 22nd.—The Grenadiers commenced crossing at
5.30 a.m., the Commander Officer going over with the
last party at 10 a.m.   The Boers tried to come up, but were
kept off by shell fire.   The column marched off and arrived
at Standerton at 4 p.m.   Scott-Kerr and Shafto met the
Battalion.   Cavendish had a bad fall from his horse.
Boswall went to hospital.

March 23rd.—The 4th Battalion Imperial Yeomanry,
who have been with us since the beginning of the campaign, left for Kroonstadt on their way home.

March 24th.—A patrol went out in the middle of the
night towards Kat Bosch, as there was a rumour that De
Wet intended to cross the river.

March 26th.—H.R.H. The Colonel's* birthday was
celebrated by running the 2nd Battalion race (Manners'
Cup), the programme having been arranged by Cavendish.
There were 19 starters, Douglas-Pennant 1st, Cavan 2nd,
Cholmeley 3rd.   Boswall went to the general hospital with
jaundice.

---

* H.R.H. The Duke of Cambridge.

CHAPTER VIII.

Major Gordon-Gilmour Commanding (Harrismith).

March 28th.—Lieutenant-Colonel Lloyd went to hospital with fever. Major Scott-Kerr, and 2nd-Lieutenant Cary went by train to Ladysmith with their companies. The remainder of the Battalion sent patrols down the line by night to the south.

March 30th.—Cavan and his company went by train to Ladysmith.

April 2nd.—No. 8 and one squadron Gloucester I.Y., arrived at Mount Prospect station, on the Natal side of Langs Nek, at about 2 a.m. Another train going north was waiting to pass, which it did. When the latter had gone about half a mile, it was blown up in a defile. Heavy Boer firing commenced. A patrol of 25 men of No. 8, under Shafto, was at once sent out and engaged about 300 Boers. The enemy had, in the meantime, detached three trucks which they let go down the railway on to Mount Prospect station, smashing the rear-van of the troop train. They then cleared off to the heights above. Day dawned at about 5 a.m., but the fog was so thick that it was impossible to see more than a hundred yards. We now occupied all available positions. When the mist dispersed the enemy opened a heavy fire from the heights, and from Neil's farm, where the Peace of 1881 was signed. This fire was silenced and the ridge below Majuba captured. Two guns now opened on us from Langs Nek, and fired a few shots, which luckily did no harm, though one burst near a truck-load of horses. These guns proved to be two of our naval ones. At about 10 a.m. General Campbell arrived, and at much the same time the Boers cleared. In doing so, they ran into a patrol of the 5th Dragoon Guards, who killed three and made five prisoners. A considerable number of Boers were picked up and buried by the 5th Dragoon Guards. We had no casualties. Neil was made a prisoner.

April 3rd.—The last of the Battalion arrived at Lady-smith, the whole being camped at Tin Town.

April 5th.—The Battalion trekked at 7 a.m. on a very muddy road to Arcadia, about 10 miles. General Campbell, with his staff, except the Brigade-Major, went by train to Harrismith. Lieutenant-Colonel Martin, Leinster, commanding the column.

April 6th.—Marched at 6.30 a.m. to a camp near Old Blue Beck. Glorious weather.

April 7th (Sunday).—Marched at 6.30 a.m., a very heavy tug-up for about 2,000 feet. Camped in the actual pass of Van Renan. The hospital and supplies went on to the top.

April 8th.—All the oxen went down the pass, so as to double-span the transport. The column, therefore, did not march until 10 a.m. A very long and slow climb. The rear-guard arrived in camp at 3.30 a.m. Camped at Van Renan's station.

April 9th.—Marched at 9 a.m. to Albertina. Wind and dust terrible.

April 10th.—Blew a hurricane. Tents badly knocked about. The column marched to Bloomfield in the worst of it.

April 11th.—The Battalion marched into Harrismith and took over the defences, with the exception of Natal Hill, which was held by the Leinster. There was much sniping early in the day at the Reitz road outposts.

April 20th.—Generals Rundle and Campbell, with all troops, including the Scots Guards, went on trek, leaving the Battalion with three companies of Leinster, and four guns to defend Harrismith. The Honours " Gazette " came out; Lieutenant-Colonel Lloyd was made a C.B., to date 29th November, 1900.

April 24th.—Lieutenant Tryon died of enteric at Harrismith, probably contracted at Vrede or Standerton. He was buried the same day at Harrismith.

May 31st.—Nos. 1, 2, and 3 companies concentrated at head-quarters. A draft of 200 Scots Guards took over their outposts under Major Erskine.

June 3rd.—The column, under Major Gilmour, consisting of four squadrons Imperial Yeomanry, two guns, and 2nd Battalion Scots Guards, marched at 9 a.m. to Mount Paul. The advance-guard engaged a small party of Boers on Mount Paul; one Yeoman was hit in the foot. Heavy firing was heard from Generals Rundle and Campbell.

June 4th.—The Battalion marched to Strath Enick. On the road the right flank-guard found 2,500 rounds of Martini ammunition in a kraal and destroyed it.

June 8th.—The Battalion marched into Harrismith.

June 10th.—Nos. 1, 3 and 7 companies took over their former outposts from the Scots Guards' draft.

CHAPTER IX.

Lieut-Colonel Lloyd Again in Command.

June 20th.—Lieutenant-Colonel Lloyd rejoined the Battalion from Durban, where he had been ill.

June 25th.—General Rundle arrived in Harrismith with his column, having cleared a considerable tract of country.

June 27th.—General Campbell returned to Harrismith with his column.

July 2nd.—Football match between 2nd Battalion Grenadiers and the South Staffordshire Regiment; drawn—two goals each. Bad wind and dust storm.

July 4th.—Generals Rundle, Campbell, and Harley started with columns. General Elliott arrived at Majors Drift with four columns, 17 miles from Harrismith.

July 8th.—Cavan, with No. 7 Company, took over the blockhouses on the Natal road from the Imperial Yeomanry.

July 17th.—The Battalion gave a concert to the hospital, which was a great success.

July 19th.—A Military Court was held, of which Lieutenant-Colonel Lloyd was president and Major Gilmour one of the members. Mrs. Dinah Wassels was tried for sending out supplies to her sons, who were on commando with the Boers. The Court sat from 10 a.m. to 4 p.m. and convicted her. The defendant was sentenced to pay a fine of £100, or in default to be imprisoned for six calendar months. The finding and sentence were confirmed, with £25 or two months remitted.

July 20th.—No. 7, under Cavan, was inspected by Lieutenant-Colonel Lloyd.

July 21st.—The block-house in charge of No. 7 on the Natal road was inspected by Lieutenant-Colonel Lloyd. Captain Bonham and 2nd-Lieutenants de Crespigny, Meeking, and Lord Alan Percy all arrived from England.

July 24th.—Lieutenant-Colonel Lloyd inspected half of No. 1 company.

July 25th.—Lieutenant-Colonel Lloyd inspected half of No. 2 company.

July 26th.—Lieutenant-Colonel Lloyd inspected second half of No. 2 company.

July 27th.—Lieutenant-Colonel Lloyd inspected second half of No. 1 company.

July 29th.—At 12.10 a.m. Lieutenant-Colonel Lloyd was woke up by Lieutenant-Colonel Morrison, commanding troops, and ordered to send a company out to make up a small column under a Major. This marched at 7 a.m. under Major Scott-Kerr, and consisted of 70 Imperial Yeomanry, No. 2 company Grenadiers, and a machine-gun, with transport.

July 31st.—Major Scott-Kerr's column returned.

August 1st.—Generals Rundle and Campbell came in with the Scots Guards.

August 5th.—The Scots Guards went by train to Pietermaritzburg. The two battalions—2nd Grenadiers and 2nd Scots Guards—which had been together ever since they landed in the country, were now finally separated.

CHAPTER X.

MAJOR GORDON-GILMOUR AGAIN COMMANDING.

August 8th.—The Battalion marched 11 miles to Ardtully, under Major Gilmour, about 620 strong, exclusive of No. 4 company, which remained under Captain Lord Ardee, and Lieutenant Shafto, as head-quarter company. The entire country was found burnt. Lieutenant-Colonel Lloyd was not allowed to go, as he was on the Compensation Board.

August 9th.—Marched at 7 a.m. Our advance-guard was engaged shortly after the start, near Elands River bridge, but, brushing away the opposition, we continued the march and camped at Osfontein.

August 10th.—The Imperial Yeomanry started two hours before day-light to occupy Tiger Kloof and anticipate opposition through the defile. We followed at daybreak, followed by the Leinster Battalion with baggage two hours behind us. The Imperial Yeomanry were just in time, as they saw the enemy coming, to occupy the position at daybreak. There being parties of from 50 to 100 Boers hanging about the right, two companies were sent up the hills on that flank. They, with the Imperial Yeomanry, kept the enemy clear of the road. The column camped in the defile, with five companies on outpost.

August 11th.—Marched at daybreak, the Battalion providing rear and left flank-guard. About two miles on we were held up in a defile for a short time, but the guns soon cleared the way, and we got to camp near Liebenberg Vlei bridge. The Imperial Yeomanry lost one man and three horses.

August 12th.—Marched at 8 through Bethlehem, camped three miles south of that town, No. 6 (Bonham) on outpost; were nearly burned out, losing two tents and a lot of blankets.

August 13th.—Sat still. Seventy-five quail were shot.

August 14th.—Marched at 8 for Retiefs Nek which was reported occupied by Boers. Colonel Hartley's column was to co-operate and clear the hills on the left of the Nek. This column, however, did not appear, so we deployed three companies, which, covered by artillery-fire, cleared the Nek without casualty, and the column passed through, but it encountered a considerable amount of rifle-fire from the high ground on the right, when we entered the Brand-water Basin. No. 7 company (Cavan's) cleared the hills, remaining there on outpost. The column camped three miles S. of the Nek, the waggons not getting in till midnight.

August 15th.—Marched at 10 a.m., and had a running fight all day. Quilter was shot through the thigh, his pony and several horses being killed. Camped at One Tree Hill for the first time. The Boers were using black powder almost entirely.

August 16th.—After marching for about a mile, we found the road closely commanded by high hills on the right. Scott-Kerr was sent with two companies and a mountain gun to clear the right flank while the column passed. We only made about three miles, although we were on the march from 7 a.m. till 7 p.m. The Imperial Yeomanry reconnoitred Fouriesburg, losing two wounded and six taken prisoners.

August 17th.—The three companies of Grenadiers, which, with one and a half squadrons Imperial Yeomanry and two guns, formed the rear-guard, were kept very busy all day by about 150 Boers, who, on one occasion, under cover of a grass fire, got within 200 yards. The rear-guard did not get into the camp at Brindisi till 10 p.m. We had two casualties.

August 18th—25th.—Remained about Brindisi reconnoitring and fixing positions for block-houses. No. 1 company holding Reinveld Kop. Considerable snow on the hills.

August 26th.—At midnight marched to surprise Fouriesburg, Gilmour commanding the advance-guard, and at daybreak occupied the town. The Boers, having got wind of the expedition, retired to the hills.

August 27th.—Lieutenant-General Rundle saw Lieutenant-Colonel Lloyd and Lieutenant-Colonel Morrison, who had been at issue with regard to Guards' privileges. The Lieutenant-General ruled—(1) that when a Guardsman is tried, one member of the D.C.M. should always be an officer of the Brigade of Guards; (2) that all Guards' details should be attached to Guards; (3) that a senior Guards' officer should settle C.O. reports irrespective of his rank. Sniping mostly all day, but at extreme ranges.

August 29th—September 1st.—Battalion employed reconnoitring, and escorting convoys from Brindisi.

September 2nd—6th.—Marched to Steynesberg Kop, and were occupied until then in making raids into the Witterbergen mountains, destroying waggons and forage, and bringing in about 60 white people, who were living in caves in the recesses of the hills. These expeditions were attended by incessant snipings, but we had few, if any, casualties.

To November 2nd.—The same procedure continued till the Brandwater Basin was comparatively cleared, and the line of block-houses from Brindisi to Retiefs Nek completed, there being a good many Boers still remaining in the almost inaccessible parts of the mountains.

September 12th.—Lieutenant-Colonel Lloyd sat as President on a Court of Enquiry on a Yeoman who surrendered on the 28th July.

September 25th.—The Court of Enquiry finished.

CHAPTER XI.

LIEUT.-COLONEL LLOYD RESUMES COMMAND.

October 4th.—Lieutenant-Colonel Lloyd, with a few details, left Harrismith to join the Battalion, *viâ* Ladysmith and Elandsfontein to Bloemfontein.

October 13th (Sunday).—Lieutenant-Colonel Lloyd left Bloemfontein to ride to the Brandwater Basin.

October 22nd.—Lieutenant-Colonel Lloyd arrived at Brindisi, on the Caledon River, in the Brandwater Basin, and found the Battalion absent.

November 2nd.—Lieutenant-Colonel Lloyd left Brandisi and rode to Fort Davidson, where he found two companies of Grenadiers under Major Gilmour.

November 3rd.—Lieutenant-Colonel Lloyd, Major Gilmour, and the two companies, marched to Retiefs Nek, about 16 miles, where the remainder of the Battalion was encamped.

November 5th.—The Battalion occupied the Nek and adjoining heights without opposition, in order to meet Colonel Briggs and his Light Horse, who were coming in.

November 6th.—The Battalion started at 7 a.m., and reached Brindisi at 5 p.m., 24 miles.

November 8th.—Marched at 12.30 p.m. and reached Fort Davidson about 5 p.m.

November 13th.—A force, including four companies of Grenadiers, under Major Gilmour, went out under the Major-General to a farm to hunt for hidden papers, about which information had been received. They returned to camp at 4 p.m., having dug up two large boxes full. There was a certain amount of sniping, but no one hit. No. 6 company fired 700 rounds.

November 15th.—Marched at 12.30 p.m. Arrived at Brindisi at 4 p.m.

November 18th.—A steeplechase between six " Gunners " and six Grenadiers. The Grenadiers won by one point, the race itself being won by Captain Davis, R.A.

November 19th.—Marched at 9 a.m., arriving at Fort Davidson about 2 p.m. A most fearful thunderstorm, which lasted well into the night.

November 20th.—Starting at 4.30 a.m., the column marched right across to Slap Krantz. A considerable number of Boers opposed our advance, and followed up our rear-guards. Camped on Surrender Hill.

November 21st.—Started at 5 a.m. along the Spur, towards Naawpoort Nek.

November 22nd.—General Campbell moved out at 5 a.m. with a mountain-gun, two squadrons, and two companies of Grenadiers, under Major Marshall. Some farms were rounded-up. Two Intelligence men came in from Basutoland, under a flag of truce.

November 23rd.—Marched at 5.30 a.m. The cavalry had left at 4 a.m. to occupy positions. Cavendish and

Bonham, with Nos. 6 and 5 companies and a field gun, evacuated their position at 4 a.m. The convoy and main body were commanded by Lieutenant-Colonel Lloyd, Major Marshall being in command of the advance-guard, and Major Gilmour of the rear-guard. Surrender Hill and Slap Krantz were passed by the greater part of the force without trouble; not so by the rear-guard. Here Marshall occupied a high kopje with two companies and one mountain-gun, covering the convoy, which turned to the left, not the road by which it had come. A very difficult road ran along the banks of the Caledon River, by which the route was continued. Tuinplatz was finally reached without difficulty by the main body, while the rear-guard were having a very hot time of it. On reaching Surrender Hill, Major Gilmour halted to allow the rear-guard cavalry to come in. The Boers made a determined attack, coming on and shooting freely. One man, Corporal Clarke, No. 5, was shot through the head, but not killed. Private Brown was slightly wounded. The enemy, who came on persistently, must have lost men. The retirement from Surrender Hill on to Slap Krantz was skilfully made. After about one-and-a-half hours, Major Gilmour withdrew, the cavalry still holding the high positions. As soon as the cavalry had withdrawn, the Boers followed up, getting on to the same kopje as Marshall's company. They also followed on to some rocks at Slap Krantz, but were driven back by the rear-guard gun. As the rear-guard arrived in camp, some Boers showed on the top of Marshall's kopje. The gun was brought into action, and made good shooting, driving the Boers off, but not before a sniper had hit a horse and a gunner. Very heavy wet and thunder came on, which lasted all night. No. 7, under Marshall, on the kopje, had a bad night. The R.F.A. gun of the rear-guard

G

fired 87 rounds during the day; the mountain-gun, 49; Nos. 5 and 6 companies, 3,996 rounds; the Maxim, which did good service under Sergeant Clay, 3,100. A sharp fight.

November 24th (Sunday).—Marched at 3.30 a.m. A fearfully wet morning. Turning to the right, the column gained the old road and reached Blackwood Farm by 9.30 a.m., without difficulty, there being only a few snipers. Yesterday's position was a nasty place to get away from, especially for Marshall. Camped at Blackwood Farm, being tired out after two heavy days. It cleared about 5 a.m., the sun came out, and a fine day followed.

November 25th.—Marched at 6.30 a.m. and reached Fort Davidson without any fighting. A nasty drift was the only difficulty.

November 26th.—Marched at 7 a.m. Reached Brindisi at 10 a.m. The men in rags. None of the expected clothing had arrived.

November 28th.—Murray-Threipland went to hospital with a bad stoppage. Austin, though anxious, did not think badly of him.

November 29th.—Murray-Threipland very ill.

November 30th.—General Campbell and Staff left for Ficksburg, and Lieutenant-Colonel Lloyd took command of the column. All means having failed to alleviate Murray-Threipland, an operation was decided on, and was performed by Civil Surgeon Dawes, assisted by Major Austin. The operation took $2\frac{1}{2}$ hours, his inside being removed and replaced. Very little chance of his living, though his coolness, courage, and strength were remarkable. Condition very critical.

December 1st.—Threipland's strength well maintained. Slight improvement. Fearful thunderstorm. Deluges of rain.

December 2nd.—Threipland's condition still very grave, but improved.

December 3rd.—Marched at 6 a.m. Met at Fouriesburg by Major Davidson, who pointed out the ridge where General Campbell wished block-houses. Lieutenant-Colonel Lloyd selected the site, and the column camped near it and got men working. Heavy thunderstorm.

December 4th.—Block-house built. Hot and fine weather. Threipland much improved.

December 5th.—Block-houses finished.

December 6th.—Marched at 5 a.m. The drift under Stene Kamp being completely washed away, the column had to re-make it. Owing to the good work done by Captain Craven and the Engineers, the column was only delayed an hour. The Boers attempted to snipe the right flank, but were shelled away. Retiefs Nek being reached, dispositions were made to attack the Nek, which was taken without opposition. The column camped east of the pass, and began to send up block-house material on to the peak, which was a heavy climb.

December 7th.—A long search for water, which could not be found. Block-house commenced on the western peak, the top of which was about 15 feet square, and about 500 feet above the pass. In the afternoon General Campbell and Major Gilmour arrived. A good account of Threipland.

December 11th.—Block-house completed and garrisoned with 35 N.C.O's. and men, under Seymour.

G 2

December 12th.—Moved at 8 a.m. through the Nek to a camp about 3,000 yards beyond. Two block-houses were commenced.

December 13th.—Thunder and wet all day, which interfered considerably with the progress of the block-houses.

December 14th.—No. 1, under Lieutenant Quilter, occupied the ridge. They saw either a baboon or a Boer watching them—were uncertain which! A telegram arrived, " Threipland removed from the dangerous list."

December 16th.—Marched at 7.30 a.m., Lieutenant-Colonel Lloyd took the convoy into Bethlehem. Much delay owing to a drift, which had to be repaired.

December 17th.—General Dartnell's column arrived, having been hunting De Wet.

December 18th.—General Dartnell's column left. Later a telegram came in that he was heavily engaged with De Wet on the Langberg. Some Imperial Yeomanry went out, and later the Grenadiers marched out seven miles and took up a position to cover the retirement of the Imperial Yeomanry. De Wet having attacked Dartnell and killed eight men, retired. The Battalion arrived in Bethlehem at about 7 p.m., after a stiffish day. Boers lost four men killed and some wounded.

December 19th.—The Battalion took over the defences of Bethlehem from the E. Yorks.

December 21st.—Heavy thunderstorms all day.

December 25th.—De Wet attacked Colonel Ferman's Yeomanry at 1 a.m. and practically annihilated it at Twee-fontein. The men of the Battalion had no Christmas dinners, as they had not arrived.

December 26th.—Lieutenant-Colonel Lloyd and Major Gilmour were visiting the advanced block-houses when Civil Surgeon Wright came in with the account of Tweefontein. Among the prisoners taken by the Boers was Douglas-Pennant, who was the only man left alive in the gun-pit, which he was assisting to hold.

December 27th.—Telegram arrived from Regimental Adjutant ordering Sergeant-Major Rolinson to be examined for the Quartermastership of the 1st Battalion, which was done.

December 31st.—Telegram arrived from the Lieutenant-Colonel proposing Acraman as Sergeant-Major of the Battalion, *vice* Rolinson. Quartermaster-Sergeant Loasby was to succeed Sergeant Brown (deceased) as Quarter-Master-Sergeant at the regimental orderly room, but to remain out until the end of the campaign, his duty to be done at the regimental orderly room by Sergeant Carter.

CHAPTER XII.

THE END IN SIGHT.

January 1st, 1902.—Lieutenant-Colonel Lloyd sent a runner to Brindisi acquiescing in the Lieutenant-Colonel's proposals and nominating Colour-Sergeant Jones, Drill-Sergeant, and Colour-Sergeant Teece, Assistant-Drill Sergeant to the Battalion.

January 6th.—Convoy started for Brindisi.

January 8th.—Lieutenant-Colonel Lloyd and Major Gilmour went to Retiefs Nek. As they were arriving at the block-house, the mountain gun was fired, killing two Boers.

January 17th.—Brigade head-quarters, three companies of Grenadiers (Nos. 1, 2 and 3, under Major Gilmour), all the Imperial Yeomanry, less one troop, and all the guns less one moved out at 5.30 a.m., to relieve the East York-shire, who went on to Dacres Kloof. Lieutenant-Colonel Lloyd took over the command of Bethlehem. General Rundle's column were nearing Bethlehem, building block-houses as they came.

January 19th.—Lieutenant-Colonel Lloyd moved his head-quarters to Vogelsfontein. General Campbell moved into Bethlehem, taking all the guns with him. The draft of Grenadiers under Colby and Colston arrived. The Grenadier block-houses now ran from Retiefs Nek to Drie-fontein, about 25 miles in all.

January 20th.—The blockhouses were now complete between Harrismith, Bethlehem, and Brindisi, 82 miles in all. The Grenadiers took over 15 more.

January 26th.—Two lieutenants, Meeking and Cary, in hospital with enteric. Six officers on the sick list, *viz.*, Blackett, Cary, Meeking, and Shafto, enteric; and Forester sickening for something. Sergt. Daniel, who had died of enteric, was buried.

January 27th.—Forester returned to duty. There was some shooting at night.

January 28th.—The 4th Battalion K.R.R. took over the block-house line from Driefontein nearly to Vogelsfon-tein, from the Grenadiers. Some Boers attempted to cross the line.

January 30th.—Colour-Sergt. Acraman arrived and took over the duties of Sergt.-Major.

February 1st.—Meeking declared dangerously ill. Lieutenant-Colonel Lloyd appointed to command the block-house line, (1) Retief-Bethlehem, (2) Bethlehem-Vogelsfontein, (3) Bethlehem-Om Draai, about 30 miles in all.

February 2nd.—The column returned to Bethlehem from Vogelsfontein. Meeking died at 10.30 p.m.

February 3rd.—Meeking buried in Bethlehem cemetery.

February 4th.—Lieutenant-Colonel Lloyd moved at 7 a.m. with Nos. 1 and 3 companies, head-quarters of the Battalion, pom-pom, and two troops of Imperial Yeomanry, and marched about eight miles down to Om Draai block-house line and camped near Major Kenna's column.

February 5th.—Major Kenna marched at 1 p.m., thus rendering Lieutenant-Colonel Lloyd's camp untenable, there being too few men to hold it. As it was probable that the enemy would try to cross the flats, Lieutenant-Colonel Lloyd marched into them and filled up the gap, entrenching himself as best he could. The Boers attempted to cross the line between Vogelsfontein and Bethlehem, but were turned back by No. 3, under Stucley. Two Boers rode down the block-house line firing from their horses, but were quickly sent about their business. Rolinson gazetted Quartermaster to 1st Battalion.

February 8th.—Colston's block-house line attached and he slightly wounded.

February 9th.—Captain Lord Ardee arrived at Bethlehem from Harrismith.

February 10th.—The block-house line, consisting of 46 block-houses, between Bethlehem and Om Draai and Norde Kopje, was completed, thus closing the Kroonstadt-

Bethlehem line. Colonel Lloyd marched into Bethlehem with his column. .

February 17th.—General Brooke arrived at Harrismith and took over command from General Rundle, who was going to England.

February 19th.—Lieutenant-Colonel Lloyd started for the Brandwater Basin in command of a small column, to put up block-houses. It consisted of No. 4, under Ardee, a pom-pom, and some Engineers, and also a draft of 50 Leinsters. The column encamped near Fort Maroni.

February 23rd.—The column employed in covering block-house building. The mountain gun fired a few rounds at some burghers. The column marched on to Stene Kamp.

February 25th.—At 8.30 a.m. intelligence came in that a large force of Boers was advancing on the camp at Stene Kamp, distant about 800 yards. All the tents were dropped and the men stood to arms. A few shots were fired, on which the enemy moved away, their intention having been to effect a surprise, which had failed. A few star shell were then fired but nothing could be seen.

February 28th.—Some sniping during the night.

March 4th.—The column marched at 8 a.m., and camped near Upper Haarlem block-house. Sergt. Craven and Pte. Fuller died of enteric.

March 7th.—Some Boers crossed the as yet unfinished block-house line. The Leinsters fired heavily but with no result.

March 10th.—Column marched to Reineveld. General Campbell left Bethlehem for England. Colonel Kenyon-Slaney took over the command.

March 12th.—Heavy firing was heard from Fort Davidson, between 8.30 and mid-night, which continued in a desultory fashion till 4 a.m. The Leinsters fired 20,000 rounds, at what they thought were 100 Boers. They had two gunners wounded, a horse, a mule, and a cock and hen! Boers' casualties not known, probably nil.

March 17th.—The column marched into Brindisi.

March 29th.—The Brindisi camp was heavily sniped. Everybody moved into the fort until the moon rose, when the sniping stopped. One native wounded, and a bullock killed in the Grenadier Lines.

March 30th.—Camp moved to where it could not be sniped.

March 31st.—Heavy firing was heard on the block-house line between Fort Davidson and Rennifeld, the Boers failed either to cut the wire, or to cross, but made a determined attempt. Every available man went out under Major Scott-Kerr to cut wood. Some Boers were driven off. 28 Waggon loads of wood brought in. Some firing.

April 4th.—The column marched at 7 a.m. to Haarlem.

April 5th.—The column marched to Driekop.

April 8th.—Owing to some of the Leinster block-houses having been captured in the Brandwater Basin, Lieutenant-Colonel Lloyd's column was unable to march into Bethlehem as had been arranged.

April 11th.—Material having been collected, Lieutenant-Colonel Lloyd moved into the Brandwater Basin with his column, which included a company of Grenadiers, for the purpose of re-building the block-houses.

April 17th.—The block-houses having been completed, Lieutenant-Colonel Lloyd marched into Bethlehem.

April 18th.—The remainder of the Worcester block-houses were taken over by the Grenadiers.

April 23rd.—De Wet crossed the block-house line at Tweefontein with a pass to visit Langberg.

April 25th.—At 9 a.m. a flag of truce was reported at No. 25 block-house from the Langberg. In about half an hour it arrived and proved to be Christian DeWet and staff. General Elliott and his staff, together with Lieutenant-Colonel Lloyd, went out to meet them. Christian DeWet was taken to Colonel Slaney's hut, his staff going to the Grenadier Mess. They had left Langberg at daybreak and were very glad of a meal.

Christian DeWet talked a great deal with Lieutenant-Colonel Lloyd and other officers. He was a fine personality, a man of about 5 ft. 10 in., of fine build and strong face and a most determined chin. He was dressed in a blue serge coat, cord breeches, putties, and a slouch hat. He said he was 48, he spoke very little English and said he had only been to school for three months when he was a boy. Some of the others seemed good fellows, but not particularly intelligent. Clothes and other comforts were given to them. About 11 o'clock they in-spanned and went on to the Kafar Kop, going down the Om Draai line.

April 27th (Sunday).—General Brooke, commanding at Harrismith, presented Major Scott-Kerr with the D.S.O.

April 28th.—Major-General Brooke inspected the Bethlehem-Retief line held by the Grenadiers, and was pleased to say he approved of it.

April 29th.—Major-General Brooke inspected the Om Draai line, and was much satisfied.

May 3rd.—Major-General Brooke presented Major Gordon-Gilmour with the D.S.O.

May 13th.—An order was received that the Boers were not to be fired on unless they committed acts of aggression.

May 15th.—The opening of the Boer conference at Vereeniging.

May 16th.—Colonel Lloyd-Payn and some officers of the Imperial Yeomanry came over from Kaffir Kop to bury one of the officers of the Inniskilling Fusiliers. The funeral was arranged by the Grenadiers.

May 19th.—Three block-houses between Bethlehem and Retiefs Nek taken over by the Imperial Yeomanry.

May 31st.—Peace signed at Pretoria.

CHAPTER XIII.

AFTER THE PEACE.

June 2nd.—A telegram was received ordering one officer, three N.C.O's., and 8 men, to go at once in order to sail on the " Bavarian," to attend the Coronation. Major Scott-Kerr, D.S.O., and the following N.C.O's. and men were selected by lot :—

> Colour-Sergt. A. Broad,
> Sergt. Newton,
> Lance-Sergt. F. Aldred,
> Pte. W. Wheeler,
> Pte. H. Simon,
> Pte. H. Herwan,
> Pte. J. Egan,
> Pte. J. Roberts,
> Pte. J. Brown,
> Pte. W. Leaky,
> Pte. S. Smith.

June 4th.—Names were sent in by Lieutenant-Colonel Lloyd for despatches.

June 9th.—Pulling down the wire and filling up the ditches on the block-house line was commenced. Burghers were surrendering freely. From their own account, they appeared to have been in a worse case than we thought, for all seemed extremely glad that the war was over, and many said that they hoped to be as loyal to their new as they had been to their old Government.

Sunday, June 22nd.—The Battalion concentrated at Bethlehem, from the Om Draai and Retief lines, leaving three men in every third block-house as caretakers.

June 23rd.—The Battalion marched as far as the iron bridge, starting at 7.30 a.m., leaving Captain Lord Ardee behind in charge of the caretakers, also Lieutenant Stephen.

June 25th.—The Battalion arrived at Harrismith.

June 27th.—The Major-General (General Brooke) inspected the Division. The Division was formed up in line of quarter columns in the following order, from the right :

> 3rd Dragoon Guards, Harrismith Light Horse, R.F.A., mountain gun, and R.E.

> 1st Brigade, Lieutenant-Colonel Grogan. 2nd Battalion Grenadier Guards, 1st Battalion Black Watch, 2nd Battalion Black Watch.

> 2nd Brigade, Lieutenant-Colonel Reay, C.B. 2nd Battalion East Yorks, 2nd Battalion Manchester, 1st Battalion South Stafford.

> The Imperial Yeomanry on the left of the whole line.

June 29th.—Order received that the Reservists of the Battalion were to go to England.

June 30th.—Reservists paraded at 9.30 a.m. and marched to the station, headed by the bands of the Manchester, Stafford, and East Yorkshire. They left by the 11 o'clock train. Lieutenant-Colonel Lloyd remained with head-quarters and 320 men.

July 3rd.—Captains Cavendish and Lord Cavan, Lieutenant Cholmeley, and 240 Reservists embarked on the P. and O. ss. " Sicilian " and sailed.

July 7th.—The remainder of the Reservists embarked on the " Mohawk " and sailed in the evening. They were seen off by Lieutenant-Colonel Lloyd.

July 21st.—Colonel Blomfield, commanding the Harrismith District, inspected the five battalions south of the Wilge River, among which were the 2nd Battalion Grenadiers.

July 28th.—Lieutenant Douglas-Pennant left for England.

July 31st.—Telegram received from the Regimental Orderly Room, that Lieutenant-Colonel Lloyd, C.B., D.S.O., Lieutenant-Colonel Gordon-Gilmour, D.S.O., Sergt.-Major Acraman, Colour-Sergt. Teece, Sergt. Glee, and Ptes. Johnson, Rose and Hayter were mentioned in despatches dated 30th July, 1902.

August 9th, 1902.—King Edward the Seventh crowned. Lieutenant-Colonel Lloyd telegraphed to the King from the Battalion, " God save the King." Coronation parade in the same order as for the inspection by Major-General Brooke. Colonel Blomfield took command.

August 11th.—A telegram was received from the Equerry-in-Waiting : " The King commands me to thank you and all ranks for the kind telegram of congratulation."

August 24th.—General Lyttleton arrived at Harrismith and inspected the troops. The parade was formed up in the same way as the Coronation parade.

August 30th.—A telegram was received ordering Lieutenant-Colonel Lloyd to hold the Battalion in readiness for embarkation.

September 3rd.—A telegram was received ordering the Battalion to start at once.

September 4th.—The Battalion paraded at 12.30 p.m. and marched to the station headed by the bands of the E. Yorkshire, S. Stafford, Manchester, and K.R.R's., and arrived at Ladysmith at 7 p.m.

September 5th.—Arrived at Pietermaritzburg at 8 a.m. and went into the Rest Camp.

September 6th.—Private Evan Thomas was found dead near the railway with his skull broken. The police were most dilatory in making the investigation. The result of a search proved that there was no doubt that he had wandered out of camp and been knocked down and killed by the cow-catcher of a passing train.

September 11th.—The Battalion left Pietermaritzburg at 8.45 p.m.

September 12th.—The Battalion arrived at Durban at 5.30 and went on board the Union s.s. " Galeka " (Captain Wolford). The North Staffordshire were also on board. What remained of the Brigade Division R.F.A. under Lieutenant-Colonel Boothby, also embarked, together with several details.

September 13th.—Sailed at 4 p.m.

September 16th.—Arrived at Cape Town.

September 17th.—Sailed at 6 p.m.

October 2nd.—Arrived at Las Palmas at 6 a.m., where the ship coaled.

October 3rd.—Sailed at 2.30 a.m.

October 8th.—Arrived off the Needles at 9.30 a.m., attended by fog. We were met in Southampton Water by the Lieutenant-Colonel (Colonel Ricardo), the Regimental Adjutant (Captain Earle, D.S.O.), and Major Scott-Kerr. Landed at Southampton about 1.30 p.m., and were taken to London by a special train arriving at Nine Elms at 6 p.m., whence the Battalion marched to Chelsea Barracks, where they were met by many friends and large crowds. The men had dinner in the recreation room, and were dismissed and allowed to go out of barracks. All officers of the Battalion who were at home met the Battalion in the new uniform with sash round the waist, etc.

October 20th.—H.R.H. the Duke of Cambridge, Colonel of the Regiment, sent for Lieutenant-Colonel Lloyd and asked him many questions about the war.

October 24th.—Lieutenant-Colonel Lloyd was invested by the King at Buckingham Palace with the C.B.

October 27th.—The King inspected the Battalions of Guards which had been in South Africa on the Horse Guards' Parade; the 2nd Battalion Grenadier Guards under Lieutenant-Colonel Lloyd, C.B., D.S.O.; the 3rd Battalion Grenadier Guards, under Lieutenant-Colonel St. Aubyn; the 1st Battalion Coldstream Guards, under Colonel Codrington, C.B.; the 2nd Battalion Coldstream Guards, under Colonel Henniker-Major, C.B.; and the 1st Battalion Scots Guards, under Lieutenant-Colonel Harbord. The 2nd Battalion Scots Guards were not present, not having arrived from South Africa. The Grenadier Regiment made rendezvous in Wellington Barracks before the parade, the 1st Battalion keeping the ground.

After the parade all the C.O.'s and the Seconds in Command went to luncheon with the King at Buckingham Palace. In the evening the officers, past and present, of the regiment attended a dinner at the Whitehall Rooms, Hôtel Métropole, 203 being present. Lieutenant-Colonel Crabbe, C.B., who had commanded the 3rd Battalion during the war, sat on the right, and Lieutenant-Colonel Lloyd, C.B., D.S.O., commanding the 2nd Battalion, on the left of the Duke of Cambridge. They each replied to the toast of the health of their Battalions.

The following is a complete list of all the officers who served at any time with the 2nd Battalion Grenadier Guards during the South African War of 1899-1902 :—

Lt.-Col. F. Lloyd, D.S.O. ...	(Commanding) wounded 29 May, 1900; rejoined 11 Oct., 1900.
Major R. Gordon-Gilmour ...	(Second-in-Command), brevet Lt.-Col. 1902.
Major R. Scott-Kerr	Captain No. 1, afterwards No. 5.
Major W. Marshall	Capt. No. 8, employed for short time on Intelligence Staff.
Capt. The Hon. W. Cavendish	Capt. No. 6, employed as Intelligence - officer to 16th Brigade.
Capt. E. G. Verschoyle ...	Capt. No. 3, died of wounds at Thabanchu, May, 1900.

Capt. The Viscount Kilcoursie	Capt. No. 7, became Earl of Cavan, July, 1900.
Capt. W. Murray-Threipland	Capt. No. 2, invalided home Dec., 1901.
Capt. The Lord Ardee	Capt. No. 4.
Capt. G. L. Bonham	Capt. No. 5, wounded 29 May, 1900, rejoined 21 July, 1901.
Capt. C. E. Corkran	Adjutant, wounded 29 May, 1900, rejoined 29 June, 1900.
*Capt. W. S. Blackett	Succeeded Capt. Verschoyle as Capt. No. 3.
Lt. F. L. Swaine	Transport-officer till Nov., 1900, then Acting-Capt. No. 5 vice Bonham, Acting - Adjt. during Corkran's absence.
Lt. M. R. A. Cholmeley ...	Machine-gun-officer, then No. 5.
Lt. G. D. Jeffreys	No. 8, then Acting-Capt. No. 6 vice Cavendish, Intelligence-officer.
Lt. J. A. C. Quilter	No. 1 Acting-Capt. while Scott-Kerr Acting 2nd-in-Command.
Lt. E. Seymour	No. 6, wounded 29 May, 1900, invalided home.
Lt. H. St.L. Stucley	No. 4, then Transport-officer vice Swaine.
Lt. The Hon. G. H. Douglas-Pennant	Signalling officer.
Lt. The Hon. A. Weld-Forester	No. 7.

---

* Promoted.

*Lt. L. R. V. Colby	No. 2.
*Lt. The Hon. M. B. Parker	No. 1, temporary A.D.C. to Maj.-Gen. B. Campbell.
*Lt. A. H. Murray	No. 5, died of wounds, Senekal, 31 May, 1900.
*Lt. The Lord H. Seymour	Joined with 1st draft, 29 June, 1900. No. 6.
*Lt. G. R. Houstoun-Boswall	No. 4.
*Lt. E. B. Loraine	No. 8.
Lt. S. D. Shafto	Joined with 2nd draft, No. 8.
2nd Lt. G. T. Tryon	No. 5, died of enteric, Harrismith, 24 April, 1901.
2nd Lt. The Lord F. Scott ...	No. 3.
2nd Lt. The Hon. L. Cary (Master of Falkland)	No. 7, invalided home, enteric, ? 1901.
2nd Lt. E. B. G. Foster	Joined with 2nd draft, No. 2.
2nd Lt. D. C. L. Stephen ...	Joined 8 June, 1900, No. 6.
2nd Lt. K. C. E. Meeking ...	Joined 21 July, 1901, Signalling officer when Douglas Pennant became Brigade-signalling officer, died of enteric, Bethlehem, 2 Feb., 1902.
2nd Lt. C. R. C. de Crespigny	Joined 21 July, 1901. No. 7.
2nd Lt. The Lord Alan Percy	Joined 21 July, 1901. No. 6.
2nd Lt. E. M. Colston	Joined 19 Jan., 1902.
†Major J. H. Austin, R.A.M.C.	Surgeon attached:
†Capt. W. G. A. Garton ...	Quartermaster.

* These officers were promoted from 2nd Lieut. during 1900.
† Promoted.

LONDON.

J. J. KELIHER & CO., LIMITED,
32, New Bridge Street, E.C.

1907.

SOUTH AFRICAN CAMPAIGN,
1899-1902.

3rd Bn. GRENADIER GUARDS.

Roll of Honours to which the Battalion is entitled for active share in the various actions.

DATE.	HONOUR.	REFERENCE.
23rd Nov., 1899	"Belmont"	Page 1 and 23
28th Nov., 1899	"Modder River"	„ 7 „ 23
10th Mar., 1900	"Driefontein"	„ 24
29th May, 1900	"Johannesburg"	„ 26
12th June, 1900	"Diamond Hill"	„ 12 and 26
26th Aug., 1900	"Belfast"	„ 12 „ 27

PREFACE.

THE narrative portion of this book was written by the late Brigadier-General E. M. S. Crabbe, C.B., who only completed the work two days before he died.

It had been General Crabbe's intention, had he lived longer, to have written a preface in order to specially draw attention to two particular points.

. These points were as follows:—

    (i) Owing to the recent nature of the events chronicled in these pages and the scope of this work (which makes no pretence to be more than a mere collection of facts), any criticisms of the operations would have been in the highest degree undesirable.

    (ii) When all Grenadiers worked with such unremitting zeal, such cordial and never-failing co-operation, and such conspicuous success, to apportion praise to any particular individual, or individuals, appeared to him to be invidious and unfair.

Owing to his innate modesty General Crabbe entirely declined to make any reference to his own share in the Battle of Belmont. It must therefore be stated here, though it is well known to all, that to his high skill and intrepid leading the complete success of the Grenadiers' advance on that occasion was greatly due.

General Crabbe was twice wounded before the end of the battle, and in his account, therefore, the final stage of the action is not described.

The Tabular portion of this work was made out during the campaign in the 3rd Battalion Orderly Room (if the word "room" may be applied to so constantly changing, so frequently unenclosed and so undefinable a locality), and is almost entirely attributable to the industry of O.R. Sergeant (now O.R. Quartermaster-Sergeant), F. Acock, 3rd Battalion Grenadier Guards.

ALICK RUSSELL, *Captain and Brevet Major,*
formerly Adjutant 3rd Battalion Grenadier Guards.

Grenadier Guards' Orderly Room,
Buckingham Gate, S.W.
April, 1905.

3rd Battalion Grenadier Guards.

SOUTH AFRICA, 1899-1902.

THE 3rd Battalion Grenadier Guards left Pirbright Camp early on the morning of the 23rd September, 1899, and travelled in two special trains round London to the Royal Albert Docks, Woolwich, where they embarked on board the S.S. " Nubia." The embarkation elicited complimentary remarks from Major Fearon, the Embarkation Staff Officer, who expressed a wish that all troops at that station would embark as quickly, and in as orderly a manner as that Battalion had done.

The Lieutenant-Colonel of the Regiment, Colonel Hon. H. F. Eaton, together with many old officers, were present to wish the Battalion godspeed, and with them were Sergt.-Major Fowles and most of the senior non-commissioned officers of the Regiment.

The weather was propitious, and the only event which took place on the voyage was the arrival of a little son to Paymaster-Sergeant Jones, who, however, only survived his birth a few hours. The ship arrived at Gibraltar on the 27th September with the same number of passengers as left Woolwich.

The Battalion was met on arrival by Major-General Sir Henry Colvile, K.C.M.G., C.B., Commanding Infantry Brigade, Gibraltar, and other officers of the Headquarters Staff.

Quickly disembarking, the main portion of the Battalion were marched to Buena Vista barracks, leaving No. 3 Company to escort the baggage and accompany the transport to barracks as soon as all was clear.

The 2nd Battalion, marching down to embark, passed the 3rd Battalion on the way to barracks.

The situation in South Africa at this time caused deep excitement in all corps who had any chance of seeing active service.

In accordance with War Office orders the change of station from Gibraltar to England was to take place on the 1st September, but owing to the critical state of affairs in South Africa, the 2nd Battalion had been kept at Gibraltar until nearly the end of September, in order that, if required, they might sail direct for South Africa. Negotiations had, however, been prolonged, and it was decided that the annual relief should take place without further delay, hence the arrival of the 3rd Battalion.

Colonel Lloyd, Major Gilmour, and officers of the 2nd Battalion, heartily welcomed the 3rd Battalion, while envying them their good luck at coming first on the roster for active service, by their arrival at Gibraltar.

During the night a telegram arrived ordering the 2nd Battalion on board the " Nubia " to stand fast. This might mean South Africa direct, or England, as the case might be, and great was the relief of the 3rd Battalion early on the next morning to see the " Nubia " steam homeward.

A month was passed at Gibraltar much as other battalions had passed it, except that everyone was alert for the latest news from South Africa, with hopes that the Battalion might soon be ordered to that country.

On the 15th October the looked-for order came for the 3rd Battalion Grenadier Guards and the 1st Battalion Coldstream Guards to embark for South Africa and form part of the First, or Guards' Brigade, under Sir Henry Colvile, which again was the first Brigade of the First Division, commanded by Lieut.-General Lord Methuen. From that date everyone was alert and anxious that the Battalion should embark as complete as possible, and fit in every way to do credit to the traditions of the Regiment. At length the order was received that the S.S. "Goorkha" would arrive at Gibraltar on 25th October with 471 reservists, officers and men to make up the Battalion to war strength; she duly arrived, and on the 26th October, 1899, the 3rd Battalion Grenadier Guards, at war strength, steamed slowly out of the harbour on its way to active service. The numbers and names of all who started will be found in the appendix. The Battalion received a hearty send off, not only from the wives and relations of those on board, but from all in Gibraltar who had interested themselves in making their stay on the Rock pleasant.

Twenty-four hours sufficed to get over sea-sickness, and then the routine of the voyage began.

Physical drill at 6 a.m.; Lieutenant Fryer, the Adjutant, drilled the officers, while company officers later on superintended the work of their individual units.

The ship's stores were requisitioned for empty bottles and boxes; the former were slung from the rigging, the latter were towed astern, and each company was exercised in musketry at these improvised targets, prizes being given when bottles were broken.

On the 29th October we reached Teneriffe, anchored in Santa Cruz Bay. The ship was coaled, and at 1.30 p.m.

we steamed out of the harbour.   A New Zealand ship heartily cheered us and their band played " God save the Queen."

The advantage of troops going to a hot climate being inoculated against enteric fever had been very strongly impressed on all in authority; officers, drummers and as many men as could be induced to undergo the operation were inoculated. The immediate result was a painful stiffness for one or two days which, however, speedily passed away leaving no bad effects behind. As far as has been ascertained the result throughout the campaign was that although a certain number of men who had been inoculated contracted enteric fever, they suffered much less severely than those who had not taken the precaution, while no deaths are recorded of men who had been inoculated.

Signalling by semaphore was practised by officers and proved useful in later days.

In addition to the work before mentioned, sports and concerts helped to while away the days which seemed all too long for lack of news.

At 4 a.m., 15th November, we anchored in Table Bay, and at 10.30 a.m., having been brought alongside, the Battalion commenced disembarking.

Numbers 1, 2, 3, 4 and 5 Companies, with Major Kinloch in command, entrained at once and started at 2.30 p.m. for Orange River, followed one hour later by the remainder of the Battalion.

The whole arrived at Orange River fairly early on the 17th and found the 2nd Battalion Coldstream Guards and the 1st Battalion Scots Guards already there.

Lord Methuen with his A.A.G., Colonel Mainwaring and his A.D.C., Major Streatfeild, Grenadier Guards, met the Battalion at the station and gave them a hearty welcome.

The Scots Guards entertained the officers of the Grenadier Guards on arrival.

The latest news was that a patrol of the 9th Lancers and other mounted troops, with Colonel Hon. G. Gough in command, had located the enemy in the neighbourhood of Belmont, and after a protracted reconnaissance had lost Major Hon. Keith Falconer and five officers wounded.

Everyone's great ambition, from the General downwards, was that the men who had been so long without exercise on board ship should be got thoroughly fit for the marches which were before them, and with this end in view the battalion went route marching twice daily for comparatively short distances, but opening out and covering a large tract of rough country. A night march formed part of the programme with a view to ascertaining whether it would be possible to advance in the same extended order at night over the rough and stony country; the result was not altogether satisfactory, but it afforded a considerable amount of instruction from which good results were afterwards obtained.

On 21st November, at 3.40 a.m., the Battalion moved out, following the Scots Guards, who formed the advanced guard of the Division. A march of twelve miles brought us to Fincham's Farm at 8.45 a.m. No one fell out, although before we arrived the sun had got up and the heat was considerable. The Battalion bivouacked, the men quickly established themselves under shelters made with blankets and sticks, and all was quiet for the rest of the day.

The object of the force under Lord Methuen was the early relief of Kimberley, which it was hoped would be effected without serious opposition, except on the Spits Kop position, some eighty miles north of Orange River, and about fifteen from Kimberley. On arrival at Orange River the officers were ordered to remove their swords and to march equipped like the men, the majority carrying rifles, while a few were content with sticks. The swords were packed up and sent from Orange River to Cape Town, whence some two-and-a-half years afterwards they were returned to the Battalion at Hanover Road none the worse for their long disuse.

On leaving Orange River the troops marched in light order, tents and heavy baggage were left behind, two blankets per man was all that accompanied the relieving force.

November 22nd: Stood to arms 5 a.m. and then remained in bivouac till 4 p.m., when the whole force marched for Belmont, some seven miles distant. On the way the artillery duel ahead and the bursting shells could be heard and seen.

Just before dusk the force arrived in camp. Its left was at Belmont Farm and the bivouac lay in a valley, covered from the enemy by ridges in front, under which the army rested in comparative peace, although within two miles of the foe.

About 10 p.m., Lieutenant Matheson, Adjutant of 1st Battalion Coldstream Guards, rode into camp ahead of his Battalion to ascertain their camping ground. No staff officer being available at the moment, they were brought in next to the 3rd Battalion Grenadier Guards, who were able to supply both officers and men with refreshment which was much needed after the forced march they had made of twenty miles from Orange River.

Orders had been received while in bivouac at Fincham's Farm for a daybreak attack on the enemy's position, and a sketch-map had been shewn to C.O.'s. This map, however, was so inaccurate as only to mislead those responsible for the direction of the final advance.

The ground was reconnoitred by Major Ruggles-Brise, the Brigade Major, who was accompanied by Lieutenant-Colonel Eyre Crabbe, Lieutenant Hon. A. Russell, and Lieutenant Hervey-Bathurst.

The following account of the battle of Belmont, with the orders which preceded it, was written by Lieutenant-Colonel Eyre Crabbe, Commanding 3rd Battalion Grenadier Guards, soon after the battle, and is, from his point of view, a correct account of that much-debated engagement.

Captain M. Earle arrived with the 1st Battalion Coldstream Guards in time to take his place in the battle, having arrived by train and forced marches from Cape Town. He was posted to command No. 2 Company.

THE BATTLE OF BELMONT,

November 23rd, 1899, from the point of view of the 3rd Battalion Grenadier Guards.

On 22nd November, the Battalion, in company with the rest of Lord Methuen's force, was bivouacked at Fincham's Farm, and about 11 a.m. the three commanding officers of the Guards' Brigade, Lieutenant-

Colonels Eyre Crabbe, Grenadier Guards; H. Stopford, 2nd Battalion Coldstream Guards; and A. Paget, 1st Battalion Scots Guards, were sent for by the Brigadier, Major-General Sir H. E. Colvile, K.C.M.G., C.B., and the plan of the intended attack was explained to them.

The 1-inch scale was the only map available, except a sketch which had been prepared by Lieutenant-Colonel Verner, of the Intelligence Department, the previous evening, from a long-distance reconnaissance of the position, and it proved inaccurate and misleading.

The general orders for the attack were for the Guards' Brigade to seize Gun Hill, Middle or Grenadier Hill, as it was afterwards named, and Mont Blanc from the west, while the 9th Brigade moved along Table Mountain from the north. The 9th Lancers being in reserve in the level ground north-west, awaiting their opportunity, and the Field Artillery due west, ready to prepare Mont Blanc if necessary for the infantry attack.

The orders for the Guards' Brigade were for the 3rd Battalion Grenadiers and 1st Battalion Scots Guards to attack Gun Hill at 3 a.m. When that was taken the Coldstream Guards were to take Middle or Grenadier Hill, and then the combined Brigade was to assault Mont Blanc. From the sketch it appeared that Middle Hill was like Gun Hill, a detached kopje. The Brigadier distinctly stated that as far as he had been informed and could judge, Gun Hill was long enough to permit of its being attacked by the two above-named Battalions. Instructions were given that after Gun Hill had been taken the Battalions were to re-form under the western side, which it was stated would afford cover. The two Battalions were to be led by the Brigade Major, Guards' Brigade, to a ganger's hut on

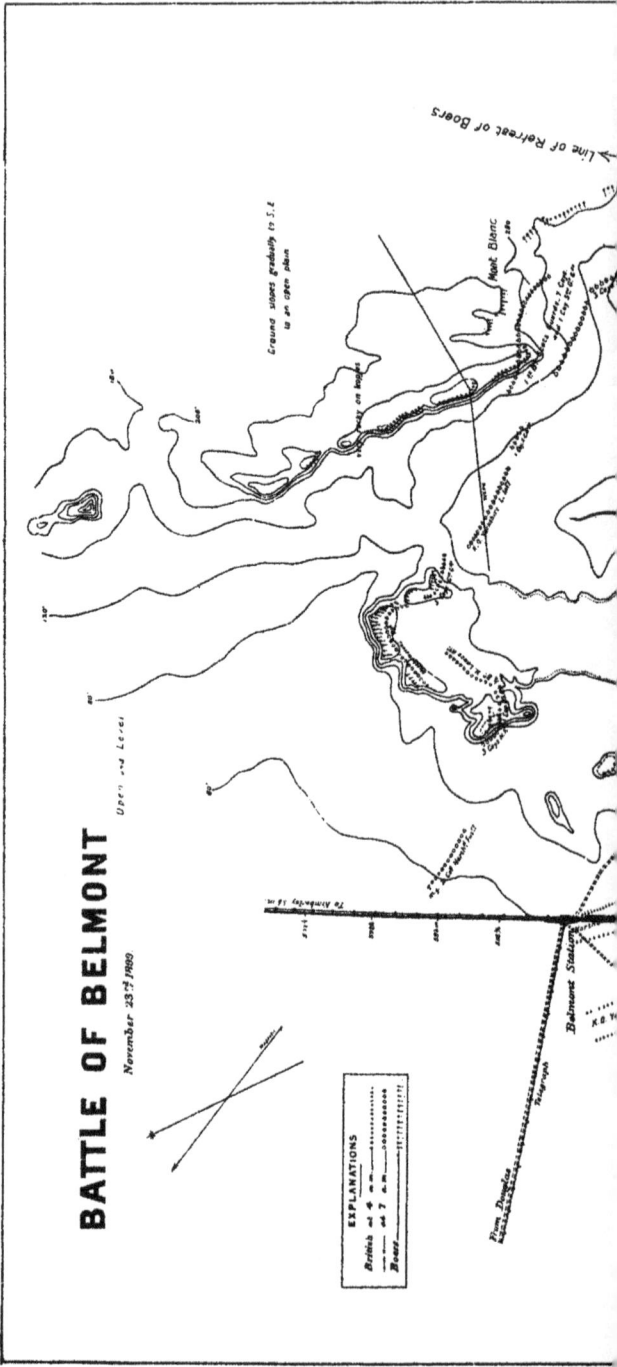

BATTLE OF BELMONT

November 23ʳᵈ 1899

Line of Retreat of Boers

Ground slopes gradually to S.E. to an open plain

Mont Blanc

Open and Level

To Kimberley 14 m.

Belmont Station

From Douglas

Telegraph

EXPLANATIONS

British at 4 a.m. ——————
        at 7 a.m. ——————
Boers ——————

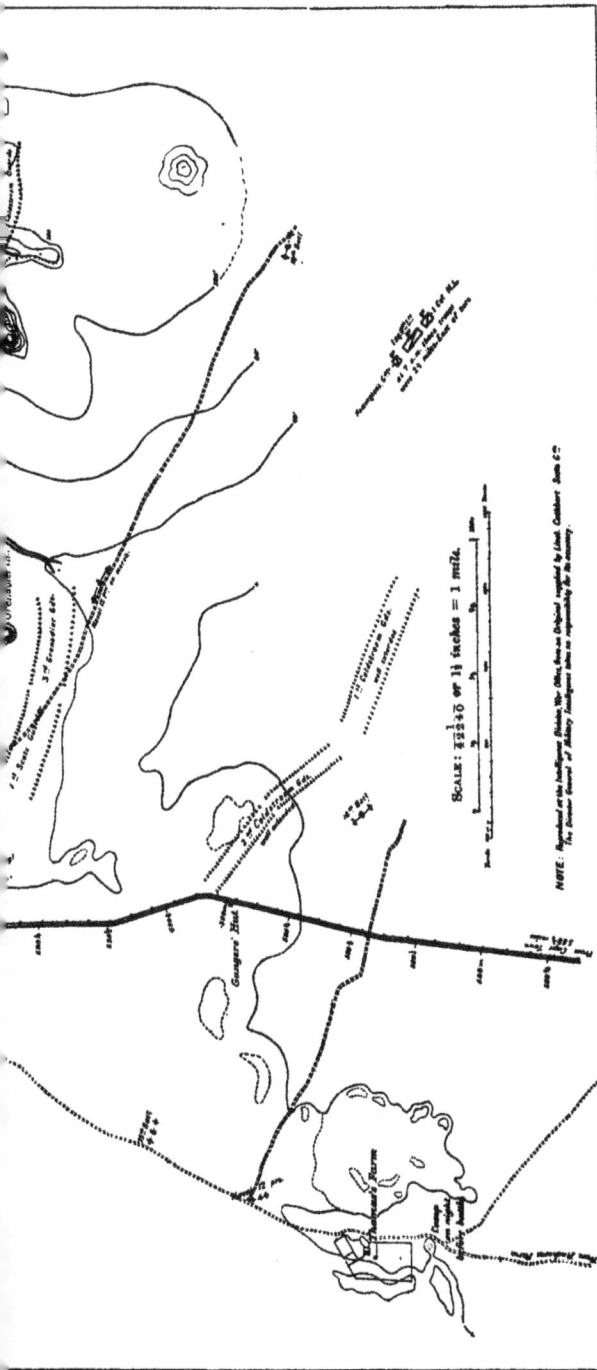

SCALE: $\frac{1}{42240}$ or 1½ inches = 1 mile.

NOTE: Reproduced at the Intelligence Division War Office, from an Original supplied by Lieut. Cuthbert, from 6th...

the railway, marked on the sketch, which was to form the centre of the deployment.

The Battalions were led with accuracy to their positions at the ganger's hut and extended. The Grenadiers extended from their left backwards on No. 4. The right half companies advanced ten paces, the whole then extending to one pace interval. This gave the attacking and supporting lines, each consisting of two companies, with the companies in proper order from the right. The left half battalion was in reserve under Major D. A. Kinloch.

The advance commenced at 3.35 a.m. on the 23rd, and was continued without opposition till 3.50, and it began to be freely anticipated that the Boers had left their position.

A heavy burst of fire gave the denial to these ideas and proved at the same time the inaccuracy of the sketch-map. The Brigade found themselves at the base of a long and steep line of kopjes, lined from end to end by the enemy, while Gun Hill proved only a small excrescence on the plain, enfiladed by Middle Hill, which jutted out as the advanced feature of the main ridge and showed up clearly as the key of the position.

Gun Hill was speedily taken by the Scots Guards and half a company of Grenadiers, who more than covered it, and the Scots Guards lapped over considerably to the left. The fire from Middle or Grenadier Hill was destructive alike to the troops in front and to the Scots Guards on Gun Hill. It was therefore necessary at all hazards to clear this, more especially as there was no room on Gun Hill and no cover in the open plateau over which the Grenadiers had advanced. Grenadier Hill was a steep kopje of ironstone boulders. This hill was taken in about a quarter of an hour by the Grenadiers, and the result was felt at once all along the line in the reduced fire of the enemy, who immediately retired to a second range to the eastward. Meanwhile, on the extreme right, the Coldstream were pressing the attack on Mont Blanc, the artillery preparing the way, and assisted by the capture of Grenadier Hill they speedily crowned the heights and the enemy were soon in full retreat to a third ridge covering their laager. The 9th Brigade on the left cleared the plateau from the north, and the enemy began to leave his position in haste, and his laager, which was immediately to the south-east of it. Had the 9th Lancers been fresh enough to pursue, the damage inflicted must have been greatly increased.

Between the first and second positions held by the Boers, there was a deep valley which was crossed by the Grenadiers and Scots under heavy fire, and it was only when the enemy saw that, as in the first attack, these troops would not be denied, that they quitted the whole Belmont position and made for the north-east. As they fled, they were further intimidated by long range volleys from the Grenadiers and Scots, while the Coldstream made for the laager.

In the Grenadiers the casualties were :—

Killed   .. $\begin{cases} 1 \text{ officer} \\ 21 \text{ non-commissioned officers and men} \end{cases}$

Wounded .. $\begin{cases} 8 \text{ officers (2 of whom died afterwards)} \\ 107 \text{ non-commissioned officers and men (12} \\ \text{of whom died afterwards).} \end{cases}$

A Boer flag, which is now preserved in the Regimental Orderly Room, was taken during the battle by No. 5693 Private John Lewis of No. 4 Company.

Captains Corry and Earle were the first to reach the

top of Grenadier Hill, while the whole Battalion maintained both in this, their first action, and in the many engagements of this campaign, the noble traditions of their beloved Regiment.

The rest of the 23rd was passed in searching for the missing, all of whom were found to have been killed, and in preparing for the sad ceremony of the evening, when just before sunset the Brigade of Guards buried their dead in one large cemetery in the veldt, close to where they had bivouacked.

Sir Henry Colvile, Commanding the Brigade, and all available officers were present; the service was conducted by the Rev. T. F. Falkner, who had joined the Brigade at Orange River, and remained its chaplain until its arrival in Pretoria. The death of their Adjutant, whose bright spirits and untiring zeal had endeared him to all, was a deep blow to the Battalion in this their first engagement.

24th November : Lieutenant-General Lord Methuen expressed a wish to see the 3rd Battalion and to say a word to them after the hard fight of the previous day. At 10 a.m., the Battalion formed up and was first addressed by Sir Henry Colvile; Lieutenant-Colonel Eyre Crabbe followed with a few words, and then Lord Methuen having arrived, expressed his satisfaction at the way the 3rd Battalion had fought on the previous day. The remarks of these three officers, taken as nearly verbatim as possible, were as follows :—

Lord Methuen's remarks :

" I feel that I should like to say a word this morning to you officers, non-commissioned officers and men of the 3rd Battalion Grenadier Guards after the noble way you acquitted yourselves yesterday. With troops like you no General can fear for the result of his plans, and I am confident that this is only the first of the successes with which we shall be associated.

"I am a man of few words, but I should not like to leave you this morning without expressing regret at the death of your Adjutant, Lieutenant Fryer, and the other brave men who fell yesterday morning. I only regret that it was impossible for me to be present last evening to pay the last mark of respect to him and to them."

Sir Henry Colvile's remarks :

"Officers, non-commissioned officers and men of the 3rd Battalion Grenadier Guards, I have always been proud that I was a Grenadier, but I have never felt so proud of it as I do at this moment when I recall the gallant deeds you performed yesterday morning."

Lieutenant-Colonel Eyre Crabbe's remarks :

"Comrades, I have only one word to say, I am satisfied with you."

Lieutenant Blundell, who died late on the evening of the 23rd, was buried in the cemetery at Belmont at 11 a.m. next day ; Lord Methuen, Sir Henry Colvile and all officers being present. A true sportsman and a gallant officer, whose place it was hard to fill.

At 2.45 p.m. the whole force paraded and marched about 10 miles, where they bivouacked for the night. There were scares of the enemy on the right during the march, but no opposition.

The command of the Battalion after the battle of Belmont devolved on Major Kinloch, Lieutenant-Colonel Eyre Crabbe having been wounded in the right arm and left leg and sent to Cape Town.

Lieutenant Hon. E. Lygon succeeded Lieutenant Fryer as Adjutant of the Battalion.

Lieutenant G. Trotter succeeded Lieutenant Blundell as Transport officer.

November 25th: The Guards' Brigade were in reserve and consequently, although they came under long-range fire and marched a considerable distance, they were not called upon to attack at Graspan, or Enslin as it is sometimes called, in which action the Naval Brigade suffered severely, and were most justly awarded the chief honours of the day.

The turning movement by the Guards' Brigade however contributed very considerably to the early flight of the Boers.

The camp that night was at Enslin Siding.

The day had been hot and the fatigue considerable, but the Battalion acquitted itself as well as it had done during its previous marches.

November 26th: The Battalion remained in Enslin Siding in bivouac.

November 27th: Marched to Witkopslaagte or Du Toit's farm. Advanced patrols were in slight contact with the enemy near Modder River, otherwise there was no collision.

Lieutenants Hon. A. Russell and Gurdon-Rebow, who had been wounded at Belmont, rejoined the Battalion in the evening from Orange River Hospital.

November 28th: It was reported that the enemy had left Modder River, and the General consequently hoped to occupy this important place without opposition, but these hopes were speedily dispelled. The Division moved off at 4.30 a.m. and the Battalion extended for attack about 6.30 a.m. The enemy was in line on both banks of the Modder River. The right half companies of

B

Nos. 1, 2, 5 and 6 Companies formed the attacking line, the left half companies and remainder of the Battalion was in reserve. The enemy's fire was very heavy.

Ammunition ran out about 12.30, and any further advance was impossible. At this time the Maxim gun, under Lieutenant Hon. Alick Russell, did good execution, threatening the enemy's left flank and compelling them to abandon the attack which was enveloping our right. The Battalion still lay under heavy fire, unable either to advance or retire. Ammunition was brought up under great difficulties by the men whose names will be found in the appendix.

When the sun at last went down the troops were collected to rest on the field with the prospect of renewing the attack at daybreak.

Lieutenant-General Lord Methuen having been wounded, Major-General Sir Henry Colvile assumed command of the Division, and Colonel A. Paget was given command of the Guards' Brigade.

An attack with the bayonet was ordered for daybreak. However, on the Brigade forming up and moving out, it was discovered that the enemy had had enough of it on the previous day, and had left their position, retiring north and east towards Spitzkopte and Jacobsdal.

During the battle of Modder River, Captain Count Gleichen called for volunteers to bring in a wounded man from the front, he and three sergeants started out, but Count Gleichen alone returned, the three sergeants and the wounded man having all been killed.

November 29th : As soon as it was ascertained that the enemy had evacuated Modder River, the troops were given a short rest and the first food they had had since the night of the 27th-28th. At 1 p.m. the force crossed the Modder River and bivouacked on the northern bank, leaving parties behind to collect the wounded and bury the dead.

No record appertaining to any part of the Brigade of Guards would be complete without mentioning the loss which the Brigade sustained on the 28th November by the death of Lieutenant-Colonel Stopford, Commanding 2nd Battalion Coldstream Guards, and Captain S. Earle of the same Regiment, who was attached to the Mounted Infantry.

November 30th to December 10th: The force lay at Modder River, the outposts being in touch with the Boer forces on the heights of Magersfontein, some three miles to the north. On Sunday, 10th December, Lord Methuen shelled the Boer position with his 4·7 naval guns, howitzers and all his artillery. It was hoped that this bombardment would so paralyse the Boers that the daybreak attack decided on for the 11th would carry the position.

At dusk on the 10th, the Brigade moved out across the Modder to the north, and after a march of about one-and-a-half miles lay down till 1 a.m.

The Highland Brigade and a brigade of artillery had been sent forward, the former to attack with the bayonet at daybreak, the latter to support the attack as soon as light permitted. The Guards' Brigade moving on at 1 a.m. found themselves in a country covered with scrub and boulders on a pouring wet night with a gale of wind blowing. Although various portions of the column had lost each other in the dark, the whole came together with the first streak of dawn, and were formed up in quarter-column out of range but in support of the Highland Brigade, when the stillness of the morning was broken by one of the heaviest bursts of fire on record. Everyone waited for the cheers which accompany a successful charge, but they waited in vain ; and soon the order came for two Battalions to advance and cover the front to protect the Highland Brigade from an attack on their right flank. The two Battalions of the Coldstream Guards were detailed for this duty, the Scots Guards were at the time detached to the left, while the Grenadiers were in reserve. The latter were formed in four lines of double companies at intervals of some 300 yards, and thus remained the whole day except when the lines were changed to enable each in turn to get water and refreshments while in the fourth line, the leading line being under sniping fire.

No. 1 and half No. 5 were sent in support of the Coldstream and remained with them throughout the night ; during the afternoon Lieutenant-Colonel Eyre Crabbe received orders that he was to command a force consisting of his own Battalion, the 1st Battalion Scots Guards and various detachments from other corps, who were to go in with the bayonet at nightfall. This order was subsequently cancelled.

December 12th : The position occupied by the Coldstream, who had gallantly borne the brunt of the fighting on the previous day after the repulse of the Highland Brigade, was taken up by the 3rd Battalion early in the morning. A truce was held from 9 a.m. till 12 noon, during which time the General Officer Commanding decided to retire his force to the Modder River and the 3rd Battalion was ordered to cover the retreat. This they did, retiring in four lines alternately one through the other. During the retirement they were heavily shelled by the enemy, who, however, made no attempt to follow them up with rifle fire. Their retirement received high approbation from the G.O.C., while the rest of the force congratulated them on their bearing throughout this trying movement. The battalion retired to bivouac, where it remained until 16th February, 1900.

Tents had been brought up from the base and efforts were made to make the men as comfortable as the adverse circumstances of the climate permitted. Dust storms were frequent, generally from 4 to 6 in the afternoon, when it was easily possible to lose one's way through the clouds of dust.

The Battalion was on outpost every fourth day, and on the last night of the old year they started a new fort in advance of the line previously held. This fort was called 2 A, and from it skirmishes with the enemy were of almost daily occurrence.

Lord Roberts arrived at Modder River on 12th February, and received a hearty welcome from the troops, who were eagerly awaiting the order to move.

On the afternoon of the 15th February, a large force of horsemen could be seen moving rapidly north some ten miles east of our position. This was the celebrated ride to the relief of Kimberley, so gallantly carried out by the Cavalry Division under the intrepid Sir John French.

On the morning of the 16th February it was ascertained that the enemy had left their position at Magersfontein and all their laager fell into our hands.

The 3rd Battalion was ordered to encamp on the forsaken position, and to examine the trenches and the baggage left behind by the Boers.

A large quantity of ammunition was found and destroyed, while provisions of all sorts proved an acceptable addition to the daily ration.

A flag of honour presented to Cronje by the inhabitants of Ficksberg, with "E BEN HAZAR" in silver
filigree on it, was found among the loot left behind
by the retreating enemy, and is now in possession of
Captain G. Trotter.

February 16th: We were warned that a considerable
number of Boers were at Schwartzkopte on the north-
east between Magersfontein and Kimberley, and were
likely to attack our forces during the night; strict
precautions were taken, but the report proved incorrect.

February 17th: We made an examination of the
Boers' positions and located their laagers. In the afternoon orders were received to return to Modder River,
where the force was complete by 5 p.m. After dinner
an order arrived for the Guards' Brigade to march to
Klip Drift. About 1 a.m. the Brigade, under the
command of Major-General Pole-Carew, moved east-
ward along the south bank of the Modder River.
After about one mile march there was a considerable
halt to allow the baggage to come up, and it was
3 o'clock before we got fairly on the way. From
Modder River to Klip Drift is 19 miles. At 9 a.m.
the Brigade arrived at its destination. Not a man had
fallen out of the Battalion, and we were within 25 miles
of the main army encircling the Paardeberg position.
Here we remained until the 28th February, when after
the Paardeberg surrender the Boer prisoners were
brought to Klip Drift on their way to Modder River;
here they were placed in charge of the 3rd Battalion
Grenadier Guards, assisted by a squadron of the C.I.V.
Mounted Infantry, and at 3.30 p.m. the march to
Modder River was commenced. The formation was
as follows: A few of the Scouts of the C.I.V. preceded
the column, then came all the Commandants and

Field Cornets mounted on ponies and escorted by mounted men, following them came the dismounted Burghers in a square surrounded by the Battalion; the rear consisted of some wagons carrying the Boer women and men unable to march, the whole being brought up by No. 8 Company.

General Cronje, who was escorted by General Pretyman, and had his own escort, travelled independently, accompanied by Mrs. Cronje. He was received with a Guard of Honour furnished by the Coldstream Guards, and lunched with General Pole-Carew, as did Major Albrecht, who had commanded the Boer Artillery. The latter endeavoured to escape, so was sent back to join the other prisoners. In consequence of this he received special attention on the march, and at night he had a sentry of his own, with orders to take effective steps should he propose moving off. The four men who formed this guard were :-

> Lce.-Sergt. R. Rea.
> Private T. Fitz-Maurice.
> ,,   T. A. Budge.
> ,,   D. O'Shea.

About 6 p.m. information was received that the enemy on the south had been watching our movements and proposed to attack us in order to rescue the prisoners. The force was brought up in rear of a slight rise in the ground and bivouacked for the night.

The C.I.V. Mounted Infantry, with the ponies of the mounted Boers, were sent to a separate bivouac some quarter-mile in rear.

The prisoners were formed into a rectangle, surrounded by the Battalion at one yard interval, but a space of 15 yards was kept clear between the prisoners and their guards in order to prevent any sudden surprise on the part of the former. The orders to the Battalion were that one man out of every three was to be standing alert on his post throughout the night. Company officers patrolled their sections every hour, and the Commanding Officer and the two next senior officers watched the whole bivouac every two hours throughout the night.

No attack was made, and at 5 a.m., 1st March, the force continued its march. In an hour we were at Brown's Drift, where the Boers were allowed to go down to the river and wash, the north side of the square being opened out for that purpose. Meanwhile a flat plain close handy had been selected and arrangements made for the morning meal.

Thanks to the efficiency of supply under Quarter-Master May, three-quarters of an hour sufficed to feed the 4,000 prisoners, and the march was then resumed. At 10 a.m. Modder River was reached and the prisoners were handed over to General Douglas and the garrison at Modder River. Ample provision had been made for them, and very soon our defeated enemies were enjoying the luxury of tents in a pouring rain ; their escort, however, were lying in the open.

At 3 o'clock next morning, 2nd March, the Battalion started on the return journey, reaching Klip Drift in good time without casualties.

On the afternoon of the 4th March the welcome order came to move east and join the main army under Field-Marshal Lord Roberts.

For several days the weather had been most inclement. Storms of rain with wind had made life in bivouac intolerable, and when the morning of the 5th arrived and the force paraded at 5 o'clock, the whole camp was a swamp. The blankets, owing to the

rain, weighed double their regulation weight, and the
mules in consequence were unable to draw them.

We had hoped to reach Stinkfontein that evening,
but instead we were obliged to bivouac at Brandt
Vlei without blankets and almost without food, but
hoping for the best.

The Scots Guards' wagon was first to arrive,
and they divided their rations with us. Next morning
there was an alarm of Boers from the south. The
Battalion went out, but nothing of importance occurred,
and when we got back we found that the larger portion
of the baggage had arrived. At 2 p.m. the Brigade
moved on, leaving Major Surtees and a half battalion
of Coldstream Guards to bring on the baggage.
Stinkfontein was reached just before dark. Lord
Roberts came out to meet us some two miles from
Camp and the Brigade defiled past him on their way
to bivouac. A short night and we were off at 2.30
a.m. to what was rumoured to be a general engagement, from which great things were hoped. The
Brigade, with a battery of 4·7 guns, was halted at
Le Gallais Kopje, where Lord Roberts made his Head
quarters throughout the day. The general disposition
was as follows: The enemy, 15,000 strong, were
occupying a ridge of kopjes about 15 miles long,
split in the centre by the Modder River. On the
right were the Cavalry, next to them the 6th Division,
then the Guards' Brigade and Head-quarters. The 7th
Division reached to the Modder River, while on the
north of the river were 9th Division and Mounted
Infantry.

It was intended that the Cavalry should move
round the enemy's left flank during the night and
threaten his rear at dawn; but by daybreak on the 6th

they were only within striking distance of the ridge of kopjes known as the Seven Sisters. Owing to the darkness of the night they had been unable to get into position before dawn, and when the Field-Marshal ordered one of the 4·7 guns to be fired to commence the battle about 5 a.m. the Cavalry had still some distance to go before being able to get round the enemy's flank.

At 8 a.m. the Boers were seen on the Seven Sisters and the 4·7 guns fired three rounds. On the first round no movement took place, on the second round fear caught them, and when the third was fired the force retired for all they were worth.

At 9.45 a.m. the Brigade was ordered to advance. They deployed in column of half battalions at some three hundred yards interval, and their movements caused much favourable criticism from the Attachés who were present with the Head-quarters Staff.

In this order and with constant halts we travelled some 14 miles to Poplar Grove. The enemy had bolted in sufficient time to save themselves, and Kruger for the first and only time during the war had a narrow escape of being taken prisoner. One gun, wagon and ammunition fell to our lot, but the much wished-for prize was gone.

We remained at Poplar Grove till the morning of the 10th, when the 9th Brigade and Head-quarters moved to Driefontein by the centre road.

General Kelly-Kenny with the 6th Division had moved the day before on our left to Abraham's Kraal, while General Tucker, with the 7th Division, moved south to Petrusberg. Thus the three roads to Bloemfontein were covered and the general advance commenced. General Kelly-Kenny with the 6th Division, and the cavalry under

Sir John French, found the enemy in position at Abraham's Kraal, or Driefontein, where a severe action took place. We only arrived at Driefontein in the evening to hear the last gun of what had been a real stand-up fight.

We had marched 19 miles, and on arrival were first of all ordered to take some kopjes about two miles distant, which were supposed to be still occupied by the enemy, and later a half battalion was ordered on outpost with the other half battalion in reserve about a mile away.

It was a rough country and very difficult for outposts to get connection. On returning to the reserve after going round the outposts, Colonel Crabbe, accompanied by Captain Trotter, met Major Congreve, V.C., a brigade-major in the 6th Division, who informed them that they had had a very hard day, and whilst they had lost considerably, they had counted 200 Boers laid out in a row and had won a complete victory. Whilst riding into camp, Major Maude, our brigade-major, got a nasty fall, which resulted in serious damage to his right arm.

Next morning we followed up the enemy, who, however, were not anxious to meet us again, and retired on their position at Quaggasfontein without firing a shot. About 3 p.m. we bivouacked east of Asvogel Kopje, near a large dam, our only water, embellished with many carcases of mules, mostly, fortunately, of a very recent date. We remained here till 3 p.m. next day, March 12th, when, in company with both Battalions Coldstream Guards, we commenced the now historic march to Bloemfontein. Our cooks, under the orders of that most excellent provider, Quarter-Master May, had gone on in the morning with the Scots Guards with instructions to have a meal ready for us whenever we arrived.

At 9.15 p.m. we halted for refreshments. Thanks to Surgeon-Major Magill, our excellent P.M.O., we were able to water the men from hospital carts, while the General gave orders that the supply wagons should be indented on for rations.

At 10.30 p.m. we marched on, arriving at Venters Vlei at 2 a.m. Tired as the men were they decided with one voice to attack the hot dinner which was waiting for them. They then lay down for a short rest.

At 5 a.m. 13th, we marched again after a good breakfast in addition to the 2 a.m. meal. A hot march of 6 hours brought us to a dam of very questionable water, which, however, was most gratefully partaken of, and as soon as we had re-started we received orders to press on for Bloemfontein and that Lord Roberts intended to lead us into the town.

At 1 p.m. we halted in a shady grove attached to a large house some four miles from Bloemfontein, and the men had a wash. We had thus covered 41 miles in 21 hours.

At 4 p.m. the drums were massed in front of the Brigade, and in Brigade order of march, the 3rd Battalion leading, we moved down the road to the Capital of the Orange Free State, already in view. It must here be put on record that this Brigade at the end of their forced march, as soon as the drums began to play, stepped out as though they were marching past in Hyde Park, having apparently forgotten all dangers and fatigues in the honour of being the first British Infantry to enter Bloemfontein.

Lord Roberts was unable to meet us, but none the less the spectacle afforded to the inhabitants of the Orange Free State was one they did not forget, and they were never afterwards anxious to meet the Brigade of Guards in the field.

INTO BLOEMFONTEIN 13TH MARCH,

STAFF OFFICERS of DIVISIONS and BRIGADES & FOREIGN MILITARY ATTACHES WHO MARCHED

LT. COL. COMMdt D'AMADE..... FRENCH MIL. ATTACHE
CAPT. BARON VON LUTTWITZ GERMAN... DO....
MAJOR GENTILINI - ITALIAN
DO.... CAPT MIRADIA... JAPANESE
MILITARY ATTACHES.

1900.

LIEUT. COL. STAKHOVITCH... RUSSIAN MIL. ATTACHE.
MAJOR ESTABAN, SPANISH MILITARY ATTACHE.

7TH DIVISION.
LIEUT. GEN. C. TUCKER, C. B.
MAJOR LUMLEY & MAJOR WILLIAMS A.D.Cs
LT. COLONEL, H. HEGAN, A.A.G.
MAJOR, H. G. FITTON, D.S.O. D.A.A.G.
LT. COL. RICE, A.S.C. D.A.A.G.

MARTYR'S M. INFTY
LT. COL. C. G. MARTYR.
MAJOR SHAW,
BENGAL LANCERS,
STAFF OFFICER.

GUARDS BRIGADE
MAJOR-GEN. R. POLE-CAREW, C.B. COMMANDING.
CAPT. F. ST.G. HUGHES, S.W. BORDERERS, A.D.C.
LIEUT. F. D. FARQUHAR, COLDSTREAM GDS A.D.C.
MAJOR, F.S. MAUDE, COLDSTREAM GDS B. MAJOR

ALDERSON'S M. INFTY
LIEUT. COL. E. A. H. ALDERSON.
CAPT. H. McMICKING STAFF OFFICER.

CAVALRY DIVISION
LIEUT. GEN. J. D. P. FRENCH
LT. COL. D. HAIG, A.A.G.
MAJOR LORD EDMUND TALBOT D.A.A.G
MAJOR G.O. WELCH, A.S.C. D.A.A.G.
MAJOR HON. C. C. BINGHAM,
A.D.C.
CAPT. HON. T.W. BRAND A.D.C.

RIDLEY'S M. INFTY
LT. COL. C. P. RIDLEY B! COL.
BT LIEUT. COL. B. R. MITFORD STAFF. OFF!

9TH DIVISION.
LIEUT. GEN. SIR. H. E. COLVILLE K.C.M.G. C.B.
CAPT. G. C. NUGENT, GRENADIER GUARDS, A.D.C.
BT. LIEUT. COLONEL, J. S. EWART, A. A. G.
MAJOR, H. G. RUGGLES- BRISE, D.S.O. D.A.A.G
CAPT. H. L. HUMPHREYS, A.S.C. D.A.A.G.

LE GALLAIS' M. INFTY
LT. COL. P. W. J. LE GALLAIS,
CAPT. G. F. BRASIER-
CREAGH I.S.C.
STAFF OFFICER.

6TH DIVISION
LIEUT GEN. T. KELLY-KENNY, C.B.
COLONEL. F. W. BENSON, A. A. G.
MAJOR, C. C. MUNRO, D.A.A.G.
MAJOR, D. WEBB, A.S.C. D.A.A.G.
CAPT. W.H. BOOTH, A.D.C.

CAPT SLOCUM... AMERICAN MILITARY ATTACHE
CAPT TRIMMEL... AUSTRIAN ... Do.

HEAD QUARTER - STAFF

MAJOR GENERAL E. WOOD, C.B. CHIEF ENGINEER
MAJOR E.H. BETHELL, R.E. STAFF OFFICER.
MAJOR R.S. CURTIS R.E.
A.D.C. TO C.E.

MAJOR GEN: W.F. KELLY C.B. D.A.G.
LT. COL: GRIERSON A.A.A.G.
LT. COL: R.B. GAISFORD A.A.G.
STAFF LT. W.S. CAUVIN A.S.C.
STAFF LT. J.H. POETT A.A.G.

COL: LORD STANLEY, PRESS CENSOR
COL: VISCOUNT DOWNE, C.I.E.
REV: H. COREY, C.F.
MAJOR EARL OF DUDLEY
CAPT. HON WARD.
STAFF LIEUT.
J. BOWERS,
A.S.C.

COLONEL E. RHODES, S.O.
COLONEL: E. SIGNALLING
LIEUT. H.T. SAWYER, R.V.D.
SENIOR NAVAL OFFICER.

MAJOR GENERAL
G.T. PRETYMAN
C.B. R.A
COMMANDANT H.Q.
CAPT. C.H.N. GOUGH 12TH BEN: CAV.
STAFF OFFICER.

MAJOR
CAPT. LORD SCOTT. A.D.C.

D.A.G's DEPT

A.D.C.
LIEUT. THE EARL OF KERRY, EXTRA A.D.C.
LIEUT. HIS GRACE THE DUKE OF WESTMINSTER
LIEUT. MAXWELL 6TH BENGAL CAV.

COLONEL N. CHAMBERLAIN PT. SEC.

FIELD MARSHAL
LORD ROBERTS
V.C.&c.
C. IN C.S. AFRICA

LIEUT. COL: H.V. COWAN, R.A. M. SEC:
LIEUT. COL: J.J. BYRON R. ASST. ART:
MAJOR S.J.A. DENISON, R. CANADIAN RA
CAPT. WATER MEYER, C.T. HIGH?

CAPT. A.G. WATERFIELD I.S.C.
CAPT. HIGH?

MAJOR
GENERAL SIR W.G.
NICHOLSON K.C.B.
DIRECTOR OF TRANSPORT
CAPT. FURSE R.A
STAFF OFFICER
MAJOR R.M.
POORE
P.M.

CAPT. A. WATERFIELD I.S.C.
CAPT. J. BEARCROFT, R.N.
LIEUT. COLONEL

CAPT. LORD SETTRINGTON A.D.C.

MAJOR GEN: G.O.C. G.H.Q. A.D.C.
MAJOR GEN: D. OF A.A.G.
COL: G.R. DK. R.B.
LIEUT. CAPT. A.D.C.
COMMANDER? DE CIE
HON NAVAL A.D.C.

C.B. D. OF SUPPLIES
P.M

COLONEL, W.D. RICHARDSON, A.S.C.
Q.P.M? & MAJOR R.E.D. OF TELEGRAPHS
LT. COL: R. L. HIPPISLEY, R.E.
CAPT. E. GODFREY – FAUSSETT, R.E
TELEGRAPH – DEPARTMENT, R.E.

COL: STEVENSON, R.A. M.C. P.M.O.
MAJOR SYLVESTER R.A. M.C.
CAPT. BEACH R.A.M.C.
KENDAL FRANKS ESQ.
WATSON CHEYNE ESQ.

H.A. SCLATER
T.H. C. SCLATER

MAJOR MILNE
CAPT ROBERTS

LIEUT. COL. J.L. MACKENZIE, D.A.A.G.
LIEUT. COL. EVANS, D.A.A.G.
MAJOR HUME, D.A.A.G.

D.M.I.
A.G.

We bivouacked half a mile south of the town, anticipating a certain amount of rest after the labours of the past fortnight.

On the following morning Lord Roberts inspected us, and the remarks he then made will be found in the Appendix.

Next morning, 15th March, we were once more on the move. The Brigade of Guards with a battery of artillery were entrained for the south to open up communication with Sir William Gatacre and General Clements at Norval's Pont. In the evening we were detrained at Edenburg and took up a position in case of attack.

At 10 p.m. Lieutenant-Colonel Crabbe, Lieutenant Hon. E. Lygon and Sergeant-Major Cook proceeded into Edenburg to make a house-to-house search for arms and ammunition ; the result was immensely satisfactory, many thousands of rounds of ammunition were seized and carried out into open spaces and arranged for destruction. The number of arms found was 14 cases of new Martini-Henry rifles and five cases of Martini-Henry carbines, besides many other rifles of all sorts.

At daybreak considerable interest was caused by the explosion of the ammunition above referred to, those not in the know imagining a heavy attack by the Boers.

The troops entrained and proceeded to Spring-fontein. Here Sir William Gatacre met us and told us he could cross at Bethulie without any difficulty. We trained on to Norval's Pont and found that the Boers had evacuated that part of the Orange Free State altogether and that General Clements could join hands with Sir William Gatacre. Having accomplished our mission, we returned to Edenburg that night and to Bloemfontein on the morning of the 17th, where we remained till the 22nd March, on

which day we were ordered to join the 1st Battalion
Coldstream Guards, who had preceded us to Glen
Siding, a bridge over the Modder River some 18
miles north of Bloemfontein. The force assembled
here consisted of the 1st Battalion Coldstream Guards,
some Colonial Mounted Infantry, and a party of
Engineers. The instructions were to repair the rail-
way and search the country for arms and ammunition.
On the morning of the 23rd Lieutenant-Colonel Crabbe,
Lieutenant-Colonel Codrington, Lieutenant G. Trotter
and Lieutenant and Adjutant Hon. E. Lygon with an
Orderly proceeded round the country to effect the order.
All were armed with rifles except Colonel Codrington,
who carried a Mauser pistol.

A few arms were found and several farms visited.

After reaching Karee Siding the order for home was
given, but immediately afterwards four Boers were seen
on a kopje to the south. Colonel Crabbe determined
to attack them, and the party galloped down to within short range. It was then found that instead of
four Boers there were seven. They kept well under
cover, and the result was Lieutenant Lygon was killed
and the rest of the party wounded.

The Boers behaved well and helped the wounded
to a neighbouring farmhouse, after which they took
their arms, saddlery, etc., and left them, giving them
leave to send to Glen for ambulances. These arrived
late in the afternoon, but the Doctor declined to allow
the wounded to move until dawn, when they were taken
back to Glen in the ambulances and thence by rail
to Bloemfontein. A funeral party came down and took
the body of Lieutenant Lygon back to Glen, where it
was buried the next evening in the presence of the
whole Battalion.

Unit	Officers	W.&N.C.O and Men	Horses	Guns	Unit	Officers	W.&N.C.O and Men	Horses	Guns
Army Hq Qrs Staff	50	65	73	"	Le Gallais M.I.				
					Staff	3	10	13	..
Cavalry Divn					6th M.I. Regt.	13	391	330	..
Divisional Staff	13	40	66	..	8th M.I. Regt.	15	511	254	..
1st Cav. Bde. Staff	6	14	22	..	City Imp. Vol.	11	185	145	..
6th Dragoon Gds	20	333	300	1x	Kitcheners H.	26	402	270	2+
2nd Dragoons	19	311	321	1x	Nesbitts H.	8	119	136	..
6th Dragoons (Det)	4	46	49	..	N.S. Wales M.I.	22	408	345	..
14th Hussars (Det)	7	108	74	..	H.Co Transp. A.S.C.	2	23	317	..
N.S. Wales Lcrs	6	89	90	..	Supply Det. A.S.C.	1	2	1	..
"Q" Batt: R.H.A.	5	147	154	6	Martyrs M.I.				
"T" Batt: R.H.A.	5	148	139	6	Staff	3	–	6	..
"U" Batt: R.H.A.	5	142	154	6	2nd M.I. Regt.	16	483	489	..
Ammunition Coln.	4	72	32	..	4th M.I. Regt.	15	327	251	..
Field Hospital	2	20	30	..	Burmah Co M.I.	17	292	332	..
Bearer Company	2	15	23	..	1st Queensland M.I.	8	184	211	..
Bde Dn Staff R.H.A.	4	16	18	..	2nd Queensland M.I.	8	128	158	..
1st Australian H	5	112	101	..	Ridleys M.I.				
2nd Cav Bde Staff	4	13	20	..	Staff	3	1	9	..
Household Cavy	22	291	292	..	5th M.I. Regt.	12	287	276	..
10th Hussars	26	386	414	1x	7th M.I. Regt.	17	337	262	..
12th Lancers	20	268	263	..	1st C Grahamst. Vol.	12	245	231	..
Staff Bde Dn R.H.A.	4	15	21	..	Ceylon M.I.	6	86	109	..
G. Batt: R.H.A.	5	147	139	6	F.Co Transp. A.S.C.	2	31	20	..
P. Batt: R.H.A.	5	145	130	6	Supply Det A.S.C.	1	8	–	..
Ammunition Coln.	2	43	36	..					
Field Hospital	3	16	25	..	Rl. Naval Bde	33	393	10	7+
Bearer Company	3	46	--	..	G in Cs Body Gd	1	43	53	..
Field Hosp. (Attd)	2	15	19	..	Staff Howitzers	6	15	14	..
					5 (St) Co S.D. R.G.A.	5	138	7	4‡
3rd Cav. Bde: Staff	4	10	15	..	Ox Amm. Reserve	1	2	2	..
9th Lancers	21	397	316	1x	9th Field Co R.E.	7	161	14	..
16th Lancers	24	373	368	2x	1st Tel. Dn R.E.	4	112	34	..
Staff Bde Dn R.H.A.	4	10	15	..	Guards Bde				
"O" Batt: R.H.A.	5	154	142	6	Brigade Staff	4	26	11	..
"R" Batt: R.H.A.	7	163	153	6	3rd Bn Gren Gds	26	899	8	1x
Ammunition Coln.	2	94	40	..	1st Bn Coldst. Gds	25	927	8	1x
Left Sn No II. Field Hp	2	16	2	..	2nd Bn Coldst. Gds	20	858	8	1x
No 9. Bearer Cy	3	42	6	..	1st Bn Scots Gds	15	516	6	1x
C.C. A.S. Corps	2	28	13	..	Gds Bde F. Hosp.	4	33	7	..
Field Troop R.E.	7	117	104	..	Bearer Co.	2	52	4	..
B. Co Transport	3	21	12	..	Supply Det.	1	16	2	..
C. Do Do	2	11	13	..	Hn Co A.S.C.	2	19	19	..
D. Do Do	1	12	8	..	VIth Division				
L. Do Do	3	9	6	..					
S. Do Do	2	33	20	..	Divl Staff	15	55	54	..
					Bde Dn Staff R.F.A.	3	2	5	..
Aldersons M.I.					76 Batt: R.F.A.	5	46	88	6φ
1st M.I. Regt	21	404	423	5x	81st Batt: R.E.A.	4	79	73	6φ
3rd M.I. Regt	12	195	228	..	82nd Do Do	5	89	94	6φ
Roberts Horse	35	553	587	..					
N. Zealand M.R.	5	60	72	..					
Rimingtons Guides	7	102	110	..					

+ 4 – 4.7 Guns
   3 – 12 Pr
‡ 4 – 6" Howitzers
φ 15. Pr
x Machine Guns

TEIN ON ITS SURRENDER... 13TH MARCH 1900

Unit	Officers	W.&N.C.O. and Men	Horses	Guns
65TH How: Batt:	5	169	162	6
R.E. Staff	2	5	4	..
38TH Co R.E.	6	131	19	..
13TH Bde Staff	3	19	7	..
2ND Bn E.Kent R.	10	560	8	1+
2ND Bn Glouce R.	22	563	8	..
1ST W.Riding R.	18	593	5	..
1ST Oxford L.I.	15	424	7	..
13TH Bearer Co	2	39	4	..
Supply Det: A.S.C.	1	15	2	..
18TH Bde Staff	4	37	7	..
2ND R.Warwick R.	20	834	7	1+
1ST Yorks: R.	12	705	..	1x
1ST Welsh: R.	11	654	7	1+
1ST Essex: R.	12	738	4	1+
18TH Field Hosp:	4	32	1	..
18TH Bearer Co	2	24	..	..
VII Division				
Divl Staff	11	77	43	..
Bde D: Staff R.E.A.	4	6	18	..
18TH Batt: R.F.A.	5	134	113	6+
62ND Do. Do.	5	128	113	6+
75TH Do. Do.	5	141	122	6+
No1 Ammn Col:	3	102	78	..
A.Sec: J.Pn Maxims	2	27	29	3+
26TH Co F. R.E.	7	126	18	..
Divn Supply Det.	1	30	21	..
14TH Bde: Staff	3	15	7	..
2ND Norfolk R.	16	763	5	1+
2ND Lincoln R.	19	752	6	1+
1ST K.O.S.Bord:	22	803	5	1+
2ND Hants R.	18	578	5	1+
14TH Bde F.Hosp:	5	31	33	..
14TH Bde Bearer Co	3	54	4	..
Supply Det A.S.C.	1	7	1	..
14TH Transpt Co.	2	25	14	..
15TH Bde Staff	4	19	8	..
2ND Cheshire R.	22	688	6	1+
2ND S.Wales Bord:	22	795	5	1+
1ST E.Lanc: R.	19	695	6	1+
2ND N.Stafford R.	19	737	6	1+
15TH Bde Bearer Co	3	48	4	..
15TH Fd Hosp:	4	31	3	..
Supply Det A.S.C.	1	9	11	..
15TH Transpt Co	2	9	8	..
IXTH Division				
Divl Staff	10	50	32	..
Staff B.D: R.F.A.	3	13	13	..
83RD Batt: R.F.A.	5	156	127	6+
84TH Do Do	5	158	131	6+
85TH Do. Do.	5	167	131	6+
Ammn Column	6	120	88	..
7TH Fd Co R.E.	6	163	35	..
Highland B: Staff	4	43	10	..
1ST A.S High: Highs	14	637	7	1+
2ND Rl High Lns	13	513	7	1+
2ND Seaforth Hrs	12	558	7	1+
Field Hospital	4	27	5	..
Bearer Compy	2	45	3	..

Unit	Officers	W.&N.C.O. and Men	Horses	Guns
XIX Bde Staff	3	26	8	..
2ND D.of Corn L.I.	15	854	5	1+
2ND Shrops L.I.	19	739	5	1+
1ST Gordon Hrs	19	738	7	1+
Rl Canadian R.	30	745	9	2+
Y.Transpt C:asc	1	33	18	..
Supply Det: A.S.C.	1	16	1	..
Bearer Compy	4	65	6	..
Field Hosp:	4	33	5	..
Supply Park A.S.C.				
No1 Section	..	5	..	..
" 22 Unit	1	5	1	..
" 25 Unit	2	6	2	..
" 29 Unit	2	8	2	..
" 5.Company	..	3	..	..
" 21. Do.	..	3	..	..
" 29. Do.	..	3	..	..
" 34. Do.	..	1	..	..
1ST Balloon Sec: R.E.	2	27	10	..
GRAND TOTAL	**1405**	**32,549**	**11,540**	

Guns: 42-12 Prs; 3-Naval 12 Prs, 54-15 Prs; 4-4.7" Naval Guns 6-5" Howitzer, 4-6" Howitzers. 39 Machine Guns

152

MAJOR-GENERAL,
D.A.GENERAL, S.A.FIELD FORCE

Major Kinloch took over command of the Battalion, which remained at Glen until 31st March, when the left half Battalion and Head-quarters were moved by train from Bloemfontein to Kaffir River, remaining there till the 2nd April, when they marched back to Bloemfontein. They were joined there by the right half Battalion on 4th April. Lieutenant Hon. A. Russell had succeeded to the Adjutancy, while Lieutenant Duberly replaced Lieutenant G. Trotter as Transport Officer.

From 4th to 7th April the Battalion remained at Bloemfontein. Orders were received on the 7th to proceed by train to Kaffir River, which was reached after dark, and considerable difficulty was experienced in placing outposts in a new country on a wet and stormy night. There was no move made till 20th. All this time the outpost duty was very heavy. The wet weather also made it very uncomfortable for the troops in camp.

On the 20th orders were received for another move. At 6.15 p.m. the Brigade moved off and reached Ferieira Siding at 2.45 a.m. Whilst the Battalion was at Kaffir River Colonel Jones assumed command of the Guards' Brigade, in place of Major-General Pole-Carew, who took command of the 11th Division. At 5.40 a.m., 22nd, the march was resumed. The Mounted Troops were engaged with the enemy most of the day; the Infantry were never actually in action. The force bivouacked at Kaffir River.

At 2.45 p.m. 23rd the Force moved on, and reached Eerste Geluk.

At 1.5 p.m. the Mounted Infantry was again engaged. The Guards furnished the outposts at night, and as they were not in till after dark some difficulty was experienced in taking up position.

The next morning the Force moved on again, and were soon once more in touch with the enemy. Though the fire was brisk very little damage was effected. The Force bivouacked that night at Damfontein, the enemy having retired in a southerly direction. A ten miles march next morning, 25th April, brought the force to Vaalbank, where it bivouacked for the remainder of the day.

Early on the morning of the 26th the force marched again and reached Reitpoort about 6.15. Orders were received here to turn back and bivouac again that night at Vaalbank.

Our 2nd Battalion was sighted the next morning some eight miles off. This was the only occasion during the war that 2nd and 3rd Battalions were in the same part of the theatre of war.

On the evening of the 27th the force bivouacked at Paardekraal on its way back.

April 28th. After a march of 15 miles reached Welgewonden by mid-day. On 29th the Brigade got once more under canvas at Bloemfontein. On coming into camp we were met by Colonel Crabbe, who had so far recovered from his wounds as to be able to ride with one arm in a sling.

Next day Major Kinloch and Major Cooper left us for England, the former to command the 1st Battalion of the Regiment, the latter to command the newly-raised 1st Battalion Irish Guards. This day, 30th April, was spent in equipping the Battalion for the general advance on Pretoria. Quarter-Master May had got everything in readiness and the result was that the Battalion started for its 300 miles march thoroughly equipped in every respect. Every man had a suit of new clothing, while socks, shirts, and under-clothing were freely given out. Boots were issued to all requiring them.

May 1st. The Battalion paraded with the rest of the Brigade and defiled past Lord Roberts in the Square on a grey cold morning, which heralded an advance which will ever be memorable in history for its rapidity and decision. That night we bivouacked at Karee Siding, after marching 21 miles, the advanced guard being furnished by the 3rd Battalion.

Next evening after a quiet day the Brigade moved just before sun-down about two miles to the front, and occupied a position in a defile opening on to the great plain stretching north to Brandfort. This evening Private Jones left the Battalion, and was never seen again. This was the only case of desertion throughout the campaign. No . fires were allowed owing to the proximity of the enemy, although the weather was exceedingly cold.

At 6.15 a.m. we marched to Allemans Dam, where a halt was made for breakfast. The Mounted Infantry under General Hutton reconnoitred the front and found the enemy in position south-west of Brandfort. Meanwhile on our right General Tucker with the 7th Division was also engaged ; however, the advance to Brandfort met with little opposition, a few shots were fired at the advanced guard of the Brigade, but no damage was done, and the force encamped at Brandfort early in the afternoon.

We remained at Brandfort 4th May. Captain Corry was sent down to Cape Town in charge of Lord Roberts's mail.

On the 5th May the advance was renewed, the immediate objective of the day's march being the position occupied by the Boers north of the Vet River.

About mid-day we halted at Eengevonden Station and gave the men tea.

Distant firing had been heard, which rapidly became heavier. At 4 p.m. the force was engaged south of the Vet River. The Artillery came into action, including the 4·7, which was moved in a marvellous manner by the Naval Brigade. The Infantry were extended. Nos. 5 and 6 Companies of the Battalion were in the firing line, but beyond a few spent bullets and a few harmless shells, received little attention.

At dark we were ordered to send two Companies to the kopje on the river which the Boers had left after a gallant attack from the Australian Contingent. Major Crompton-Roberts took Nos. 3 and 4 Companies, the remainder being bivouacked some 1½ miles south of the river, finding four more Companies, Nos. 1, 2, 7 and 8, for outpost.

Next morning, 6th May, the passage of the Vet was accomplished. The height of the bank and the sandy roads made this a matter of no little difficulty, even in the absence of the enemy. By night-fall the whole force was collected at Smalldeel Station, the junction for Winburg, where we remained until the 9th to enable the damaged bridges in rear to be repaired, and stores brought up. While here we heard of the death of Captain Verschoyle, of the 2nd Battalion, who was shot on outpost on the 5th and died next day.

On the 9th the Battalion marched to Welgelegen Siding, 13½ miles. On the 10th, to Reit Spruit, 13½ miles, crossing the River Zand, where the Boers were in position. On our right General Ian Hamilton had a serious action, but although in strong position in front of us the enemy retired in face of our heavy Artillery. This river, like the Vet, had steep banks, and it was 11 p.m.

before the baggage got into camp. Meanwhile on our arrival about 5 p.m. a homely pig was seen, and after giving a sporting half-hour to Lieutenant Hamilton and four Privates was duly brought in. A copper was purchased from the natives and in it some 12 lbs. of pig with all our Liebig and preserved soups soon made a smoking mess, the soup of which stayed our appetites until the arrival of our baggage at a late hour.

May 11th: Marched at 7 a.m., following the 18th Brigade. After crossing a drift and the railway line, we moved along on a somewhat uneventful march, halting at mid-day near Holfontein Siding and completing 19 miles to Dispruit.

May 12th: Marched at 5.45 a.m., hoping to find the enemy on the Boschrand position, south of Kroonstadt; we were ordered, in company with the rest of the Brigade, to make a right flanking movement; this took us through high fields of mealies, which were heavy going. At the end of five hours information was received that the enemy had abandoned the Boschrand position, and we were ordered to the left on to the railway, where we halted, the men were watered, and instructions were received that we were to march into Kroonstadt with drums beating. The Battalion consequently took its place at the head of the Brigade, arrived at Kroonstadt at 2 p.m., and defiled past Lord Roberts and the Head-quarters Staff. The Boers had disappeared and Kroonstadt was in the hands of the British. Though the Boers had evacuated it, it was evident that they had at one time intended to hold this position. An elaborate line of entrenchments was found, and a considerable number of tools fell into our hands. We passed through the town, and bivouacked some mile and a half to the east, close to the Valsch River.

May 13th to 22nd : The Head-quarters Army, of which the Battalion formed part, remained at Kroonstadt from the 13th to the 22nd. The men were employed on heavy fatigue making a deviation of the railway, necessitated by the Boers having blown up the main bridge. The Cavalry Division were encamped to the north of us, and their advanced squadrons were more or less in continual touch with the enemy, but nothing of importance occurred and the Boers showed no signs of attack.

May 22nd : Left Kroonstadt late, having waited for supplies; marched to Honing Spruit Siding, 15 miles, arriving in bivouac at 4 p.m.

May 23rd : Marched at 6 a.m. in full expectation of meeting the enemy at Rhenoster River. Again discretion had proved the better part of valour; there were no Boers, but they had left unmistakable marks of their presence in a filthy camp, littered with the remains of their slaughtered cattle. The drift over the Rhenoster River was narrow and impracticable, and the 1st Battalion Coldstream Guards spent some hours in improving it, but even then it was impassable for the main portion of the baggage.

May 24th : Our Most Gracious Majesty Queen Victoria's Birthday. A short march to Vredefort Road Station, greatly impeded by the difficulty of getting the transport over the Rhenoster River. Although the distance was only 16 miles it was 8 p.m. before the second line transport arrived. An issue of rum was ordered but could not be supplied. The officers drank to the health of their Sovereign from two or three flasks of long-preserved brandy.

May 25th: Moved on to Grootevlei Station. Nothing of importance occurred.

May 26th: Marched to Taaibosch Spruit. The crossing of the spruit caused much delay. The banks were steep, with a left angle turning, and the Battalion, which was on rear guard, was delayed for some hours.

May 27th: The Brigade marched at 6.45 a.m. and reached Viljeon's Drift at 8.30 a.m., crossed the Vaal River by a pont at 9.30 a.m., and bivouacked north-east of Vereeniging at noon.

May 28th: The advance was continued at 7 a m. Several checks occurred, as the 18th Brigade, which was leading, crossed the Klip River twice unnecessarily. We marched into our bivouac at Klip River Station at 4 o'clock in the evening, just as the last trainload of Boers was leaving. Sir Ian Hamilton's guns were heard firing all the afternoon. The night was very cold, with 15 degrees of frost.

May 29th : The Brigade marched at 6.45 a.m. The crossing of the railway bridge over the Klip River caused some opening out, and the head of the column was halted. This halt was considerably lengthened by one of the Naval guns going through the bridge which the transport were crossing by, and causing a block. The Brigade was ordered to move on again at 8.45 a.m. as fighting was going on in front. After a somewhat long march we reached Elandsfontein Junction, where the line from Pretoria divides into three, the eastern branch going to Natal, the centre one to Bloemfontein, and the western one to Johannesburg. As the Brigade were going into bivouac shortly before 4 p.m. firing broke out from the neighbourhood of Germiston, and the Battalion was ordered to attack. Nos. 3 and 5 advanced in double time, captured Germiston Station, and with it 50 Boer prisoners, together with several hundred rifles and a quantity of stores, while No. 6 was sent into the town and returned with between 40 and 50 prisoners under charge of Lieutenant Gurdon-Rebow. Nos. 3 and 5 bivouacked in the station that night. The remainder of the Battalion, after clearing the mines north of the station, returned through the town and bivouacked with the rest of the Brigade about a mile to the south of it. Although the firing had been somewhat heavy on both sides there were no casualties among the Grenadiers, and the day's work was distinctly creditable to the companies in action. This affair obtained for the Brigade the clasp of "Johannesburg," which was shared with General Ian Hamilton's and Sir John French's troops. The night was dark and it was with considerable difficulty that the Battalion found its allotted bivouac. The second line transport, which had come by another route, was some distance behind, and did not reach camp till nearly midnight.

May 30th: Remained in bivouac. Colonel Davies, of the Grenadiers, attached to the Head-quarters Staff, went into Johannesburg under a flag of truce and persuaded the Burgomaster and Town Council to surrender, and come out to Lord Roberts's camp. News was received this day of the battle of Biddulphsberg, and that Colonel Lloyd and Lieutenant and Adjutant C. Corkran had been severely wounded, and 2nd Lieutenant Murray killed.

May 31st: The whole force made a triumphal entry into Johannesburg, marching past Lord Roberts in the Market Place. After clearing the town they marched along the Pretoria Road and bivouacked some six miles out near the Orange Grove. It was dark when the troops got to their camp, and the second line transport did not arrive until the middle of the night.

June 1st and 2nd: The Brigade remained in bivouac. Five per cent. of the men were allowed to visit Johannesburg each day. Officers shaved their beards off and their example was followed by the men.

June 3rd: Marched to Leeuwkop. Some of our young officers went out shooting Koran in a wood near, which resulted, early next morning, in an alarm throughout the camp.

June 4th: Marched at 7.30 a.m. Arrived at Six Miles Spruit about 11.30 a.m. and after advancing another couple of miles, orders were given to attack the Boer forces defending Pretoria. The Brigade was told off to attack the Boer left, but the enemy gradually retired. There was very little fighting, although at one time the Battalion came under a heavy fire from the Boer guns, while crossing a defile in rear of our Naval guns. At dusk the order was received to bivouac where we stood, which unfortunately was on ground that had recently been burnt. Strong outposts were furnished.

June 5th: The early morning brought rumours of the surrender of Pretoria. Cheering was heard in the distance, and Lord Setrington, cne of Lord Roberts's A.D.C.'s, came round to inform us that the Burgomaster of Pretoria had brought the keys of the city to Lord Roberts during the night. It was also reported that Botha had surrendered. This latter remark was evidently not correct, and we were yet to hear more of this redoubtable Boer leader. At 6.50

a.m. the Battalion was ordered to march with the rest of the Brigade into Pretoria, where it arrived about 8.30 a.m. and was immediately ordered to picket the important places throughout the city, being relieved about mid-day by troops from the 18th Brigade. The Battalion was then instructed to clear and hold the Market Square, preparatory to a review of the troops by Lord Roberts, No. 1 forming a guard of honour to His Excellency. After the Union Jack had been hoisted on the Raadzaal, and the troops had marched past, the Battalion, in company with the rest of the Brigade, bivouacked on the west of the town.

June 6th; Remained in bivouac. Half the officers and ten per cent. of the men were allowed to visit the town.

June 7th: The Brigade marched at 1.15 in the afternoon to Silverton, some six miles east of Pretoria. Although the distance was short there were many stoppages on the road, and the second line transport did not get in until nearly 9 p.m.

June 8th: The enemy at Pienaarspoort opened fire with one of their Long Toms on some Mounted Infantry Transport returning from the front. The shells fell a quarter of mile short of the Battalion camp and were replied to by our 5-inch guns. Beyond this there was no collision. Several congratulatory telegrams on the capture of Pretoria were received from Her Majesty, the Prince of Wales, the Secretary of State for War and the Commander-in-Chief.

June 9th: Remained in bivouac.

June 10th: Thanksgiving service in the Cathedral at Pretoria.

June 11th: Marched some four miles to Strubens Farm, whilst Ian Hamilton and the Cavalry Division attempted to turn the enemy's left out of their position on the Donkerhoek Ridges.

June 12th: General Ian Hamilton's attack developed into the battle of Diamond Hill. The Brigade, with the exception of the 1st Battalion Coldstream Guards, was not engaged until late in the afternoon, and then only comparatively lightly. The Battalion had one man dangerously wounded, who subsequently died.

June 13th: Stood to arms at 5.30 a.m. at our bivouacs on the battlefield. After placing outposts on the top of the ridge, the Battalion, together with the rest of the Brigade, came down off the hills to the shelter on the south side. The wind was bitterly cold.

June 14th: Two companies, with the Field Company Royal Engineers, were sent to improve the drift at Koodoespoort, to facilitate the return of the Army to Pretoria. They bivouacked at the drift and joined the Battalion next day.

June 15th: The Brigade returned and bivouacked east of Pretoria near the Yeomanry Hospital.

June 16th to 20th: Remained in camp at Pretoria. On the 19th, two companies from each Battalion of the Brigade were sent by train to Watervaal to bring back, for the use of the Brigade, the corrugated iron huts, which had been erected by the Boers for their British prisoners.

June 21st: Brigade moved to Marks' Farm, about half way to Donkerhoek. Mr. Marks, a very rich Dutch merchant, with a nice house, allowed officers to go there and enjoy the luxury of a hot bath, which was much needed. He also had a distillery in which, according to his overseer's report, he manufactured brandy, whiskey and all liqueurs from the same in gredients and in the same way, adding a little flavouring for the distinguishing mark.

June 22nd: Remained in camp.

June 23rd: Advanced to Donkerhoek and took up our old camping ground where we had lain after the battle of Diamond Hill.

June 24th to July 23rd: Remained in camp at Donkerhoek. There were constant alarms of Boers from all quarters, but our outposts proved too tough a nut and they did not endeavour to crack it. The Battalion received fresh clothing, and was served out with sun hats, helmets being stored and sent to Pretoria. The corrugated iron from Watervaal arrived and officers and men made themselves fairly comfortable in shelters and lean-to's. The outpost work was considerable, but on off days the Battalion was exercised in running and free gymnastics under the Adjutant. During this time a draft numbering four Officers and 100 N.C.O.'s and men arrived under command of Captain G. D. White, accompanied by Lieutenants Leslie-Melville, Vivian and Brooke. While at Dunkerhoek £8,000 in gold, 22 rifles and some books of correspondence were dug up in the garden attached to the Head-quarters of the Brigade.

July 24th: Brigade marched to Bronkhorst Spruit, 16 miles, the scene of the massacre of the British in the '81 Boer War. The Battalion found the outposts, which were very scattered and very difficult to visit.

July 25th: Crossed the Wilge River and reached our bivouac some three miles east, about 4 p.m. in tropical rain, which lasted nearly all night. The men were soaked and the cold wind and rain made it one of the most trying days of the whole campaign.

July 26th: The bright sun and strong wind helped to dry the clothing, and the Brigade made a short march of five miles in the afternoon to Hartebeestefontein.

July 27th: Marched to Bruig Spruit Station, escorting an ox convoy and halting 2½ hours at midday.

July 28th to August 15th: Remained at Bruig Spruit. Continuous alarms of enemy. This being a tin village, a good many houses were utilized for making tin huts for Officers and men. Paymaster Sergeant Jones died of pneumonia and was buried near the line under a mimosa tree on the 6th August. Train loads of Boer women and children, sent from Pretoria to join their relatives in the field, passed through Bruig Spruit continually. On the 15th August the Battalion was ordered to send one Company to Howard's Colliery and one to Whitbank. While at Bruig Spruit the Battalion was served out with quinine as a preventive against malaria fever, and elaborate instructions were issued to cure snake bites. On the 14th the Battalion received the Yorkshire Regiment, who had come to relieve them, and entertained both Officers and men.

August 16th: Battalion marched to Oliphants River, taking over charge of the post from the 1st Battalion Coldstream Guards. While the exchange was being effected, the grass in the neighbourhood of the camp caught fire, and a heavy report of musketry quickly succeeded. Lieutenant A. Russell, the Adjutant, galloped off to ascertain the cause. His pony made a mistake, he had a heavy fall, cutting open his forehead. After 24 hours' rest, however, the gallant officer was as hard at work as ever. Two guns of the 85th Battery, and some Mounted Infantry were attached to Colonel Crabbe's command.

August 17th : Remained in camp.

August 18th : The Battalion marched to Middelburg, and rejoined the remainder of the Brigade.

August 19th : Sunday at Middelburg. The Battalion held a large open fort on the high ground south-east of the town.

August 20th : The Battalion marched at 8.30 a.m. for Pan Station, a distance of 12 miles. A very dusty road, and a hot day, and on arrival there water and wood were scarce, while the wind raised clouds of dust throughout our stay.

August 21st : Moved to Wonderfontein, another dusty march and bad bivouac. The striking force was to assemble here preparatory to an advance against Belfast and Machadadorp.

August 23rd : The 11th Division had now assembled at Wonderfontein.

August 24th : Marched at 6.45 a.m., and at noon Belfast appeared with a high monument directly in our front, and high ground to the right and left. The Battalion was ordered to seize the high ground south of the town, supported by the rest of the Brigade. The position was seized without opposition and entrenched, and the enemy then opened a heavy shell fire which, however, was ineffective.

August 25th : The enemy kept up a hostile fire at intervals throughout the day. The Battalion still furnished a portion of the outposts. Sir Redvers Buller arrived in camp to confer with Lord Roberts.

August 26th : The Brigade moved out early as far as the monument, with the exception of the 3rd Battalion, who were in charge of the baggage, and did not move

until it was decided to make a general advance. During
the afternoon, the Coldstreamers and Scots were involved
in a heavy action some mile and a half to our front.
Stray bullets reached the Battalion and caused a few
casualties. Late in the afternoon, Nos. 3 and 5 Companies
were ordered to support the remainder of the Brigade,
and the Boers retiring shortly before dusk, the baggage
advanced, and the whole Brigade bivouacked more or less
on the scene of the battle. Our casualties were one man
killed and one man wounded. A signal message was
received in the course of the afternoon, stating that
Lieutenant the Honourable A. Russell had received
promotion to Captain.

August 27th: The Brigade remained in bivouac.
The Battalion shifted camp twice during the day in
consequence of the fire of the Boer Long Tom, which
landed one shell exactly where the officers had, five
minutes before, finished their breakfast. The shells
were somewhat frequent all day, and the Battalion
amused themselves by digging them up after they had
entered the ground. Buller's guns could be heard
heavily engaged at the battle of Bergendal.

August 28th and 29th: A long and somewhat
tedious march, owing to difficulties with the supply
column. The Head-quarters of the 11th Division bivouacked close to the Battalion, the remainder of the
Brigade having gone on to Elandsfontein. The
Battalion consequently became practically a guard for
the Naval 12-prs. and the supplies. General Carew
sent for Colonel Crabbe, and explained his hope that
next day he would bring the Boers to bay. With
this view, the Battalion marched at dawn on the
29th. One company was escort to the Naval 12-prs.,
and the whole joined the remainder of the

Brigade about 7 a.m. in a dense fog on the top of a high plateau, some six miles from Helvetia. About 8 a.m. the fog lifted, and the main body moved on. The Battalion formed the rear-guard, and was entrusted with working the whole of the transport down a precipitous hill some quarter of a mile long. The execution of this difficult task met with high approval from General Pole Carew. The whole country was mountainous and rugged. Parties of the enemy were seen and fired at with long-range volleys, but no serious attack took place. The Battalion arrived in bivouac with the 2nd Battalion Coldstream about 10 p.m., some four miles short of Helvetia, after a particularly heavy day.

August 30th : The Battalion brought all the convoy into camp at Helvetia by 9 a.m. and rested there about two hours. The Natal army, under Sir Redvers Buller, was bivouacked side by side with the 11th Division. The former were tented, and appeared generally to have been in better circumstances during the last few months than we had. Late in the morning an advance was ordered to Waterval Onder, which at that time was occupied by the Boers. They, however, moved off as soon as our force approached, with the exception of a few snipers, who remained hidden in the rugged cliffs and were the cause of considerable annoyance throughout the afternoon. The Brigade remained on the top of the hill looking down on Waterval Onder.

August 31st : Remained in camp on the top of the hill. The British prisoners from Nooitgedacht, having been released by the Boers, were seen wandering back towards our lines. Some 1,800 of them came into camp, and were there temporarily accommodated, being eventually sent back to Pretoria.

September 1st: Half a Battalion of the Coldstream were ordered, early in the morning, to clear the hills south of Waterval Onder, and in the afternoon the Battalion followed them into the town, which was situated in a hollow entirely surrounded by hills, with a narrow outlet east and west.

September 2nd: The Battalion proceeded to make themselves as comfortable as possible in Waterval Onder. The outposts were heavy and necessitated an hour-and-a-half continuous climb from our bivouac to the top of the plateau south of the town. Four Companies were on outposts daily. Arrangements were, however, made for sending up food and blankets.

September 3rd: The West Australian Mounted Infantry, under Colonel Pilkington, were ordered to burn some farms south of Waterval Onder. They were supported by half a Battalion each of the Grenadiers and the 2nd Battalion Coldstream.

September 4th to 9th: Remained at Waterval Onder. Fine warm weather, and nothing of importance beyond the daily outposts.

September 10th: Half the 3rd Battalion, with a Field Company Royal Engineers and the West Australian Mounted Infantry, under the command of Lieutenant-Colonel Crabbe, advanced along the Nooitgedacht road, but met with no opposition and bivouacked half way to Nooitgedacht.

September 11th: Remained in bivouac. The Adjutant was sent back to Waterval Onder, with despatches to the G.O.C. 11th Division.

September 12th: Moved on early in the morning and occupied a camp close to Nooitgedacht. The remainder of the 11th Division followed in the afternoon.

September 13th: Advanced to Godwan River.

September 14th: A 12 miles march to De Kaapsche Hoop. This march was equal to 25 miles, being from start to finish up the face of a precipitous mountain. The Boers had calculated on it being impracticable for the British to bring their baggage by this almost impossible route.

September 15th: Marched down the eastern slopes of the hill to North Kaap River, passed through a good deal of scrub with practically no road. Engineers hard at work, but a difficult and tiring day for the transport, which arrived late.

September 16th: Marched on to Murray's Store.

September 17th: North Kaap Station. A short march, but very bad road.

September 18th: Honey Bird Creek. Very difficult road.

September 19th: Loouws Creek. A very trying march. Battalion on rear-guard. Second line transport not in until 10.30 p.m.

September 20th: Marched to Kaap Muiden. A very bad road, but the transport was considerably lightened by halving the loads on reaching the railway, and sending them forward by train. On arrival at Kaap Muiden, we were informed that the Brigade was to push forward as rapidly as possible to Komatipoort, leaving one Company per Battalion and nearly all the baggage at Kaap Muiden. Major Crompton-Roberts, and Lieutenant Gilbert Russell, were left with a detachment of the 3rd Battalion, which was made up of those least capable of a long and arduous march.

September 21st: A long march to Broken Bridge. The road was non-existent, and, before the transport could move, had to be made by the Engineers, through a sub-tropical forest. The Infantry marched along the railway. We had now descended from the hills, and the plain stretching eastward was full of vegetation, hot, stuffy and damp.

September 22nd: Moved on to Hector Spruit in the afternoon. Bivouacked near the Crocodile River.

September 23rd: Marched at 1 p.m. As there was no water between Hector Spruit and Komatiepoort, the Battalion presented a somewhat curious sight on leaving bivouac. Every man was carrying a bottle, a jar, or a camp kettle full of water, in addition to his water bottle. The cooking pots were all filled with water and carried in wagons, but the result of this latter experiment did not fulfil our hopes, as they leaked considerably between the lid and the kettle. The men behaved splendidly, and when in sight of Komatiepoort, about 11 a.m. next morning, nearly everyone had a small reserve of water left. A halt was made about 7 p.m., where it was intended to bivouac, but in less than an hour we moved on to Ten-bosch, arriving there at 10 p.m., and bivouacking till 5 a.m.

September 24th: Occupied Komatiepoort unopposed, and after a much-needed and refreshing drink in the Komati River moved to an excellent bivouac in the angle of the Crocodile and Komatie Rivers, in a grove of palm-trees, with excellent bathing, and general tropical sur-roundings.

September 25th and 26th: Remained in bivouac. One of the peculiarities of this place is that it is the frontier between the Transvaal and Portuguese territory. The hills separating the two countries were lined with Portuguese troops in white duck dress. They were prepared to be friendly with us when they saw that the British had indeed arrived in force. Some Officers visited Ressano Garcia, the Portuguese Station on the East of the Komati River. This was, however, afterwards prohibited. An enormous quantity of railway stock was found here, which had been run up the Selati Railway by the Boers, and had in some cases been fired. It was quite evident that a large number of Boers had escaped through Portuguese territory, having burnt their supplies and their railway stock before leaving the Transvaal.

Although there were only a few razors in the Battalion, the men turned out shaved the day after the arrival at Komatiepoort, and were thus clean, but ragged, Officers and men alike having but few whole garments between them.

The arrival of Lord Kitchener was the signal for renewed activity. The Selati railway was required to deliver up its spoils, the burnt carriages were thrown off the line and trains were rapidly made up out of the workable stock for the return of the invaders to Pretoria. As far as the Brigade of Guards were concerned, they were told that their journey to Pretoria was only the forerunner of their return to England, and willing were the hands that made up the trains to carry us the first stage on our homeward journey.

September 27th to 30th : The Battalion entrained at 7 p.m. but did not move until 5 a.m. on the 28th. The engines were in a bad state and there were practically no engine-drivers. Volunteers were called for, and any man who had driven a stationary engine at home was considered fully qualified to take a train safely along the steep gradients of the Netherland Railway. Water was only to be obtained at distant intervals, and fuel was also scarce. Notwithstanding all these drawbacks, the Battalion embarked in the best of spirits and proceeded leisurely some 20 miles, when the engine gave out, there was no more water and we were at a standstill. Another train came up from Komatiepoort, detached its engine, and pushed us on to the first siding. There our engine was cast adrift, the second train was put into the siding, and their engine proceeded to take us on. A good day's run of 30 miles brought us to Kaarpmuiden, where we picked up our Reserve Company, remained the night, and started again early on the 29th, but our engine was not equal to the task, and it soon became apparent that the only way to get ourselves home was to push our train up all the inclines. This we did with considerable success, and eventually reached Waterval Onder late in the evening. From Waterval Onder to Waterval Boven is a very stiff incline, worked on the cog-wheel system, consequently there is always a stop at Waterval Onder till special engines are ready to take the train up the incline. An ordinary train is divided into two, and thus some considerable time must naturally elapse before the journey can be resumed at Waterval Boven. In our case this was considerably accentuated by the want of experience of the Railway Staff Officers. However, on the morning of the 30th we got away from Waterval Boven about 10 o'clock and reached Olifants River as it was growing dusk. While stopping in camp at Machadadorp, we found Lieutenant the Marquis of Douro, who had come out with a draft (200 men) for the Battalion. This draft was then forming part of the garrison of the town. We also there picked up the little pug dog belonging to our Quartermaster, which he had last seen at Waterval Onder more than a fortnight before.

October 1st : Arrived at Pretoria. Detrained at the

siding east of the town and camped near our former
bivouac just below the Yeomanry Hospital.

October 2nd : Lieut.-Colonel Crabbe and Captain and
Adjutant Russell visited General Tucker, who commanded
in Pretoria, and lunched with him. They afterwards
went to Head-quarters, where they were met by Colonel
Rawlinson, who informed Colonel Crabbe that Lord
Roberts wished to see him at once. The Commander-
in-Chief detailed an expedition of which Colonel Crabbe
was to be in command, and which was to consist of
the 3rd Battalion Grenadiers, 1st Battalion Coldstream, a
Battery of Field Artillery and some 300 Mounted Infantry,
who were to occupy a position on the Six Miles Spruit
to connect the forces covering Pretoria from the south.
This order was, however, cancelled the same evening,
and the next morning the Grenadiers moved to a
bivouac west of the town which had been vacated by
the C.I.V.'s.

October 3rd to 24th : Remained in bivouac and re-
fitted. The Brigade Staff and the Divisional Staff
remained on the east of the town, and the Battalion
was practically on detachment. A considerable amount
of steady drill was carried out and preparations were
made for, as it was hoped, an early return to England.
On the 20th October, the Battalion, in company with a
mixed force, marched out to Uitzacht in the Magaliersberg
Valley, as intelligence had been received that Steyn
might attempt to break through from the south. The
baggage did not arrive until early next morning and the
night was altogether a somewhat dreary one. No enemy
was seen; the Battalion remained there until the 24th
October, when it returned to its camping ground west of
Pretoria.

October 25th : The Battalion took part in a review in the main square of Pretoria, when the Proclamation of Annexation was read.

October 26th : No. 1 Company, Captain N. Corry, Lieutenants B. N. Brooke and R. H. Hermon-Hodge, relieved No. 1 Company 1st Battalion Coldstream Guards as personal escort to Lord Roberts.

October 28th : The Battalion was ordered to move to Cape Town on the morrow and to embark on the " Canada," as Lord Roberts's escort on his return to England.

October 29th and 30th : The Battalion, less two Companies, entrained and their destination was changed to Bloemfontein ; the remaining two Companies were ordered to escort the body of the late Prince Christian Victor to Cape Town the following day, but on the 30th this order was cancelled, as it was decided that the Prince should be buried at Pretoria.

October 31st : These two Companies entrained to rejoin the remainder of the Battalion at Bloemfontein.

November 1st to 3rd : The Battalion remained at Bloemfontein until the 3rd, when it was ordered down the line to Springfontein. The night of the 3rd was passed at Edenburg, and on the morning of the 4th November, Springfontein was reached.

5th to 21st November : The Battalion remained at Springfontein. The defences were somewhat narrowed in consequence of the departure of the Coldstream Guards. Sir Hector MacDonald, who was in command of that section of the line, came down and expressed general approval with the defence arrangements. The enemy was active on the railway between Edenburg and Springfontein, and on two occasions so-called armoured trains were sent up with detachments from the Battalion. These armoured trains consisted of ordinary trains of trucks, with sandbags and compressed forage packed round them to form a temporary defence. On one of these occasions Lieutenant Travers, who was in command of the detachment, met the enemy near Jagersfontein Road, and drove them back into the hills.

On the 15th, Nos. 2 and 4 Companies, under Major White, were ordered to join Colonel Herbert's column at Edenburg, as escort to his baggage. The officers accompanying this detachment were: Sir Robert Filmer, Lord O'Hagan, and Lieutenant Churchill.

By this time it had fully dawned on us that England was not within reach, and that we were likely to be yet for many months in South Africa, and eventually Lord Roberts returned in the " Canada " without his promised escort of Grenadiers.

Reports from Major White and Lieutenant Churchill, giving in detail their doings while on detachment, are appended.

While at Springfontein, Sergeant-Major Cook, who had been absolutely indefatigable ever since the arrival of the Battalion in South Africa, went sick. At first he was reported to be suffering from enteric fever, but almost before he became convalescent, rheumatic fever supervened, and it was some weeks before he was pronounced out of danger. No report of the work of the 3rd Battalion in South Africa would be complete without an expression of the debt the Battalion owes to Sergeant-Major Cook, who, by his firmness and consideration for all ranks, had earned the universal affection of the Battalion and the absolute confidence of its Commander.

On the 20th November, instructions were received

that the Battalion was to line the drifts of the Orange River, on the south, from Orange River Station to Norvals Pont, and on the 21st the move commenced. The dispositions of the Battalion along this line are given in the Appendix.

The Battalion being now split up along about 120 miles of river, the Commanding Officer decided to make his headquarters at Colesberg Road Bridge, some 30 miles north-west of Norvals Pont, with No. 1 Company, the drums and regimental transport being also located there.

23rd November: The headquarters proceeded by march route from Norvals Pont to Colesberg Wagon Bridge. After a long and tiring march they arrived there before dark.

24th November: A small detachment, consisting of Corporal Mainwaring and eight men, left Norvals Pont for Hamelfontein. More will be heard later of this detachment, which gallantly upheld the honour of the Regiment.

On reconnoitring the Orange River, from Norvals Pont to Orange River Station, the Officer Commanding the Battalion modified the dispositions for which instructions had been given by the General Officer Commanding the Brigade of Guards, in order to cover, as far as possible, all the drifts, several of which were not noted on maps, and were therefore unknown until personally reconnoitred. Having visited all stations, the Commanding Officer returned to Colesberg Wagon Bridge, and all being quiet, visited the town of Colesberg, some 18 miles to the south, remaining there 24 hours.

About the 10th December, a second expedition, consisting as before of the Commanding Officer; Captain and Adjutant the Hon. A. Russell; Lieutenant Duberly, the transport officer, with a small escort of Nesbitt's Horse, and accompanied by Captain Wylde, Coldstream Guards (the Brigade signalling officer), moved again along the drifts. On arrival at Sand Drift, which was occupied by Captain Fisher-Rowe with 15 men, they were shown the dispositions which he had made, and with which, on the 27th November, he had repelled an attempt to cross the river by some 300 Boers. In this defence Private Wardle was killed, and buried where he fell.

On the 15th December, while at Petrusville, a message came in to say that Rolfontein Drift, which was occupied by Lieutenant Weller-Poley, was attacked. The Adjutant started immediately for the scene of the encounter, followed shortly afterwards by the two Australian guns, and the 65th Coy., Imperial Yeomanry, who were in garrison at Petrusville. The Adjutant found that the action was over, the enemy had been driven off, and the casualties on our side were one man killed—Private P. Knowles, an excellent signaller. These were the only occasions on which isolated detachments were attacked on the drifts of the Orange River, and on both occasions the officers showed judgment, dash, and prudence, while the detachments under their command faithfully upheld the traditions of their Regiment.

A telegram was received this day informing us that Lieutenant Lord O'Hagan had died at Springfontein Hospital on the 13th, of enteric fever. He had accompanied Major White on detachment with Colonel Herbert's Column. In Lord O'Hagan the Regiment lost a young officer of great promise. He was quiet and retiring in manner, universally popular with all ranks, and a good soldier.

About this time it began to be noised abroad that De Wet was again attempting to cross into Cape Colony, and on the 18th December, when the Head-quarter party arrived at Petrusville, on their return journey from Orange River, they learnt that the country between them and Norvals Pont was occupied by some 3,000 Boers under that celebrated leader. It was after-wards ascerained that the crossing had been effected at a drift called Holfar, some four miles north-west of Sand Drift, which had not been notified as·a passage of the river, nor had local intelligence confirmed it as such. Under these circumstances it was impossible to proceed further in the direction of Colesberg Bridge. Lieutenant-Colonel Crabbe therefore took over the command at Petrusville, which was garrisoned at that time by two guns Royal Australian Artillery, the 65th Company Imperial Yeomanry and 60 details of Mounted Infantry, the whole under the command of Captain Boyle, Somerset Light Infantry.

It was reported and subsequently proved correct, that the advance guard of the Boer force had attacked a small garrison of Yeomanry, at Hamelfontein, under Lieutenant Fletcher, Imperial Yeomanry. In this garrison were included Corporal Mainwaring and eight men of the 3rd Battalion. Lieutenant Fletcher stated that this detachment was the backbone of his defence. Two men were wounded, Privates Rowe and Radford, while Private Mahoney received the Distinguished Conduct Medal in recognition of the services he had there rendered. This soldier went out under heavy fire to procure water for his wounded comrades.   Corporal Mainwaring was mentioned in despatches.

19th December : At 1 p.m. the following message was received from Lieutenant Travers at Daltons Pont by Mounted Orderly :—

> " All drifts from Zootpan to Sand inclusive
> " have received orders from G.O.C. Guards'
> " Brigade to concentrate at Petrusville with all
> " possible despatch.   Remaining detachments of
> " 3rd Battalion Grenadier Guards to be with-
> " drawn on Norvals Pont."

At 5.30 p.m. a duplicate message was sent to the Brigade-Major Guards' Brigade, acknowledging the message received through Lieutenant Travers, giving the situation, strength of garrison at Petrusville, and available supplies.

20th December : A half company of No. 5 from Rolfontein Drift, under Lieutenant Weller-Poley; half company No. 1, under Lieutenant Travers from Daltons Pont; half company No. 6, under Second Lieutenant Hermon-Hodge from Vissers Drift; and a half company No. 6, under Lieutenant Gurdon-Rebow from Gladde Drift, arrived at Petrusville and were at once utilised in the defence.

21st December : Half company No. 7, under Captain the Hon. G. Hood, arrived from Bosjesmans Drift.

22nd December : Half company No. 7, under Major Crompton Roberts, arrived from Zootpan Drift.

23rd December : All hands having worked with energy and determination, the defences of Petrusville were now practically complete.   The town was situated just to the north of a ridge of hills, the highest points of which were immediately above the town.   These had all been placed in a thorough state of defence, and commanded every approach. The low ridge on the east was also strongly held, while the spruit to the south, and the scrubby ground was intersected with wire entanglements, and was defended by a Half Company of Mounted Infantry bivouacked on the outskirts of the town. Towards the west and north-west, the ground was open, and any attempt at attack from that direction could be easily and successfully met. The guns were posted on a spur just south of the town, and commanded the entire country.

24th December (Monday): Continuous mounted patrols were sent out all round the country, one under Second Lieutenant Hermon-Hodge, but no sign of the enemy could be discovered, although from information received he had gone down to the neighbourhood of Phillipstown.

25th December: The following despatch was received from De Aar, having been brought by patrol from Hootkraal Station :—

> " From Lord Kitchener.—O.C. Petrusville is
> " to withdraw on Krankuil with whole force.
> " Stop. Orders will await him there. Reply."

A reply was sent stating that the Petrusville Garrison would withdraw next day (26th), and would bivouac at Wolvekuilen.

The day was employed in collecting transport and packing stores ready for an early start next morning.

26th December: At 6.30 a.m. the head of the force moved off, formed as a column, with the following staff :—

Commanding—Lieutenant-Colonel Eyre Crabbe.

Staff Officer—Captain Boyle, Somerset Light Infy.

Asst. Staff Officer—Captain the Hon. A. Russell.

Transport Officer—Lieutenant Duberly.

Signalling Officer—Captain Wylde.

Nothing of importance occurred on the march, and by mid-day the fighting force was bivouacked, followed in good time by the baggage and rear-guard.

27th December : March was continued to Krankuil. On arrival there a message was received from General Settle, Acting Chief Staff Officer to Lord Kitchener at De Aar, instructing the column to remain there.

28th December : Entrenchments commenced.

29th to 31st December : Remained at Krankuil. On the 31st a telegram was received saying that the Boers were moving north-west from Middelburg, and that the column's object should be to head them off from crossing the line, while leaving the Orange River clear for them to get back into Orange River Colony. Colonel Crabbe decided to move to Potfontein and started at 6 p.m., and arrived at Potfontein the next evening (1st January).

2nd January, 1901 : Entrenchments were immediately commenced at Potfontein. The column remained here until Tuesday (8th January), when it moved to Hootkraal under orders from General Settle to come to De Aar. It appeared, however, that there was some misunderstanding, and consequently the column remained at Hootkraal, where entrenchments were once more commenced, and a general state of defence instituted.

As will be seen from what follows, the Battalion remained at Hootkraal for a considerable time, and while there the following events took place :—

On the 23rd January news was received that Her Most Gracious Majesty Queen Victoria had died the previous day at Osborne. The Commanding Officer telegraphed to the Colonel of the Regiment asking him to express to His Majesty King Edward VII. the deep sorrow of the Battalion on hearing of the death of their beloved Queen, and at the same time to express their loyal attachment to

His Person and Throne. A reply was received signifying His Majesty's gracious satisfaction at the sentiments expressed. On the 24th January a parade of the column was held to announce the accession of King Edward VII., for whom three hearty cheers were given.

On the 29th January, Captain Boyle, having been offered the post of Commandant of Beaufort West, left the column, and was succeeded as Staff Officer by Captain the Hon. A. Russell.

On Monday, 4th February, Lieutenant and Quartermaster May was found dead in his bed in his tent. He had for some years been suffering from an internal complaint, which had never been absolutely diagnosed. He was in his usual health on Sunday evening, but passed away quietly in the night.

Lieutenant-Colonel Crabbe wishes to place on record his very high opinion of this officer, whose good work in earlier years at the Regimental Orderly Room was known to every Grenadier, while the health and comfort of the Battalion in South Africa had depended on him, and to his absolute devotion to his duty, whether in or out of health, was due in a great measure the efficiency which the Battalion showed throughout the campaign. He was buried in the evening in a small walled-in cemetery near the station. His funeral was attended by the whole column, and his body was carried to the grave on a gun carriage most kindly lent and horsed by the Australian Artillery. Pending the appointment of a successor, his work was well carried out by Quartermaster-Sergeant Spearing, to whom great credit is due.

During the time that the Battalion was at Houtkraal there were continual rumours of Boers in all directions. The country was patrolled over a radius of some 30 miles. The greater portion of the column was kept in active work, while the 3rd Battalion were continually employed on outpost duty, and in placing Houtkraal in such a state of defence as would render it a formidable obstacle should the Boers come that way.

It gradually became certain that De Wet was intending a second invasion of the Colony. The Orange River drifts were mined by Major Taylor, Royal Engineers, covered by some 30 or 40 Mounted Infantry under Captain Hon. G. Hood. This work continued until February 12th, on which day Phillipstown, garrisoned by half the 65th Company Imperial Yeomanry, under Lieutenant Munn, was heavily attacked. Instructions were received that the whole force should be collected at Houtkraal as speedily as possible. Colonel Henniker's column was sent to Phillipstown and relieved Lieutenant Munn, who after a severe action, on being reinforced by some Australian Mounted Infantry, drove off the Boers, and was congratulated by General Settle on his action.

Lieutenant Muir, with the remainder of the 65th Imperial Yeomanry, was sent to patrol between Phillipstown and Petrusville, and being ambushed by De Wet, was taken prisoner with most of his force.

On the evening of February 14th, the position was as follows :—

> Lieutenant Munn, from Phillipstown, had arrived at Houtkraal.
>
> Captain Hood, accompanied by Lieutenant Weller Poley, was still out near Taaibosch.
>
> Lieutenant Muir's whereabouts were not accurately known.

Armoured trains were running between Houtkraal and Krankuil, and everything pointed to an attempt on the part of the enemy to cross the line to the west. A pouring wet night after two days of rain had put the whole country under water, and any effort on his part to move his baggage could not but end in disaster.

Late in the afternoon the 71st Imperial Yeomanry, under Captain Sir Saville Crossley, and a Company of Thorneycroft's Mounted Infantry arrived at Houtkraal and joined the column.

The Boers blew up the line and destroyed the telegraph between Houtkraal and Potfontein somewhat early on the evening of the 12th February, after which it became necessary to find means of communication with the armoured trains and with Potfontein, which lay about 12 miles up the line and beyond the spot selected by the enemy for crossing. Corporal Gorman and Private Macefield, both of No. 5 Company, volunteered for the duty, and not only suceeeded in getting to Potfontein, but also in returning to Houtkraal before daybreak. At 4 a.m. the column moved out in a northerly direction up the line to Bartmans Kopje, which was found to be occupied by the Boers, who had got most of their men across, but their baggage was stuck, both east and west of the line, in mud up to the axles. A few rounds from the 15-prs. anu a sharp attack by the 71st Imperial Yeomanry soon cleared these kopjes, and the Boers were in retreat to take up another position some eight miles further on, west of railway. Meantime our spoils consisted of one Maxim gun, some 20 wagons and 60,000 rounds of small arm ammunition.

The armoured trains had assisted in out-manœuvring the enemy, and his hasty evacuation of the kopjes was soon explained by the appearance of Plumer with his column, following hard upon his rear. The enemy halted for some hours at Nooitgedacht, our column moving to

Hennop's Kraal and enveloping his left. He then moved on to Deput, some ten miles further, where he spent the night. Crabbe's and Plumer's columns bivouacked at Rhenoster Vlackte, and were at daybreak reinforced by Henniker, who had pushed on from Houtkraal, which he had reached late the previous evening.

The chase was renewed early on the 16th, and on arriving at Deput, some 40 English were found awaiting us. These men had been taken prisoners in the fighting of the previous three days and were left by De Wet, who had neither time nor means for looking after prisoners. They all spoke of his harsh treatment; food had been scarce, and they had been marched night and day on foot through what was practically a morass.

It may now be considered that the hunt after De Wet in Cape Colony, as far as it concerned the Battalion, had fairly commenced, and it is only necessary for the moment to put on record, that three Companies under the command of Major Crompton Roberts, formed the baggage guard of Colonel Crabbe's column, which was included in the force commanded by Brigadier-General Plumer.

The Boers were continuously followed, and frequently engaged at long ranges, on each of the following days, but it was not until the 23rd February that the pursuing force can be really said to have caught up the enemy.

Moving on from Welgevonden, some ten miles south of the Orange River, and 25 miles south-west of Douglas at 5 a.m. on the 23rd, all were in high fettle at the prospect of overtaking the somewhat slippery enemy.

The order of march was as follows :—

       Advance Guard - - Crabbe.
       Main body   - - - Henniker and Plumer.

The first 15 miles were north-east to Pompoen Pan, and it was only while watering the horses there that an exchange of shots by the scouts warned us that we were nearing the enemy. Another 3 miles and they could be seen in front, making for a long ridge which, if held, promised to afford some tough fighting. The Australian gunners, however, were equal to the occasion, and their correct shooting kept the Boers down behind the ridge, while the 65th and 71st Imperial Yeomanry, and a Company of the Imperial Light Horse from Henniker's column, charged up the slope to find the enemy in full retreat in rear.

Henniker's column had now deployed to the left of ours, and swooping down to the river effected a considerable number of captures, and drove the Boers south-east along the river. Some parties were picked up on the veldt, and at 1 o'clock Colonel Crabbe's column drew up at a dam, where it was necessary to call a halt, to water the horses and collect the prisoners.

We had some 50 prisoners to our credit, besides those which had been taken by the other columns.

Henniker now took the lead, and just as it was getting dusk, after a 40-mile march, he came up with De Wet's gun and Pom-pom and captured them. A camp was formed at dusk some 10 miles north-west of Hopetown, and men and horses were glad of a few hours' rest after an exciting and successful day.

Next morning at day-break the chase was renewed, Plumer leading, Henniker on the right, and Crabbe on the left. The enemy had disappeared, and beyond the fact that Crabbe's column captured 50 more prisoners in caves near the river, nothing of importance occurred, and the whole force bivouacked at Hopetown.

Next day Crabbe and Henniker pursued De Wet to Krankuil, on the railway, and although on the following days we came up with his rear-guard, nothing more of importance occurred, and on the morning of the 1st March, when with Hickman at Bultfontein, 25 miles north of Colesberg, we learnt that De Wet had crossed the Orange River early that morning into the Orange River Colony.

Next morning all columns rendezvoused in Colesberg, and Henniker and Crabbe were ordered to return to Orange River, which was reached on the 12th March. Crabbe's column was here broken up, the Grenadiers were sent by train to De Aar, and Colonel Crabbe was ordered to Naauwpoort by Lord Kitchener's instructions to take command of another column, accompanied by Lieutenant Hermon-Hodge, his orderly officer, and followed two days later by Captain the Hon. A. Russell, his Staff Officer. Colonel Crabbe and his Staff remained with this column, which they took over on the 15th March, 1901, until the 4th March, 1902, when they rejoined the Battalion at Hanover Road.

The Battalion in March, 1901, was located as follows :—

Major the Hon. G. Legh at Norvals Pont with four Companies, one of which, No. 3, was guarding the line between Norvals Pont and Colesberg, with Head-quarters at Achtertang. Major Crompton Roberts, with Head-quarters and three Companies, was in command at De Aar. No. 4 Company was on trek with Colonel Herbert's column, from which it returned to Norvals Pont on the 9th April, and proceeded almost immediately to Hanover Road.

The Battalion was now employed on blockhouse duty, covering the line from De Aar to Naauwpoort, from

HANOVER ROAD TO ANDRIESFONTEIN
BLOCKHOUSE SECTION.

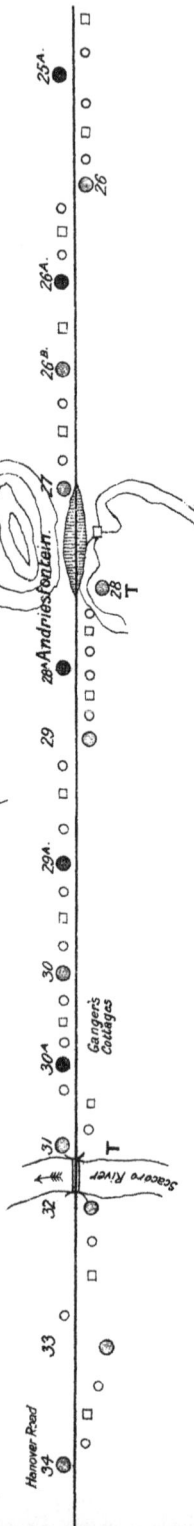

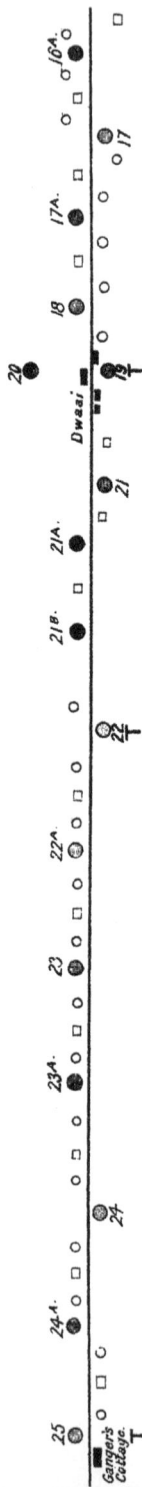

Scale 2 Inches to Mile

Blockhouses and Sangars on Wildfontein Section.

Garrisoned by Militia from
De Aar.

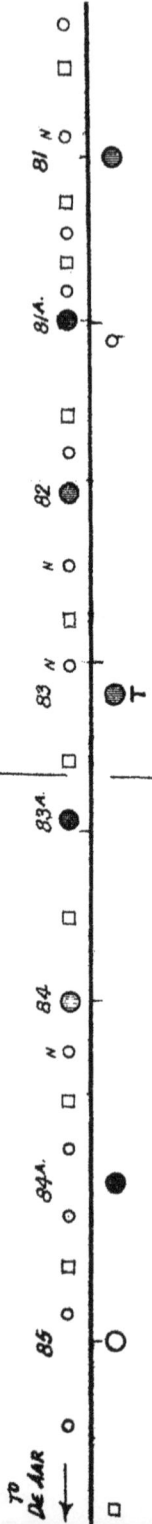

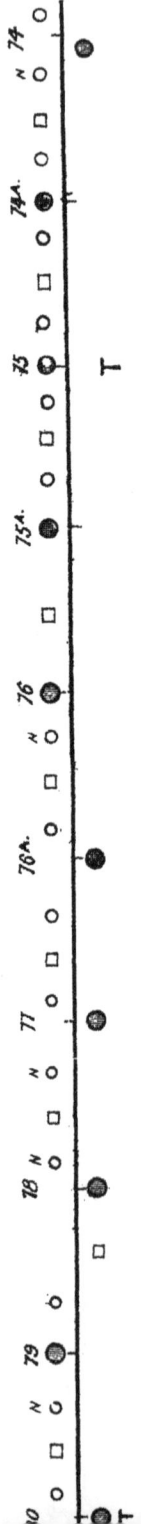

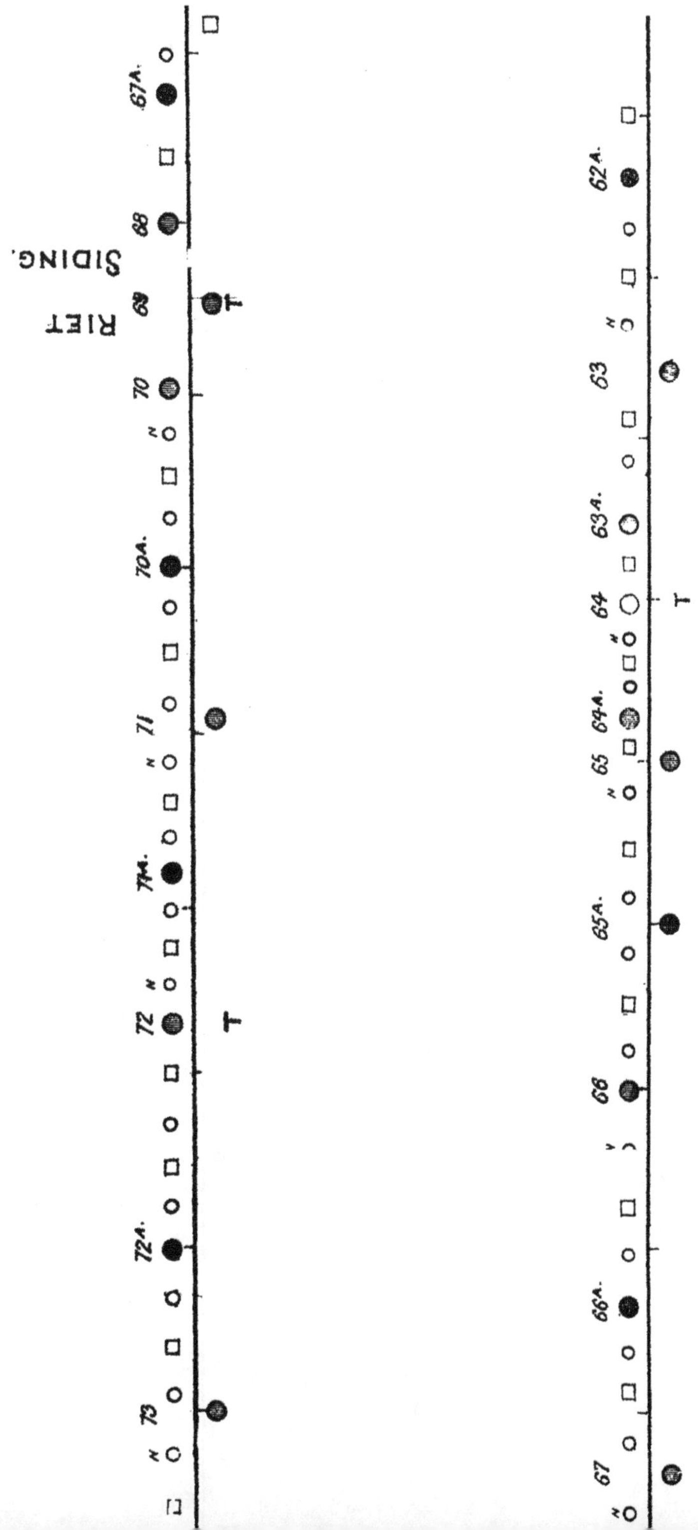
RIET SIDING.
62A.
63
63A.
64
64A.
65
65A.
66
66A.
67
67A.
68
69
70
70A.
71
71A.
72
72A.
73
T
T
T
T

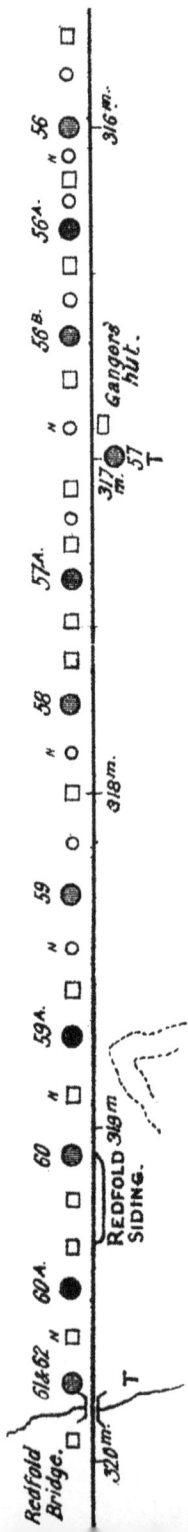

(Redfold Bridge.—Franzkop)

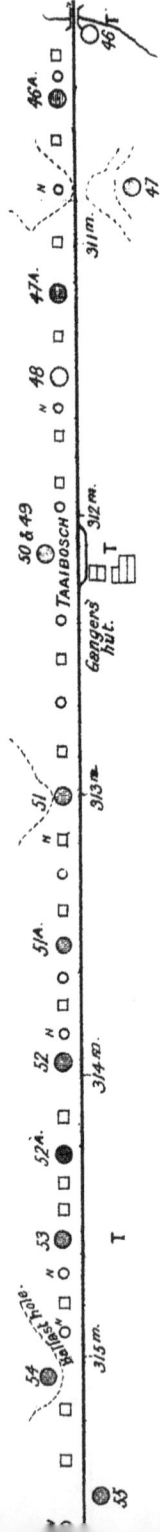

Scale.— 2 inches to 1 mile

Legend:

Original Blockhouse... ○

Intermediate... ◉

Large Sanger... □

Small Sanger... ○

T — Telephones.

HEADQUARTERS of the BATTALION

Hanover Road

$RF = \dfrac{1}{31680}$

Scale = 2 inches to 1 mile.

Scale.

2 miles.

Franz

Kop.

Ganger's hut No.77.

Ganger's hut.

Naauwpoort to Colesberg, while No. 5 was subsequently detached to the south as far as Richmond Road Station. Companies were also sent on detachment along the Steynsburg line as far east as Stormberg Junction. These were, however, temporary movements, and the Head-quarters of the Battalion remained at Hanover Road. No. 7 Company, under Captain Hon. G. Hood, was in garrison at Philipstown.

The Battalion distinguished itself during this year of comparative inactivity by the excellence of its manual labour on the blockhouse lines, with the result that their section was seldom attacked.

The following report of the incidents which led to the death of Lieutenant Gurdon-Rebow on the 16th September, 1901, is taken from that furnished by Major the Hon. G. Legh, at that time in command of the 3rd Battalion Grenadier Guards, at Hanover Road, to Major-General Inigo Jones, commanding the Guards' Brigade at Naauwpoort.

A report had been received that Commandant Malan with eight men and 31 horses was lying hidden among the farms north of the railway line between Taaibosch and Redfold. The mounted scouts of the Battalion, under Lieutenant Sir Robert Filmer, were assembled at Taaibosch, and the enemy having been located at Dedam, it was decided to try to effect a night surprise. The violent storm, however, of the night of the 15th-16th frustrated their efforts, they were obliged to halt at Helder Water, six miles north of Taaibosch, where after breakfast, the parties separated, Sir Robert Filmer taking his command back to Taaibosch and Lieutenant Gurdon-Rebow starting for Hanover Road.

Eventually, instead of going straight to camp, the latter's keenness prompted him to visit a farm called Leeuwfontein, where he found a Bywoner without a pass and decided to bring him into Riet.

Still full of energy, he sent the Bywoner under escort of one of his men and took the rest of his patrol to visit another farm, Verkraal, four miles to the west. Here the two advanced scouts signalled Boers on the right. Lieutenant Rebow and the party (five), galloped up a small rise and saw four Boers galloping away. The party was ordered to dismount and take cover. As they did so, fire was opened on them from three sides at short range. There was a fair amount of cover, and the unequal contest was therefore prolonged. Sergeant Priest, seeing they were greatly outnumbered, and knowing the country, galloped off to Riet for assistance. The Carolus River, close to Riet, was swollen by the heavy rain, and in attempting to cross it Sergeant Priest was drowned. Meanwhile it fared badly with the little party on the kopje. One man had been killed and two wounded, when Lieutenant Gurdon-Rebow, in the act of firing, was shot through the head. The remainder then surrendered. The Boers, as soon as they found out who the party were, behaved well, and allowed one of them to ride at once to Taaibosch for medical assistance. It is not possible to say how many Boers were present, but apparently there were something like 20, among them Malan and Hugo, with a considerable number of led horses.

Captain Profeit, R.A.M.C., came out with medical assistance to the kopje, and removed the casualties, but the Boers by that time were out of sight.

Lieutenant Gurdon-Rebow was a young officer of

the highest courage, and had been particularly active through the latter part of the campaign in training and working mounted men as scouts for the Battalion.

In December, 1901, Kreitzinger's column endeavoured to force a passage from the north, near Fransch Kopje, some five miles west of Hanover Road. The blockhouses at this time were nearly a mile apart, and the entanglements and other defences had not reached that stage of perfection which they afterwards attained. The column got across, but Kreitzinger and one of his men were left behind dangerously wounded. They were captured where they lay, and brought in to Hanover Road, and immediately sent on to hospital at Naauwpoort. Kreitzinger recovered, but the other man died.

While on column Colonel Crabbe surprised Van der Merve's laager near Ladismith, Cape Colony, killing him and capturing some 40 prisoners, a number of horses, and a considerable amount of stores and ammunition. This column was constantly in contact with the enemy throughout the year, and in December, 1901, took a large convoy of provisions from Clan William to Calvinia, assisted by Colonel Wyndham, with a column principally composed of 16th Lancers and Yeomanry. On this expedition there were 3 days' heavy fighting, the Boers having concentrated with the evident intention of preventing the convoy reaching Calvinia. The brunt of the fighting fell to Colonel Wyndham, and his losses were somewhat heavy, but in spite of this the convoy arrived safely, and the Boers' efforts to obtain a Christmas dinner were absolutely frustrated.

The Guards' Mounted Infantry, under Captain E. Trotter, joined Crabbe's column on the 1st January, 1902, and were with it in heavy fighting between

Beaufort West and Fraserburg. On one occasion, when acting as rear-guard to the column, they suffered severely, but entirely upheld the honour of the Brigade to which they belonged.

From March 12th, 1902, to May 20th, there was comparatively little to report. The Battalion was employed on blockhouse work along the lines previously indicated.

On the 5th May, 1902, a large draft of the Brigade of Guards passed through De Aar on its way north. The Grenadiers were represented by Major G. E. Pereira, D.S.O., Lieutenant G. D. Jeffreys, Second Lieutenant J. F. Hubbard, Second Lieutenant C. T. Clayton, Second Lieutenant H. C. Woods, and Second Lieutenant M. C. Maitland. To these officers were added Major W. Fox Pitt to command the whole detachment, and Second Lieutenant C. N. Fisher-Rowe, to act as his Adjutant.

The Grenadiers were in the first place quartered at Devondale, and afterwards at Maritzani, where they formed the garrison of a blockhouse line as far as Polfontein, and eventually on to Lichtenburg. This they occupied until peace was proclaimed, after which the reservists were almost immediately sent home and the remainder of the detachment joined the head-quarters of their various Battalions. For details of the work done by this draft see the Appendix.

On May 20th, the Battalion was ordered to the east to form part of a force under Lieutenant-Colonel Crabbe, to hold the blockhouse line from Thebus *viâ* Stormberg Junction to Veltevreden, some 16 miles north of Queenstown. The object of the concentration was to drive Fouchee into this angle, and if possible, smother him.

The line was made excessively strong, and a successful issue seemed almost assured.

The position of the Battalion was as follows :—

Head-quarters and No. 8 at Molteno,
No. 1, Bamboo to Stormberg,
No. 2, Stormberg to Molteno,
No. 3, Molteno to Cyphergat,
No. 7, Cyphergat to Bushman's Hoek,
No. 6, Bushman's Hoek to Sterkstroom,
No. 4, Sterkstroom to Veltevreden,

with numerous outposts on the mountains.

On the 26th May, Major Crompton Roberts, while riding round his line, which extended from Bushman's Hoek to Veltevreden, met with a very severe accident by the fall of his horse, from which he has ever since been a sufferer.

On the 1st June, news was received that peace had been signed the previous evening at Pretoria.

On the 4th June, orders were received for the Battalion to return to Hanover Road; this was carried out on the following days and the Battalion remained there until it received orders to proceed South *en route* for Cape Town and embarkation for England.

Lieutenant-Colonel Crabbe left the Battalion at Hanover Road on the 9th July, and was succeeded in command by Lieutenant-Colonel The Hon. J. St. Aubyn from England.

Details of
Operations with Colonel Herbert's Column.

On 15th November, 1900, No. 2 Company and No. 4 Company, with three wagons, one S.A.A. cart, one water cart, one ammunition mule, under the command of Captain J. D. White, started from Springfontein and halted at Jagersfontein Road. That evening, about 5 o'clock the Boers began firing on the trains in the station from a range of kopjes 2,000 yards off. The Grenadiers lined the opposite ridge, and after a few volleys the enemy cleared off towards Boomplatz. Strong outposts were, however, furnished by the Grenadiers, as also by other details from trains in the station.

On 16th November the Companies halted at Topfontein, midway between Kruger and Pompi Sidings, and on the 17th reached Edenburg.* Here there was a week's delay, owing to no transport or ambulances being ready, and waiting for Colonel Barker's column.† When, on 21st November, the two Columns moved forward, Dewetsdorp was known to be besieged, and by forced and very trying marches, of considerably over an average of twenty miles a day, a point was reached four miles off Dewetsdorp about 9 o'clock, on morning of 24th November. Here the Columns were stopped by

---

* Colonel Herbert's Column : 17th Lancers, one squadron 9th Lancers, two guns " R " Battery, R.H.A., one Pom-pom.

† Colonel Barker's Column : approximately remainder 9th Lancers two field guns, one Pom-pom, one company Seaforth Highlanders.

shell and rifle fire. The 17th Lancers and 9th Lancers charged the long line of kopjes and drove the enemy off them, losing Lieutenant Hon. E. Baring and one Sergeant 16th Lancers wounded and one man killed. The enemy were apparently using the two 15-pounders captured at Dewetsdorp. One of these might possibly have been captured by the 9th Lancers if Colonel Barker had allowed them to charge it, as the fire from our pom-pom was so accurate and well sustained that the enemy were not able to work it. At night-fall the enemy managed to withdraw it and post it further south. During that day the Grenadiers remained as escort to the guns, but at dusk were ordered across the valley to assist the 17th and 9th Lancers, who were holding a very extended and exposed position. A squadron of the former was so exposed that the men had to lie flat all day behind small sangars and food could only be brought to them at night. They lost one killed and two wounded here. The Grenadiers not on outpost slept with their arms beside them that night. On Sunday, 25th November, there was inter-mittent shell and musketry fire all day, both on our side and that of the Boers. The latter had a 15-pounder to the left front of the position held by the Grenadiers. The next day (Monday) shelling re-commenced at daybreak; soon afterwards the 15-pounder opposite the Grenadiers was hauled into position by horses, fired three rounds, and was then seen to be cautiously drawn down again by drag-ropes.

About 10 a.m. Colonel Barker suggested to Colonel Herbert that the Grenadiers should attack the Boer position to see if the enemy were still in position. Colonel Herbert decided that doing so in daylight might entail great loss of life, and it was postponed till nightfall. In the meantime Captain Shaw Stewart, 17th Lancers, and Lord F. Blackwood, 9th Lancers, had reconnoitred the position and proved that the enemy had retired. The force advanced at 1 p.m., and entered Dewetsdorp at 3 p.m. This presented a horrible sight, and the smell from the burning mules and horses, which the garrison had endeavoured to dispose of by enveloping them in blankets and then setting them on fire, was overpowering. Steyn and the rear guard of Boers had left four hours previously. The Grenadiers had to find a very extended outpost line on the position that had been held by the H.L.I., to that held by the Gloucesters. Out of the trenches of the former, they next morning got blankets, picks and shovels, biscuits, etc. On that day, about 12 noon, all the Column except the Grenadiers, who remained to guard the baggage, were sent off to assist Colonel Pilcher's Column, which was fighting on the right. The latter had surprised and nearly captured Steyn whilst at breakfast. After a long march of 28 miles camped at Helvetia. Here Captain White received orders to detach one Company for Colonel Pilcher's Column, and sent No. 2 Company, under Lieutenant Sir R. Filmer and Lieutenant Leslie Melville, keeping back one N.C.O. and 16 men, who were escort to prisoners taken from Dewetsdorp and from farms *en route.* The following day a very long and arduous march of quite 30 miles brought No. 4 Company into Smithfield at 9 p.m. The weather had been intensely hot for some days. By shorter marches thence to Slik Spruit, whence on 1st December the other Columns proceeded to Bethulie. Sent in Lord O'Hagan and other sick. On the 2nd, Colonel Herbert was told to proceed towards Smithfield by the New Smithfield Road. At 8 a.m. Captain White

received an order from him to park the convoy, as
there was a Boer convoy in front which the
Column were pursuing. (This proved to be the Cape
carts of De Wet's advance guard.) During this halt
a column was plainly discernible in the distance
descending from the direction of Tafelberg, but it
was impossible to make out whether British or Boers.
The natives as well as the conductor of the 17th
Lancers, a Boer who had himself been on commando,
declared that it was an English Column, as the Boers
would not be in such a regular formation. About
10 a.m. the Grenadiers got the orders to move on ;
barely had they done so when a gun was heard
about 2,000 yards off us, and shells began to come
amongst the convoy. This was ordered to trot and
it got away with only one animal killed. As Captain
White was riding across a donga to tell a section
(which had been ordered to retire) to hold on a little
longer, his horse was struck by a shell just below
the saddle, and galloping off was shot by Sergeant
Collins under a heavy fire.

Some of the enemy, 200 in number, galloped up in
extended order to the kopjes the Company had just
vacated, and poured in a heavy fire at 400 yards at the
retiring infantry. Though their distances were excellent and the bullets were going all amongst the men,
they failed to hit anyone, though they kept it up till
the Company had gone over a mile, and they must
have fired more than 1,000 rounds. The ground the
Company retired over was perfectly flat and with no
cover at all. The enemy then left to take up positions
on the ranges of hills on each side of the valley; but
before they could do the Grenadiers any harm, they
came in contact with the posts of the 17th Lancers

which had been sent back by Colonel Herbert on hearing the firing and seeing the enemy advance. Just as the convoy reached Colonel Herbert's position* the gun which had been shelling and which had now apparently been shifted further forward, began shelling the transport again and made splendid practice, being evidently one of the 15-pounders taken at Dewetsdorp. The convoy moved off to the east side of the valley at Willoughby Farm. Here it was met by a heavy fire from a pom-pom posted 2,500 yards east of the farm, and had again to shift its position. Meanwhile the Company had hurriedly been moved up on to two ranges of hills north and south of the position, which was, roughly, a large oval stretching from Strydfontein to Willoughby, about two miles from west to east, and about one and a half miles from north to south, a very extended position for so small a force. One squadron of the 17th Lancers was at a farmhouse one and a half miles in front of the line and was exposed all day to a very hot fire and most determined attacks. "R" Battery tried to shell out the Boers, but so worn and bad were the guns that they actually would not "range" far enough. At 2 p.m. the convoy again came under a heavy fire from the same 15-pounder. The water-cart of the Grenadiers was hit by a percussion shrapnel. Six mules were killed and a camp kettle on the Grenadiers' wagon riddled with holes. Captain Warner, the Transport Officer of the 17th Lancers, was wounded by shrapnel and the convoy had to trot off to Willoughby Farm. There it met a hot rifle fire from the commanding kopjes, and had ultimately to seek refuge in a donga. The Boers

---

* Loss, Colonel Herbert's Column : four men killed, two officers and 6 men wounded.

pressed the attack very hotly towards dusk on the
N.E. corner held by one troop 17th and one troop
9th Lancers, and firing went on till after dusk. At
dusk, a half Company Grenadiers was moved from the
north to an advanced position on the south side.
Very strong outposts were furnished, and the men and
officers had to sleep as they were, without blankets or
coats, the wagon having broken down at Willoughby
Farm. They had only biscuits and no water during
the day up to 5 p.m. The night was very cold, with
some rain. At dawn the Boers, who we had thought
had retired, re-commenced, and again shelled the
transport, this time from the east, making wonderful
practice, following it as it went to Strydfontein, and
one shrapnel burst in the room at that farm where
Captain Warner was lying wounded. During the
morning, General Knox from the west, and Colonel
Williams from the east, came up and materially
altered the position of affairs with the howitzers, though
the Boers still held tenaciously to the ridges. About
4 p.m. the Boer guns were seen going off, and their
large laager five miles off, which contained the 400
Dewetsdorp prisoners, to break up.*

That night rain fell in torrents and continued to
do so whilst the Column advanced to Pampasfontein
and from there back by forced marches to Bethulie,
following Colonel Pilcher's Column. The ground
meanwhile was a perfect morass and Slik Spruit Drift
nearly impassable. Thence the Column went to Aliwal
North, and on 12th December started to assist Colonel
Grenfell's Column near Klaarwater Drift, arriving there
at 1 a.m. after a most fatiguing march. The enemy

---

* Boers buried six men in their main laager alone, including De
Wet's nephew.

were in a very rugged country near Vechtkop, and the 17th Lancers had one man killed. Thence to Damers Nek, where on 14th December the Column shelled and prepared to attack Kreitzinger's strong position, near which he had the previous day captured 120 of 2nd Brabant's Horse. He had, however, retired, and the next day we marched 37 miles through Rouxville, clearing the country as we went to Smithsdal, where we were informed the commando was only twelve hours ahead of us. Another forced march brought us to Odendaal Drift, to find that the Boers had crossed ten hours previously at Rhenoster Hoek, capturing the six Cape Police there. The river was very high and great difficulty was experienced with the wagons, some of which had to be lightened and the contents taken across in boats. The crossing took from 12 noon to 3 p.m. on the following day, and a party of Grenadiers had to stay the night on the north bank, both sides finding outposts and standing to arms. The Column had passed on in pursuit of Kreitzinger. The convoy halted at Odendaalstroom for two days in very heavy rain, and Captain White then got orders to proceed to Aliwal North with all haste. The march was completed in 15 hours, despite the delay at the flooded Stormberg Spruit Drift. Left Aliwal North on the 21st, and Lieutenant Churchill with a half Company went on from Steynsburg with Colonels Grenfell and Herbert, and had a fight the next day near Roosterhoek. The other half Company, under Captain White, arriving too late, was ordered back by General MacDonald to Albert Junction, and that night an outpost on a kopje above the station was attacked, and Private Howard and one Boer wounded. The half Company remained there, doing very heavy outposts, with two field guns, till 3rd January, when it went to Aliwal North and rejoined Herbert's Column, and on the 5th left for Dordrecht by train, the Column meanwhile having started in pursuit of Myburg without wagons. On 6th, Captain White received orders to join Column south-east of Jamestown, but the country being reported impossible for wheeled transport and the enemy being all round, he left the two 15-pounders of the 83rd Battery and a half Company under Lieutenant Churchill, and after a difficult trek by moonlight over Labu-schagne's Nek reached the Column on 7th. On the 8th the Column moved to Roode Nek, crossing the Kraai River, a long march. Whilst the wagons were being pushed by hand up an exceptionally bad hill, 60 Boers were reported behind the "King's Crown" Kopjes, one mile off. The Grenadiers climbed very high mountains but the enemy did not attack; all the country was most mountainous and difficult. The 17th Lancers here de-tached a squadron to pursue Myburg, and on the 10th the whole force moved, reaching Jamestown at mid-day, the 11th. The convoy then had orders to proceed at once to Dordrecht to fill up and left at 2 p.m. At about 4 p.m. a small laager of about 14 Boers was sighted by Captain White on a hill just out of rifle range. They galloped as if to attack but did not do so. More Boers were seen where the half Company outspanned for the night at Oorlog's Poort on Holle Spruit. The next morning the convoy arrived safely at Dordrecht and were joined by Lieutenant Churchill and half Company and two guns, and after filling up outspanned at Oorlog's Poort, reaching Jamestown after a hot march (the wagons being full) at 1 p.m.

On 15th January, the Column left for Burghersdorp, arriving on the 16th. The march of the 15th was a very long and arduous one of 30 miles over very precipitous country. On the 17th, they moved in two marches viâ Joubert's Kop to Zand Drift, where the Column crossed into the Orange River Colony. The Grenadiers and convoy marched thence to Aliwal North to fill up.

On the 18th they marched, outspanning for the night ten miles west of Aliwal North on the O.R.C. side of the river and joined the column on the 19th at Dronkfontein. For a week the farms in the neighbourhood were cleared, the inhabitants being removed to Aliwal. Orders were suddenly received that De Wet with a large force was coming south and that Colonel Herbert was to proceed with all dispatch to Bethulie. On the 27th, the Column accordingly marched with all dispatch to Karreepoort Drift on the Caledon River and halted on the south bank. Barely was camp pitched when the enemy commenced "sniping" from the high hills on the north side of the river. They were silenced by the guns at 2,200 yards, but it was necessary to move the camp further back from the river. The Column escaped without casualties.

On January 28th made a long march, during which there was an alarm of a possible attack, and on 29th mid-day outspanned at Slik Spruit. A squadron of the 9th Lancers had been sent to the north to reconnoitre; they became engaged with a considerable number of Boers, and though they drove the latter from their positions, the enemy on their retirement followed them up in such strength that Colonel Herbert decided to move the whole Column into Bethulie at once. Wagons were hurriedly inspanned and by fast travelling Bethulie Bridge was reached soon after dark. The next day, starting as usual before daybreak, they reached Oliveboschfon-

tein a farm four miles south of the Rhenoster Hoek
Drift. The column, barely 300 strong, had to hold all
the drifts between Bethulie and Odendaal Drift, and
a weak troop of the 17th Lancers was posted at each.
Fortunately for the Column, De Wet, instead of coming
due south, struck westward across the railway and
crossed the Orange River west of Colesberg. The patrols
had several skirmishes north of the river, and in one,
2nd Lieutenant Russell, of the 17th (who was killed in
September, 1901, near Tarkastad) with only ten men
beat off a patrol of superior strength and killed two
Boers. During the fortnight that the Column remained
there, the outpost duty was extremely heavy and men
not on duty had to sleep on the kopjes near the posts.

On the 14th the Column moved viâ Knapdaar
Station to Burghersdorp, entrained there; proceeded to
Rosmead; whence, after being detained for some days
owing to the want of rolling stock, they proceeded by
train to Bethesda Road on the 19th and 20th.

On February 22nd at daybreak, they started towards
New Bethesda, to get in touch with Colonel Gorringe
who, with the "Colonial Defence Force" was pursuing
Kreitzinger. The wagons being full and there being a
difficulty in conveying the men, a half Company of Grenadiers were left behind and sent as escort with two
15-pounders by rail to Middelburg. The road led over
two most precipitous passes, and the Grenadier wagon
slipped over, but was recovered with the loss of a
broken "long wagon" and other parts after two hours'
hard work. The mules were only slightly hurt. Just
as the wagon was being mended, pom-pom and heavy
rifle fire was heard in front. This turned out to be an
attack by Kreitzinger with 250 men on the Column,
which was outspanned for the mid-day halt. Owing to the

coolness and presence of mind of Major Lund and his squadron of the 9th Lancers, who saddled up and seized an important ridge, the Boers were driven off. Our loss was two Artillerymen wounded, and some horses killed. The guns at the time were firing at 800 yards. This occurred four miles north of Compassberg, and later in the evening Colonel Goiringe, having come up, Herbert's Column camped on the scene of the fight. The next day, February 23rd, a surround of Smith's Kloof, where the Boers had laagered, was made. Gorringe worked round the right and Herbert went along the heights. The Grenadiers occupied successive ridges, but on arrival at Smith's Kloof it was found that Kreitzinger had left by an unknown and almost impassable bridle track to the north two hours previously. The convoy had to proceed to Roodehoogte by a devious and very bad mountain road and over the Lootsberg Range. The last ten miles had to be done in the dark over an indistinct road. The armoured train was passed in Jagtpoort Gorge, the line having been torn up by the Boers. Roodehoogte was reached at last at midnight; men and animals were thoroughly exhausted, and, it not being possible to get across some broken ground to Herbert's Camp, the convoy halted where it was, amongst the Colonial Defence Force. The railway station had been burned by the Boers at 1 p.m. and their rear-guard was still there when the Columns arrived at 4 p.m., and shelled the enemy retiring.

The next day, 24th, scouts sent out were held up by the enemy in a deep gorge three miles from camp. Two men were wounded and one native scout murdered by the Boers. Our two guns and pom-pom went out with a cavalry screen and shelled the enemy's strong position for four hours, when he retired

We had one more man wounded. On the 25th there was a desultory rear-guard action; the cavalry seized Rooinek, a strong position. The enemy's laager at Spitz Kop was reported to have formidable entrenchments.

The Columns operated in the surrounding country for three days, the convoys of the two Columns, as well as one Company Royal Fusiliers and 200 dismounted men of the C D.F., and Kaffrarian Rifles, etc., of Gorringe's Column, as well as Regulars of Herbert's Column, being left at Roodehoogte under the command of Captain G. D. White. About 40 Boers were on a farm five miles south-west, and a small patrol got in touch with them on one occasion. Their vedettes could be plainly seen on the heights. On March 1st, Captain White received helio orders from Colonel Gorringe to take as many infantry as possible to seize the high mountains near Bulhoek Farm, eight miles north of the camp, and co-operate with the Columns, which were to work from the north to try and drive Kreitzinger on to the infantry position. He accordingly took No. 4 Company Grenadiers and three sections of the Company of Royal Fusiliers, and starting at daybreak reached the summit of the mountains, after very arduous climbing, in some places on hands and knees, by mid-day. The force held the ridges all day, seeing what they took to be the enemy, but it proved to be Gorringe's Scouts, and the enemy, owing to false information, had been able to slip out and were then marching rapidly towards Pearstone. At dusk the infantry withdrew and reached Roodehoogte again at 9 p.m. During the day, which was very hot, they suffered from want of water, which it was not possible to carry to them up the mountain after their water-bottles were exhausted.

On March 4th, Captain White received orders to move the base depôts to Cookhouse; this was altered the next day to Graaf Reinet. But it being impossible to get any rolling stock or engines, he decided to go by road to Graaf Reinet. Starting from Roodehoogte at 1 p.m., the convoy outspanned for two hours at Blaauwater at the foot of the Lootsberg Pass, and starting again at 8 p.m., trekked through the night over the Naudesberg till 2 a.m., outspanned near a dam, started again at 6, and with a short outspan reached Graaf Reinet, a total distance of 51 miles, by 12 noon.

Here Colonel Herbert's convoy remained till March 17th, the men having not only heavy outpost duty, as the enemy were reported near the town, but having also to work at the defences. On that day they left for Rosmead, where they were detained four days awaiting orders and rolling stock. On 21st and 22nd, they left for Kromhoogte Station, arriving about mid-day on 22nd.

The next morning the Column, one of a large cordon comprising Colonel Crabbe's, Colonel Henniker's, Colonel Gorringe's, Colonel de Lisle's, Major Murray's and other Columns, started as usual just at daybreak. About mid-day they received orders to double back, and it was then known that a large part of Kreitzinger's force with Lotter and van Reenen had broken back that morning between Colonel Herbert's and Colonel Henniker's Columns, the latter going in pursuit, but the enemy escaped into the Zuurberg. The Column camped at Schilderkranz, where the Boers had been the previous night. A squadron of the 17th sent out to hold a nek eight miles out were fired on in the dark. They returned the fire and an engagement ensued, and they had to retire, being heavily shelled till out of range.

This proved to be Gorringe's Colonial Defence Force. The 17th had one officer slightly wounded and two men shot through their clothes, and the same casualties precisely took place in the C.D.F., as was heard afterwards. On the 25th the Column camped at Olifantsfontein, ten miles from Bethulie Bridge, filled up, and did next day a very long and trying march to Tweefontein and on the 27th to Steynsburg. They left on the 28th and arrived after two long marches in company with Lovat's Scouts under Major Hon. A. D. Murray at Slingersfontein near Colesberg, being in touch with the enemy shortly after passing Knell Farm. They left the next day and after dark on April 1st, through a deluge of rain, reached Keerom Farm. The whole of the Boers were then in front and riding hard to cross the Orange River at Krugers Drift. On the 2nd they marched to Venterstad, seeing two other Columns on the way, and there heard from General H. MacDonald that the whole of the enemy had crossed the river and that the result of the drive had therefore been attained.

This, however, was not the case, as many had broken through, but a considerable number were still crossing, and Herbert's Column, in conjunction with Colonel Gorringe's and other Columns, started in pursuit and shelled the enemy on the far bank. Lovat's Scouts had some casualties. The convoy, meanwhile, remained at a farm five miles from Knapdaar Station in a somewhat exposed position, all mounted men having gone on with the Column. They moved on April 6th, through very heavy rain, to Bethulie and camped at Constantia Farm, three miles north of the town. There, at last, the orders came for No. 4 Company to rejoin the 3rd Battalion, and on the 9th they reached Norvals Pont viâ Springfontein, having trekked for five months and covered, roughly, over 1,500 miles. There were no cases of enteric, except in the lamented case of Lieutenant Lord O'Hagan, during this time, and the admissions to hospital from other causes were very small in number, whilst in the matter of casualties in the field they had been extraordinarily fortunate.

No. 4 Company was at once sent to hold Hanover Road Station, with one Section under Lieutenant Spencer Churchill detached to hold Redfold Bridge, mid-way to De Aar. Here they remained in solitude till the arrival of the Head-quarters of the Battalion four months later, Captain G. D. White being in control of the railway line between Naauwpoort and De Aar, in addition to being Commandant, under Martial Law, of the northern part of Hanover District. As the enemy were constantly about, tearing up the railway and wrecking trains, the outpost duty was very arduous.

APPENDIX.

BELMONT.

Roll of Officers, N.C. Officers and Men Killed in Action at Belmont, on 23rd November, 1899.

Officers.

Co.	Rank and Name.
1	Lt. & Adjt. F. L. Fryer.

N.C. Officers and Men.

Co.	Reg. No.	Rank and Name.	Co.	Reg. No.	Rank and Name.
2	4431	Cpl. L. Bates.	3	5935	Pte. C. Melbourne.
3	7102	Pte. P. Curry.	1	3963	Pte. J. O'Beirne.
2	7565	Pte. P. Davies.	1	4614	L.-C. G. Pattison.
4	6697	L.-C. C. Drury.	2	5811	L.-S. F. Richardson.
1	5796	L.-C. R. Fraser.	1	6027	Pte. D. St. John.
3	5706	Pte. J. Goodson.	4	5899	Pte. J. Stevenson.
4	3135	Pte. W. Griffiths.	3	5602	Pte. J. Tolley.
3	5895	Pte. F Hewer.	6	7145	Pte. E. Underwood.
4	6889	L.-C. H. Honey.	3	6200	Cpl. E. Watson
3	6016	Pte. S. Ingham.	5	7562	Pte. M. Whelan.
4	6801	Pte. E. Mansfield.			

Roll of Officers, N.C. Officers and Men wounded in action at Belmont, on 23rd November, 1899.

Officers.

Co.	Rank and Name.	Result.	Co.	Rank and Name.	Result.
1	Lt.-Col. E. M. S. Crabbe		4	Lieut. W. B.H. Blundell	Died 23.11.99
8	Lieut. D. Cameron	Eng. 16.12.99	4	2nd Lt. E. N. Vaughan	Eng. 17.1.00
6	Lieut. M. Gurdon-Rebow		3	2nd Lt. T. B. Leslie	Died 4.12.99
5	Lieut. Hon. A. V. F. Russell		7	2nd Lt. Hon. R. Lygon	

N C. Officers and Men.

Co.	Reg.No.	Rank and Name.	Result.	Co.	Reg.No.	Rank and Name.	Result.
3	7055	Pte. H. Aldridge	Eng. 15.12.99	1	5354	Pte. D. Bowen	Eng. 14.4.00
3	7411	L.-C. A. Ansell		1	6886	Pte. J. Brandreth	
8	5043	Pte. E. Allman		1	5526	Pte. J.Burroughs	Eng. 20.2.00
4	7641	Pte. W. Brain	Eng. 5.2.00	1	5295	Pte. J. Coutts	Eng. 15.12.99
5	5000	L.-C. W. Burley		1	5603	Pte. E. Cunliffe	Died 22.12.99
5	5916	Pte. P. Bloor		1	7370	Pte. J. Cole	Eng. 6.12.99
4	3814	Pte. J. Beech	Eng. 13.2.00	2	6693	L.-C T. Carey	Eng. 2.1.00
6	5290	L.-S. J. Brennan	Eng. 6.12.99	7	5169	L.-C. F. Caunt	
3	5611	Pte. G. Brayford		7	6958	Pte. H. Cole	
3	6993	Pte. J. Baker	Eng. 6.12.99	5	3524	L.-C. A. Clifford	

N.C. Officers and Men—*continued*

Co.	Reg.No.	Rank and Name.	Result.	Co.	Reg.No.	Rank and Name.	Result.
3	5455	Pte. J. Cryer		4	3617	Pte. H. Marsh	Eng. 6.12.99
4	5461	L.-C. J. Downings	Died 2.12.99	4	3769	Pte. A. Moody	Eng. 15.12.99
3	5476	Pte. R. Dodd		4	3728	L.-C. C. Neville	
3	6008	Pte. J. Dixon		3	3916	Pte. S. Nicholls	
2	2035	L.-S. W. Dipper		4	5851	Pte. W. Pullinger	
4	5800	Pte. A. Dawes	Del 24.11.99	4	5368	Pte. W. Partick	Eng. 15.12.99
1	5828	Pte. T. Edmonds	Eng. 17.1.00	4	5902	Pte. E. Parker	
3	5394	Pte. J. Egan	Eng. 23.12.99	2	7269	Pte. F. Page	Died 1.12.99
6	3033	Pte. T. Ells		1	5340	Pte. G. Perry	Eng. 31.1.00
5	3784	Pte. G. Fcokes		1	5549	Pte. D. Packham	Eng. 15.12.99
3	3795	Pte. F. Flowd		1	5679	Pte. E. Palmer	Eng. 23.5.00
3	7138	Pte. J. Friel	Eng. 6.12.99	1	5430	Pte. T. Reynolds	Eng. 6.12.99
3	5420	Pte. C. Fowell	Died 24.11.99	1	4409	L.-C. W. Robinson	Eng. 23.12.99
1	7439	Pte. D. Fildes	Eng. 6.12.99	1	7443	L.-C. R. Rea	
1	7374	Pte. J. Fudge		1	7640	Pte. T. Roberts	
1	5697	Pte. A. Fennell		1	5663	Pte. G. Roberts	Eng. 13.2.00
1	7553	Pte. J. Freedman		3	5923	Pte. S. Roberts	
1	7348	Pte. W. Gordge		3	7350	Pte. R. Richmond	
3	5589	Pte. H. Girt	Eng. 15.12.99	3	3102	Pte. A. Royle	Eng. 15.12.99
3	5979	Pte. G. Green		4	7385	Pte. R. Robinson	Eng. 2.5.00
8	4620	L.-S. A. Hatrick	Eng. 13.2.00	6	7295	Pte. A. Rowe	
4	3405	L.-S. E. Higgott		5	7482	Pte. W. Sage	
4	4294	Sgt. R. Hughes		4	5652	Pte. W. Smith	Eng. 23.12.99
3	3397	Pte. J. Henry	Died 10.12.99	1	5336	Pte. H. Schultze	Died 24.11.99
3	3456	Pte. C. Hewitt	Died 24.11.99	8	7066	Pte. W. Stevenson	
7	3232	Pte. H. Hubbard	Eng. 2.1.00	3	6105	L.-C. G. Skinner	Eng. 31.1.00
3	6866	Pte. A. Herbert	Eng. 15.12.99	3	3305	Pte. A. Sanderson	Eng. 15.12.99
3	5606	Pte. H. Hill		1	3389	Pte. A. Stratford	Eng. 17.1.00
3	6320	Pte. A. Higgins		1	5639	Pte. W. Smith	Eng. 23.12.99
3	3711	Pte. A. Holl	Eng. 15.12.99	1	4559	Pte. A. Tiney	
3	5976	Pte. R. Howe	Died 23.11.99	1	1200	D.-Sgt. A. Thomas	
1	4468	L.-S. R. Holmes	Eng. 17.1.00	2	5645	Pte. A. Taylor	
3	7130	Pte. W. Jones		3	5511	Pte. A. Tellick	
3	2174	C.-Sgt. C. Jones	Eng. 6.12.99	3	3578	L.-Sgt. J. Thomas	Eng. 15.12.99
2	7273	Pte. J. Kilby		3	5965	Pte. W. Thain	Eng. 13.2.00
4	3836	Pte. W. King	Died 23.11.99	3	5913	Pte. C. Turner	
7	6719	Pte. H. Kersley	Eng. 6.12.99	5	5785	Pte. M. Watkins	Died 23.11.99
6	6786	L.-C. M. Leigh		2	5529	Pte. T. Westgarth	Eng. 2.1.00
2	6948	L.-C. W. Lines	Eng. 6.12.99	4	3673	Pte. A. Wait	Eng. 6.12.99
1	3152	Pte. D. Lingard	Eng. 6.12.99	4	7522	Pte. A. Watkins	Eng. 6.12.99
1	7258	Pte. W. Murrell		8	2456	Sgt. J. Wagstaffe	Eng. 5.2.00
2	6745	Pte. C. Monday	Eng. 17.1.00	8	6649	Pte. A. White	
3	7178	Pte. G. Machin	Eng. 15.12.99	8	3415	Pte. F. Waters	Eng. 15.12.99
3	3374	Sgt. A. Mellors	Died 27.11.99				

Recapitulation of Casualties at Belmont.

CO.	KILLED						WOUNDED						TOTALS					
	O.	S. & L.S.	C. & L.C.	D.	P.	TOTAL.	O.	S. & L.S.	C. & L.C.	D.	P.	TOTAL.	O.	S. & L.S.	C. & L.C.	D.	P.	TOTAL.
1	1	—	2	—	2	5	1	2	2	—	24	29	2	2	4	—	26	34
2	—	—	2	—	1	3	—	1	2	—	5	8	—	1	4	—	6	11
3	—	—	1	—	6	7	1	3	2	—	29	35	1	3	3	—	35	42
4	—	—	2	—	3	5	2	2	2	—	13	19	2	2	4	—	16	24
5	—	—	—	—	1	1	1	—	2	—	4	7	1	—	2	—	5	8
6	—	—	—	—	1	1	1	1	1	—	1	4	1	1	1	—	2	5
7	—	-	—	—	—	—	1	—	1	—	4	6	1	—	1	—	4	6
8	—	—	—	—	—	—	1	2	—	—	4	7	1	2	—	—	4	7
Totals	1	—	7	-	14	22	8	11	12	—	84	115	9	1	19	—	98	137

Out of the 115 wounded, 2 officers and 12 men subsequently died.

Strength of Battalion present   ...   ...   29 officers, 973 men.
Percentage of Casualties   ...   .   31·03 ,,   14·18 ,,

---

Extract from 1st Divisional Orders, dated 23rd November, 1899, issued by Lieut.-Gen. Lord Methuen.

"I am directed to convey to you for communication to those under "your command, the following remarks by Lieut.-Gen. Lord Methuen, Com- "manding 1st Division, on this morning's engagement."

(Signed) H. NORTHCOTT, *Lieut.-Col.,*
D.A.A.G.

"Comrades,
"I congratulate you on the complete success achieved this morning. "The grounds over which we have to fight present exceptional "difficulties, and we had as an enemy a past-master in the tactics of "Mounted Infantry.
"With troops, such as you are, a Commander can have no fear "as to the result.
"There is the sad side, and you and I are thinking as much of "those who have died in the honour of their Country, and those who are "suffering, as we are thinking of our victory."

MODDER RIVER.

Roll of Officers, N.C. Officers and Men Killed in Action at Modder River, on 28th November, 1899.

Officers.

Nil.

N.C. Officers and Men.

Co.	Reg. No.	Rank and Name.	Co.	Reg. No.	Rank and Name.
2	6711	Pte. J. Brown.	6	3185	L.-C. J. Metcalfe.
8	7111	Pte. J. Davies.	7	6716	Pte. T. Nicholson.
1	5767	Pte. H. Ellis.	1	5155	Pte. P. O'Sullivan.
1	4106	Sgt. S. E. Eastwood.	5	2509	Pte. P. Stanley.
6	7668	Pte. J. Gee.	1	6900	L.-S. F. Watmuff.

Roll of Officers, N.C. Officers and Men Wounded in Action at Modder River, on 28th November, 1899.

Officers.

Co.	Rank and Name.	Co.	Rank and Name.
4	Major Count A. E. Gleichen	1	2nd Lieut. A. H. Travers.
1	Lt. & Adjt. Hon. E. H. Lygon.		

N.C. Officers and Men.

Co.	Reg. No.	Rank and Name.	Result.	Co.	Reg. No.	Rank and Name.	Result.
1	2723	L.-Sgt. H. Brown	Died 29.11.99	1	5421	Pte. T. Newport	Eng. 6.7.00
2	3357	Pte. W. Booth	Eng. 31.1.00	3	3729	Dr. A. Payne	Eng.
2	5689	Pte. F. Burroughs		4	6179	Pte. G. Philpott	Eng. 31.1.00
7	3595	Pte. J. Bowers	Died 29.11.99	6	3099	Pte. G. Peach	
7	5838	Pte. H. Butler	Died 7.12.99	5	3197	Pte. W. Russell	
6	5342	Pte. A. Cussell	Eng. 2.1.00	3	4837	Pte. R. Riddick	
6	6912	Pte. M. Callan	Eng. 23.12.99	6	5535	Pte. J. Sheehy	Eng. 23.12.99
4	7438	Pte. J. Doran	Eng. 20.2.00	4	3251	Pte. J. Saunders	
4	3683	Pte. E. Daughtry	Eng. 17.1.00	6	7496	Pte. J. Shaw	Eng. 15.12.99
6	3088	Pte. J. Dursley	Eng. 17.1.00	5	9417	Sgt. W. Swift	Eng. 2.1.00
1	5708	Pte. M. Evans.		1	7605	Pte. P. Shaw	Eng. 5.2.00
7	3885	Pte. F. Gregoire		1	3414	Pte. T. Smith	
4	3614	Pte. G. Griffin		1	7189	Pte. W. Shepherd	
1	7464	Pte. J. Hale	Eng. 31.1.00	1	195	Sgt. R. Trotter	Eng. 17.1.00
3	3449	Pte. E. Hawker	Eng. 10.2.00	1	3163	Pte. C. Tulett	Eng. 15.3.00
4	7472	Pte. F. Hicks		1	7413	L.-C. P. Tulett	Eng. 17.1.00
5	3438	Pte. T. Julian		2	5525	Pte. R. Trevett	Eng. 20.2.00
6	6291	Pte. C. Leefe	Eng. 13.2.00	1	3230	Sgt. P. Walsh	Eng. 10.2.00
6	5982	Pte. J. Marman	Eng. 31.1.00	2	3223	Sgt. W. White	Eng. 31.1.00
7	6687	Pte. R. Martin	Died 30.11.99	7	6781	Pte. E. Woodward	
4	3563	Pte. F. Marriott		4	3526	Sgt. T. Wyatt	
6	3903	Pte. G. Morris					

Recapitulation of Casualties at Modder River.

CO.	KILLED.						WOUNDED.						TOTALS.					
	O.	S. & L. S.	C. & L. C	D.	P.	TOTAL.	O.	S. & L. S.	C. & L. C.	D.	P.	TOTAL.	O.	S. & L. S.	C. & L. C.	D.	P.	TOTAL.
1	—	2	—	—	2	4	2	3	1	—	7	13	2	5	1	—	9	17
2	—	—	—	—	1	1	—	1	—	—	3	4	—	1	—	—	4	5
3	—	—	—	—	—	—	—	—	—	1	2	3	—	—	—	1	2	3
4	—	—	—	—	—	—	1	1	—	—	7	9	1	1	—	—	7	9
5	—	—	—	—	1	1	—	1	—	—	2	3	—	1	—	—	3	4
6	—	—	1	—	1	2	—	—	—	—	9	9	—	—	1	—	10	11
7	—	—	—	—	1	1	—	—	—	—	5	5	—	—	—	—	6	6
8	—	—	—	—	1	1	—	—	—	—	—	—	—	—	—	—	1	1
Totals	—	2	1	—	7	10	3	6	1	1	35	46	3	8	2	1	42	56

Of the 46 wounded, 4 men subsequently died.

Strength of Battalion present   ...   ...   21 officers, 836 men.
Percentage of Casualties ...   .   14·27 „   6·34 „

Extract from 1st Divisional Orders, issued by Lieut.-Gen. Lord Methuen, Commanding 1st Division, dated 29th November, 1899.

"The Lieut.-General congratulates the Division on having secured
"the Modder River after one of the hardest fights in the annals of the Army.
"It is not possible, with so mobile a foe, to get round a flank, and, therefore,
"one has to accept the inevitable and attack the position in front, trusting
"to the courage and stubbornness of our troops to gain the day. The
"casualties, though heavy, are not so great in proportion as those at
"Belmont."

MAGERSFONTEIN.

Roll of Casualties in Action at Magersfontein on 11th and 12th December, 1899.

Officers.
Nil.

N.C. Officers and Men.

Co.	Reg. No.	Rank and Name.	Casualty.		Result of wounds.
8	5926	L.-C. W. Cooksey	Killed	12.12.99	
3	6748	Pte. S. Lind	Wounded	11.12.99	
2	5598	Pte. T. Martin	,,	,,	
7	7674	Pte. R. Smith	,,	,,	

Strength of Battalion present　　...　　...　　21 officers, 857 men.
Percentage of casualties ...　　...　　...　　Nil　,,　·46　,,

MISCELLANEOUS CASUALTIES.
Miscellaneous Casualties subsequent to Magersfontein :—

Officers.

Co.	Rank and Name.	Casualty.	Date and Place.	Result of wounds.
1	Lt. Col. E. M. S. Crabbe	Wounded 23.3.00	nr. Glen.	
1	Capt. G. F. Trotter	,, ,,	,,	Eng. 25.4.00
1	Lt. & Adjt. Hon. E H. Lygon	Killed ,,	,,	
6	Lt. M. Gurdon-Rebow	,, 16.9.01	nr. Riet.	

N.C. Officers and Men.

Co.	Reg. No.	Rank and Name.	Casualty.	Date and Place.	Result of wounds.
7	5487	Pte. T. Fox	Wounded 2.1.00	In trenches, Modder River.	
1	7277	Pte. F. Jones	Deserted 3.5.00	Karee Siding.	
4	5534	Pte. A. Hazelden	Wounded 12.6.00	Diamond Hill.	Died 16.6.00
5	5637	Pte. T. Donnelly	Killed 26.8.00	Belfast.	
7	6862	L.-C. F. Gray	Wounded ,,	,,	
5	2056	Pte. F. Wardle	Killed 27.11.00	Sand Drift.	
4	6823	Pte. W. Turner	Deserted 29.8.00	Capetown.	
5	3524	L.-C. A. Clifford	Wounded 27.11.00	Sand Drift.	
5	1937	Pte. H. Knowles	Killed 15.12.00	Rolfontein Drift.	
8	2333	Pte. H. Rowe	Wounded 17.12.00	Hamelfontein.	
8	2757	Pte. G. Radford	,, ,,	,,	
4	54 2	Pte. S. Howard	,, 23.12.00	Albert Junction. (In Blockhouse.)	
5	7747	Pte. A. Gasgarth	,, 22.8.01	nr. Riet.	
5	3365	Pte. A. Fackrell	,, 16 9.01	,,	Eng.24.10.01
6	7587	Pte. W. Burge	,, ,,	,,	Died 15.10.01
6	3565	Pte. H. Ham	Killed ,,	,,	
5	7034	L.-C. J. Hopkins	Wounded 30.9.01	,,	
5	3718	Pte. J. Coleman	,, 1.10.01	,,	

Table showing number present with the Battalion in the Field on various dates.

	23rd Nov., 1899.		28th Nov., 1899.		11th Dec., 1899.		13th Mar., 1900.		29th May, 1900.		4th June, 1900.		12th June, 1900.		26th Aug., 1900.		24th Sept., 1900.	
	Officers.	Men.	Officers.	Men.	Officers.	Men.	Officers.	Men.	Officers.	Men.	Officers.	Men.	Officers.	Men.	Officers.	Men.	Officers.	Men.
Total present with Battalion fit for duty.	29	973	21	836	21	857	26	917	24	801	24	781	24	778	27	826	24	717

DEATH ROLL.

Roll of Officers, N.C. Officers and Men who died of Wounds, Disease, etc.

Co.	Rank and Name.	Date and Place of Death.		Cause.
1	Lieut. W. B. H. Blundell	23.11.99	Belmont	Wounds
3	2nd Lieut. T. B. Leslie	4.12.99	Wynberg	,,
4	Lieut. Lord T. T. O'Hagan	13.12.00	Springfontein	Enteric Fever
1	Lieut. & Qr.-Mr. J. May	4.2.01	Houtkraal	Apoplexy

Co.	Reg. No.	Rank and Name.	Date and Place of Death.		Cause.
4	7873	Pte. J. Allen	24.5.00	Deelfontein	Enteric Fever
1	4762	L.-C. W. Bennett	13.7.00	Pretoria	Dysentery
1	5472	Pte. C. Ball	6.6.00	Capetown	Enteric Fever
1	2723	L.-S. H. Brown	29.11.99	Modder River	Wounds
7	3595	Pte. J. Bowers	29.11.99	,,	,,
2	5689	,, F. Burroughs	7.7.00	Pretoria	Enteric Fever
2	7571	,, M. Barry	24.6.00	,,	,,
5	3090	,, H. Brightwell	23.3.00	Kimberley	,,
7	4273	Sgt. F. Bryant	21.6.00	Pretoria	,,
7	5804	Cpl. T. Baker	13.3.00	Modder River	,,
7	5322	Pte. C. Ball	2.7.00	Pretoria	,,
7	5838	,, H. Butler	7.12.99	Orange River	Wounds
6	4046	,, H. Brindle	27.11.00	Springfontein	Enteric Fever
8	5962	,, H. Baines	21.4.00	Bloemfontein	,,
6	7587	,, W. Burge	15.10.01	De Aar	Wounds
4	4527	,, G. Belcher	16.7.01	Hanover R'd	Heart Disease
1	7809	Pte. A. Cox	30.6.00	Johannesburg	Enteric Fever
1	5603	,, E. Cunliffe	22.12.99	Wynberg	Wounds
2	4928	L.-S. W. Cater	15.7.00	Pretoria	Enteric Fever
2	6398	Pte. W. Cook	28.9.00	,,	,,
2	7408	,, T. Callan	16.5.00	Bloemfontein	,,
4	2829	,, J. Carruthers	29.10.00	Pretoria	,,
3	7667	,, G. Corder	6.4.01	Norvals Pont	,,
2	2055	L.-S. W. Dipper	15.5.00	Bloemfontein	,,
2	7407	Pte. J. Delaney	14.7.00	Pretoria	,,
4	5461	L.-C. J. Downings	2.12.99	Wynberg	Wounds
4	5800	Pte. J. Dawes	24.11.99	Belmont	,,
4	5154	,, W. Evans	17.2.00	Modder River	Enteric Fever
6	5790	,, J. Evans	2.4.00	Bloemfontein	,,
2	6043	,, H. Fisher	22.5.00	,,	,,
3	5429	,, C. Fowell	24.11.99	Belmont	Wounds
5	2193	,, W. Foster	26.12.00	Petrusville	Alcoholic Poisoning
2	3080	,, A. Fensome	9.3.00	Rondebosch	Enteric Fever
1	5038	,, J. Garbutt	10.5.00	Deelfontein	Erysipelas
6	5755	,, B. Gibson	12.6.00	Bloemfontein	Enteric Fever
8	5513	,, T. Gosden	2.10.00	Pretoria	Pneumonia
8	3500	L.-C. W. Granville	31.3.00	Bloemfontein	Dysentery
8	7079	Pte. G. Gerrard	23.5.00	,,	Enteric Fever
8	3588	,, J. Gentle	6.6.01	Norvals Pont	,,
1	5203	,, W. Harrison	9.12.00	Pretoria	Pneumonia
1	2983	,, E. Holloway	27.5.00	Kroonstad	Enteric Fever
2	5897	,, J. Holt	5.5.00	Bloemfontein	,,
1	5059	,, A. Herrington	21.6.00	Pretoria	,,

Death Roll—*continued.*

Co.	Reg. No.	Rank and Name.	Date and Place of Death.		Cause.
3	3456	Pte. D. Hewitt	24.11.99	Belmont	Wounds
3	3397	,, J. Henry	10.12.99	Wynberg	,,
3	5976	,, R. Howe	23.11.99	Belmont	,,
4	5534	,, A. Hazelden	16.6.00	Pretoria	,,
4	5335	,, C. Holland	8.7.00	,,	Enteric Fever
5	7505	,, J. Hendon	30.6.00	,,	,,
8	2769	,, T. Hopper	16.1.01	Norvals Pont	,,
1	5317	,, J. Hesketh	15.9.02	S.S. "Lake Michigan"	Pneumonia
3	6594	,, R. Inwards	15.5.00	Bloemfontein	Enteric Fever
8	7949	L. C. H. Jessop	8.6.01	Norvals Pont	,,
1	5218	Pte. A. Jenkins	7.3.00	Wynberg	Dysentery
2	9258	C.-S. J. Jones	6.8.00	Brugspruit	Pneumonia
4	7358	Pte. T Jeffs	12.6.00	Deelfontein	Enteric Fever
6	3388	,, G. Johnson	4.6.00	Kroonstad	,,
7	5367	,, E. Jones	13.5.00	Bloemfontein	Dysentery
8	7492	,, H. Jones	11.5.00	,,	Enteric Fever
1	1828	,, E. Jones	6.5.01	Norvals Pont	,,
4	3836	,, W. King	23.11.99	Belmont	Wounds
4	7356	,, C. Lee	10.6.00	Johannesburg	Enteric Fever
6	2841	Sgt. A Linwood	10.4.00	Bloemfontein	Fractured Spine
7	4007	Pte. S. Langton	4.6.00	,,	Enteric Fever
8	3412	L.-C. A. Lake	2.7.00	Donkerhoek	,,
2	5272	Pte. W. Maude	13.2.00	Orange River	Dysentery
3	3374	Sgt. A. Mellors	27.11.99	Wynberg	Wounds
3	7537	Pte. J. McDermott	2.7.00	Pretoria	Enteric Fever
3	7609	,, E. Martin	24.4.00	Bloemfontein	Peritonitis
3	2953	,, W. Mee	29.6.00	Pretoria	Enteric Fever
5	7778	,, A. Mason	1.8.00	,,	Pneumonia
7	6687	,, R. Martin	30.11.99	Modder River	Wounds
8	6723	,, G. Moule	7.5.00	Bloemfontein	Enteric Fever
2	4032	,, S. Miles	8.6.01	De Aar	,,
1	5134	,, J. Nicholas	26.4.00	Bloemfontein	,,
4	7654	,, A. Oldershaw	25.6.00	Kroonstad	,,
8	6929	,, J. O'Malley	17.12 03	Doornhoek Drift	Drowned
2	7269	,, A. Page	1.12.99	Wynberg	Wounds
4	5016	,, W. Pearce	3.12.00	Kroonstad	Enteric Fever
4	7110	,, F. Plum	10.11.00	Wynberg	Tubercular Cystitis
6	7221	,, A. Pratt	3.5.00	Bloemfontein	Enteric Fever
7	7118	,, H Powell	30.5.00	Kroonstad	,,
3	2031	,, H. Pywell	12.8.00	At Sea	Epileptic Fit
5	3566	L.-S. F. Priest	16.9.01	Nr. Riet	Drowned
4	9102	Pte. T. Poulter	27.2.02	Nr. Dwall	Accidentally Shot
1	2850	,, G. Roberts	19.5.00	Bloemfontein	Enteric Fever
2	5991	,, W. Riley	23.5.00	,,	,,
3	2932	,, S. Robinson	13.6.00	Pretoria	Pneumonia
4	5279	,, F. Reddington	29.6.00	,,	Enteric Fever
5	7948	,, F. Rowley	21.11.00	Springfontein	,,
8	7520	,, A. Rowe	14.5.00	Bloemfontein	,,
4	7622	,, T. Rex	22.5.02	Capetown	Suicide
1	5336	,, H. Schultze	24.11.99	FrazerbergRoad	Wounds
1	7980	,, J. Stammers	5.7.00	Pretoria	Enteric Fever
2	4510	,, G. Simms	9.2.00	Modder River	,,
3	7626	,, J. Stoker	30.4.00	Bloemfontein	,,
3	3990	,, G. Stevens	17.7.00	Pretoria	,,
5	7532	,, J. Shaw	13.12.99	De Aar	,,

Death Roll—*continued.*

Co.	Reg. No.	Rank and Name.	Date and Place of Death.		Cause.
8	7192	Pte A Smith	5.5.00	Bloemfontein	Enteric Fever
2	1627	Sgt. F. Tyrrell	26.4.00	„	„
5	2610	Pte. J. Trimby	26.11.00	Norvals Pont	„
7	5642	„ E. Tasker	22.11.99	Orange River	Pneumonia
2	3542	„ A. Tyler	22.2.01	Norvals Pont	Rheumatic Fever
5	4169	Sgt. T. Tudor	15.9.01	Philipstown	Drowned
1	7860	Pte. P. Vowles	10.6.00	Johannesburg	Enteric Fever .
2	5088	„ A. Villiers	7.7.00	Pretoria	„
5	4528	L.-S. F. White	15.4.00	Bloemfontein	„
5	5785	Pte. M. Watkins	23.11.99	Belmont	Wounds
7	5762	„ E. Ware	28.6.00	Pretoria	Enteric Fever
8	7489	„ R. Woods	29.4.00	Bloemfontein	Pneumonia

TABLE "A."

Recapitulation of "Deaths caused by Disease."

Co.	Officers.	Sergts. & Lance-Sergts.	Corporals & Lance-Corporals.	Drummers.	Privates.	Totals.	Remarks.
1	1	—	1	—	13	15	
2	—	4	—	—	14	18	Not including :—
3	—	—	—	—	9	9	
4	1	—	—	—	11	12	1 suicide 1 accidentally shot by comrade
5	—	1	—	—	6	7	2 drowned
6	—	—	—	—	5	5	1 accidental
7	—	1	1	—	6	8	
8	—	—	2	—	11	13	1 drowned
Totals	2	6	4	—	75	87	6

TABLE "B."

Recapitulation of "Deaths by all Causes," including killed in Action and Deaths by Wounds.

Co.	Officers.	Sergts. & Lance-Sergts.	Corporals & Lance-Corporals.	Drummers.	Privates.	Totals.	Remarks.
1	4	3	3	—	19	29	
2	—	5	1	—	17	23	
3	1	1	1	—	19	22	
4	1	—	3	—	19	23	
5	—	3	—	—	13	16	
6	1	1	1	—	9	12	
7	—	1	1	—	10	12	
8	—	—	3	—	13	16	
Totals	7	14	13	—	119	153*	

* See the Total of Table " C."

G

TABLE "C."

Recapitulation of Deaths.

Killed in Action.	Died of Wounds.	Enteric Fever.	Pneumonia.	Dysentery.	Peritonitis.	Erysipelas.	Epileptic Fits.	Alcoholic Poisoning.	Tubercular Cystitis.	Apoplexy.	Rheumatic Fever.	Drowned.	Fractured Spine.	Suicide.	Accidentally Shot.	Heart Disease.	TOTAL.
39 *	20 *	67	8	5	1	1	1	1	1	1	1	3	1	1	1	1	153

Actions.	Killed.	Died of Wounds.
Belmont	22	14
Modder River	10	4
Magersfontein	1	—
Other Actions	6	2

*

ITINERARY OF THE BATTALION DURING THE CAMPAIGN.

Date.	From	To	No. of Miles.
1899			
Nov. 15	Battalion disembarked at Capetown from the S.S. "Goorkha," and proceeded by rail up country.		
„ 18 ⎫ „ 19 ⎬ „ 20 ⎭	Orange River		
„ 21	Orange River	Fincham's Farm	12
„ 22	Fincham's Farm	Belmont	7
„ 23	**Battle of Belmont (22 killed, 115 wounded).**		
„ 24	Belmont	S. of Enslin	⎫
„ 25	S. of Enslin	Enslin Siding	⎪
	Action at Graspan, midway.		⎬ 50
„ 26	Enslin Siding		⎪
„ 27	Enslin Siding	Witkopslaagte	⎪
„ 28	Witkopslaagte	Modder River	⎪
	Battle of Modder River (10 killed, 46 wounded).		⎭
„ 29 to Dec. 10	Modder River		
„ 11	Modder River	Magersfontein	4
	Action 11th and 12th (1 killed, 3 wounded)		
„ 12	Magersfontein	Modder River	4
„ 13 to **1900** Feb. 15	Modder River		
„ 16	Modder River	Magersfontein	6
„ 17	Magersfontein		
„ 18	Magersfontein	Modder River	6
„ 19	Modder River	Klip Drift	19
„ 20 to „ 27	Klip Drift		
„ 28	Klip Drift	Brown's Drift	8
Mar. 1	Brown's Drift	Modder River	1
	Escorting Gen. Cronje and 4,000 prisoners.		
„ 2	Modder River	Klip Drift	19
„ 3 „ 4	Klip Drift		
„ 5	Klip Drift	Brandvallei	10
„ 6	Brandvallei (scouting)		4
„ 6	Brandvallei	Osfontein	9
„ 7	Osfontein	Poplar Grove	14
	Action, midway.		

Itinerary—*continued.*

Date. 1900	From	To	No. of Miles.
Mar. 8 } 9	Poplar Grove		
„ 10	Poplar Grove	Driefontein	18

Battle of Driefontein (no casualties).

„ 11	Driefontein	Doornboom	12
„ 12	Doornboom	Venters Vallei	20
„ 13	Venters Vallei	Bloemfontein	21

Entry into Bloemfontein.

„ 14	Bloemfontein		
„ 15	Bloemfontein	Edenburg	
„ 16	Edenburg	Donkerpoort	} By rail
	Donkerpoort	Edenburg	
„ 17	Edenburg	Bloemfontein	
„ 18 to „ 21	Bloemfontein		
„ 22	Bloemfontein	Glen Bridge	By rail
„ 23 to „ 30	Glen Bridge		
„ 31	Glen Bridge	Kaals Spruit	By rail

Hd.-Qrs. and Left Half Battalion only.

April 1	Kaals Spruit		
„ 2	Kaals Spruit	Bloemfontein	16

„ 3 Hd.-Qrs. and Left Half Battalion remained at Bloemfontein. Right Half Battalion remained at Glen Bridge.

„ 4	Glen Bridge	Bloemfontein	

Right Half Battalion.

„ 5 } 6	Bloemfontein		
„ 7	Bloemfontein	Kaffir River	By rail
„ 8 to „ 19	Kaffir River		
„ 20	Kaffir River	Ferreira Siding	17½
„ 21	Ferreira Siding		
„ 22	Ferreira Siding	Wellgevonden	} 17
„ 23	Wellgevonden	Karreefontein	
„ 24	Karreefontein	Damfontein	15
„ 25	Damfontein	Vaalbank	10
„ 26	Vaalbank (scouting)		16
„ 27	Vaalbank	Paardekraal } Actions	16
„ 28	Paardekraal	Wellgevonden	15
„ 29	Wellgevonden	Bloemfontein	12
„ 30	Bloemfontein		

Itinerary—*continued.*

Date.	From	To	No. of Miles.
1900			
May 1	Bloemfontein	Karee Siding	21
,, 2	Moved camp		2
,, 3	Karee Siding	Brandfort	15
,, 4	Brandfort		
,, 5	Brandfort	Vet River	20½

Action—midway.

,, 6	Vet River	Smalldeel	7½
,, 7 ⎫	Smalldeel		
,, 8 ⎭			
,, 9	Smalldeel	Welgelegen	13½
,, 10	Welgelegen	Rietspruit	13½

Battle of Zand River.

,, 11	Rietspruit	Dispruit	19
,, 12	Dispruit	Kroonstad	22
,, 13 ⎫ to ⎬ ,, 21 ⎭	Kroonstad		
,, 22	Kroonstad	Homing Siding	15½
,, 23	Homing Siding	Roodeval	14
,, 24	Roodeval	Vredefort	16
,, 25	Vredefort	Grootvlei	11
,, 26	Grootvlei	Taaibosch Spruit	16
,, 27	Taaibosch Spruit	Vereeniging	10½

Crossed Vaal River.

,, 28	Vereeniging	Klip River Station	20

Action in Germiston—no casualties.

,, 29	Klip River Station	Germiston	23
,, 30	Germiston		
,, 31	Germiston	Johannesburg	11
June 1 ⎫ ,, 2 ⎭	Johannesburg		
,, 3	Johannesburg	Leeuwkop	13
,, 4	Leeuwkop	Pretoria	15

Action outside Pretoria—no casualties.

,, 5	**Battalion marched into Pretoria and kept ground in Market Square for Lord Roberts's ceremonial parade. (Union Jack hoisted at 2.19 p.m.).**		7

,, 6	Pretoria		
,, 7	Pretoria	Silverton	11
,, 8 ⎫ to ⎬ ,, 10 ⎭	Silverton		
,, 11	Silverton	Struven's Farm	4
,, 12	Struven's Farm	Donkerhoek	10

Battle of Diamond Hill (1 wounded).

Itinerary—*continued.*

Date. 1900	From	To	No. of Miles.
June 13 „ 14	Donkerhoek		
„ 15	Donkerhoek	Near Pretoria	19
„ 16 to „ 20	Near Pretoria		
„ 21	Near Pretoria	Mark's Drift	10
„ 22	Mark's Drift		
„ 23	Mark's Drift	Donkerhoek	6
„ 24 to July 23	Donkerhoek		
„ 24	Donkerhoek	Bronkhurst Spruit	16
„ 25	Bronkhurst Spruit	Bosseman's Kraal	13
„ 26	Bosseman's Kraal	Hartebeestefontein	5
„ 27	Hartebeestefontein	Brugspruit	12
„ 28 to Aug. 15	Brugspruit		
„ 16	Brugspruit	Olifant's River	11
„ 17	Olifant's River		
„ 18	Olifant's River	Middelburg	15½
„ 19	Middelburg		
„ 20	Middelburg	Pan	12
„ 21	Pan	Wonderfontein	14
„ 22 „ 23	Wonderfontein		
„ 24	Wonderfontein	Belfast	12½
„ 25	Belfast		
„ 26 „ 27	**Battle of Belfast (1 killed, 1 wounded).**		
„ 28	Belfast	Vlakfontein	12
„ 29	Vlakfontein	Helvetia	12
„ 30	Helvetia		
„ 31	Helvetia	Waterval Onder	8
Sept. 1 to „ 9	Waterval Onder		
„ 10	Waterval Onder	Near Nooitgedacht	4
„ 11	Near Nooitgedacht		
„ 12	Near Nooitgedacht	Nooitgedacht	4
„ 13	Nooitgedacht	Godwan River	13
„ 14	Godwan River	De Kaapsche Hoep	12
„ 15	De Kaapsche Hoep	Near N. Kaap River	9
„ 16	Near N. Kaap River	Murray's Store	10
„ 17	Murray's Store	Nord Kaap Station	12
„ 18	Nord Kaap Station	Near Avoca	9
„ 19	Near Avoca	Honey Bird Creek	8
„ 20	Honey Bird Creek	Kaapmuiden	8
„ 21	Kaapmuiden	Broken Bridge	19
„ 22	Broken Bridge	Hector Spruit	3
„ 23	Hector Spruit	Tenbosch	} 22
„ 24	Tenbosch	Komati Poort	

Itinerary—*continued.*

Date. 1900	From	To	No. of Miles.
Sept. 25 to „ 27	Komati Poort		
„ 28	Komati Poort	Kaapmuiden	
„ 29	Kaapmuiden	Waterval Onder	By rail
„ 30	Waterval Onder	Olifant's River	
Oct. 1	Olifant's River	Pretoria	
„ 2	Pretoria (E. of town)		
„ 3	Moved camp (W. of town)		4
„ 4 to „ 19	Pretoria		
„ 20	Pretoria	Uitzicht	9
„ 21 to „ 23	Uitzicht		
„ 24	Uitzicht	Pretoria	9
Oct. 25	**Lord Roberts's Review in Market Square**		4
„ 26 to „ 28	Pretoria		
„ 29	Pretoria (entrained for South)		
„ 30	Pretoria	Viljoen's Drift	By rail
„ 31	Viljoen's Drift	Zand River	
Nov. 1	Zand River	Bloemfontein	
„ 2	Bloemfontein		
„ 3	Bloemfontein	Edenburg	By rail
„ 4	Edenburg	Springfontein	
„ 5 to „ 20	Springfontein {	On 15th Nov. Nos. 2 and 4 Cos. left for Edenburg to join column.	
„ 21	Springfontein	Norvals Pont	By rail
„ 21 to Dec. 17	Here the Battalion split up and proceeded to garrison various drifts south of the Orange River. Average miles companies marched		25
„ 18	Nos. 5, 6, 7 Cos. and half Co. No. 1 were, at Petrusville, absorbed in Lt.-Col. E. M. S. Crabbe's column.		
	Average miles companies marched from their drifts to Petrusville		20
	.(For Itinerary of Col. Crabbe's Column see p. 105)		
„ 18	No. 3 and half Co. No. 1 rejoined No. 8 Co. at Norvals Pont		By rail

(After this, the Battalion being so broken up—See Diary, pp. 108—110).

Date. 1902	From	To	No. of Miles.
Sept. 4 to „ 6	Hanover Road	Stellenbosch	By rail
„ 7 to „ 10	Stellenbosch		
„ 11	Stellenbosch	Capetown	By rail
	Embarked on S.S. " Lake Michigan " for England.		
„ 12 to Oct. 6	Cape Town	Southampton	

Extract from Guards' Brigade Orders issued at Silverton, near Pretoria, on 7th June, 1900, by Maj.-Gen. R. Inigo Jones, C.B., Comdg. Brigade after the fall of Pretoria.

[No. 7.]

The following telegrams have been received and are promulgated for information :—

From Her Majesty the Queen, at Balmoral :—

"Accept my warm congratulations for yourself and all under you. I shall celebrate your entry by a bonfire and torchlight procession to-morrow. Trust wounded and sick are doing well. How are the prisoners?"

From H.R.H. the Prince of Wales, London :—

"Sincerest congratulation, successful termination."

From Lord Lansdowne, War Office, London :—

"I rejoice with you at the glorious achievement, and offer to you and your brave troops my warmest congratulations."

From Field-Marshal Viscount Wolseley, London :—

"On behalf of the Army I congratulate you and the splendid troops under your command upon the well-earned success you and they have achieved."

P.S.—The above telegrams were, of course, addressed originally to the Commander-in-Chief, S. Africa.

Address by Field-Marshal Lord Roberts, C.-in-C., to the Guards' Brigade at Bloemfontein on 14th March, 1900.

"General Pole-Carew, officers, non-commissioned officers and men of the Brigade of Guards—I have come here to-day to thank you, and to say how disappointed I was I did not know how near the Brigade of Guards were yesterday.

"The information I received misled me, I kept asking, 'When are the Guards coming? Where are the Guards?' and at last I was told that they were at Bloemfontein.

"It was my intention to come and meet you on the plain and march at your head into Bloemfontein. I heard from Maj.-Gen. Pole-Carew that you started at 3 p.m. on the 12th, and were here, 40 miles distant, at 7 p.m. on the 13th, a very good performance if you had been marching the whole time, but I hear you were 4 or 5 hours in camp, and I can only say it shows what an excellent spirit must pervade Her Majesty's Brigade of Guards.

"I was thinking of you fellows yesterday and how hot you must be. It was a very close morning, much hotter than we have had lately.

"Everyone in Great Britain will rejoice at the taking of Bloemfontein, and there are a great number of persons in those islands who will rejoice that the Brigade of Guards were present to take part in it. We have done a portion of our work, and I hope well, but more yet remains to be done, and I hope that I may be told in time, and may have the opportunity, of marching at the head of the Brigade of Guards into Pretoria."

Extract from Guards' Brigade Orders, dated 24th September, 1900, issued at Komati Poort.

No. 3.—SPECIAL ORDER.

The Major-General wishes to record his high appreciation of the excellent work performed by all ranks of the Guards' Brigade during the march from Waterval Onder to Komati Poort. For 13 consecutive days the Brigade has marched through a country almost devoid of roads, and presenting considerable natural difficulties to the movements of a force of all arms.

These conditions have involved long and dragging marches from daybreak till dusk, and sometimes later—short rest at night, heavy fatigue work by day, and often lack of water during the hottest hours of the day, and under a burning sun.

The cheerfulness, keenness and zeal evinced by all ranks throughout the march, and the sterling work performed, are worthy of the best traditions of the Brigade of Guards, and have won the admiration of all who have witnessed the march.

COLONEL CRABBE'S 1st COLUMN.

Itinerary of above Column which was formed at Petrusville, Cape Colony, on 18th December, 1900.

Date.	From	To	No. of miles.
1900			
Dec. 18 to „ 25	Petrusville.	No. 6 Co. Half Co. 5 Co. and Half Co. 1 Co. arrived on 20 Dec. Half Co. 7 Co. arrived on 21 Dec. Half Co. 7 Co. arrived on 22 Dec. Half Co. 5 Co. arrived on 24 Dec.	
		The above Companies of the 3rd Bn. Grenadier Guards joined Column at Petrusville.	
„ 26	Petrusville	Leeuwfontein	15
„ 27	Leeuwfontein	Krankuil	20
„ 28 to „ 30	Krankuil		
„ 31	Krankuil	Paauwpan	12
1901			
Jan. 1	Paauwpan	Potfontein	12
„ 2 to „ 8	Potfontein	Hd.-Qr. Staff of 3rd Bn. Grenadier Guards arrived Potfontein on 2 Jan., 1901	
„ 9	Potfontein	Houtkraal	12
„ 10 to Feb. 14	Houtkraal	3 sections 6 Co. 3rd Bn. Grenadier Guards left for Norvals Pont on 11 Jan. No. 7 Co. 3rd Bn. Grenadier Guards left for Krankuil on 11 Feb. to strengthen Garrison.	
„ 15	Houtkraal	Rhenoster Vlakte (Action)	14
		No. 5 Co. 3rd Bn. Grenadier Guards left to garrison Houtkraal.	
„ 16	Rhenoster Vlakte	Vlug Pan.	22
„ 17	Vlug Pan	Geluks Poort (Action)	23½
„ 18	Geluks Poort	Leeuwberg (Action)	13¼

Col. Crabbe's 1st Column—*continued.*

Date. 1901	From	To	No. of miles.
Feb. 19	Leeuwberg	Zoutpansfontein	12
„ 20	Zoutpansfontein	Grasvlakte	14
„ 21	Grasvlakte	Elsies Vlakte	6¾
„ 22	Elsies Vlakte	Wellgevonden	19
„ 23	Wellgevonden	Distlefontein (Action)	28¼
„ 24	Distlefontein	Hopetown (Action)	13
„ 25	Hopetown	Krankuil	21¾

Section 1, No. 6 Co. was left here.

„ 26	Krankuil	Kalkfontein	21½
„ 27	Kalkfontein	Elands Kloof (Action)	26
„ 28	Elands Kloof	Derdepoort	20½
Mar. 1	Derdepoort	Kupersfontein	12
„ 2	Kupersfontein	Colesberg	13
„ 3 to „ 5	Colesberg		
„ 6	Colesberg	Gansgat	18½
„ 7	Gansgat	Karbonaatjes Kraal	25
„ 8	Karbonaatjes Kraal	Petrusville	8¾
„ 9	Petrusville	Vluitjes Kraal	23
„ 10	Vluitjes Kraal	Orange River Station	18
„ 11 „ 12	Orange River Station		

Here Col. Crabbe's Column broke up, the greater portion joining Col. Henniker's column.

Col. Crabbe proceeded to Steynsburg to take over command of Col. Donald's column.

„ 13	Detachment 3rd Bn. Grenadier Guards proceeded by rail to De Aar.

No men of 3rd Bn. Grenadier Guards were killed or wounded in this column.

DIARY

of Battalion during the Campaign.

Date.	If Battn. or what Companies.	Move, &c.
1899		
Nov. 15	Battalion ...	... Disembarked from S.S. "Goorkha" and marched intact to Brugspruit.
1900		
Aug. 15	Nos. 6 and 7 Cos. ...	Brugspruit to Witbank.
" 16	" "	... Picked up by Battalion, *en route* to Oliphant's River from Brugspruit.
	Battalion ...	... Intact to Komati Poort and back to Pretoria.
Oct. 26	No. 1 Co. ...	... Left Battalion at Pretoria as bodyguard to the C.-in-C.
" 30	Nos. 5 & 6 Cos.	... Left by Battalion at Pretoria as escort to the body of the late Prince Christian from Pretoria to Capetown.
	Nos. 2, 3, 4, 7 & 8 Cos.	Trained S. from Pretoria.
Nov. 1	H.-Qrs. & No. 8 Co....	Arrived at Bloemfontein from Pretoria.
	No. 4 Co. ...	... Arrived at Kruger's Siding from Pretoria.
	No. 7 Co. ...	... Arrived at Edenburg from Pretoria.
	Nos. 2 & 3 Cos.	... Arrived at Springfontein from Pretoria.
" 3	H.-Qrs. & No. 8 Co....	Joined at Station by Nos. 5 & 6 Cos. from Pretoria. Entrained at Bloemfontein for Springfontein, O.R.C.
" 4	" "	Arrived at Springfontein from Bloemfontein.
" 6	½ Co. No. 8 Co.	... Proceeded from Springfontein to garrison blockhouse on Bethulie Line.
	½ Co. No. 8 Co.	... Proceeded from Springfontein to garrison Botha's Farm and Prior's, near Norvals Pont.
	Nos. 3 & 5 Cos.	... Proceeded to Norval's Pont from Springfontein.
" 7	No. 1 Co. ...	... Rejoined at Springfontein from Pretoria.
" 9	No. 7 Co. ...	... " " " Edenburg.
" 11	No. 4 Co. ...	... " " " Kruger's Siding.
" 14	No. 7 Co. ...	... Proceeded from Springfontein to Kruger's Siding.
" 15	" ...	... Rejoined at " from "
	Nos. 2 & 4 Cos.	... Proceeded from Springfontein to Edenburg to join columns.
" 20	½ Co. No. 8 Co.	... Rejoined at Springfontein from Bethulie Line.
" 21	H.-Qrs.& ½Co.No.8 Co.	Proceeded from Springfontein to Norvals Pont, picking up other ½ Co. No. 8 Co. *en route.*
	No. 1 Co. ...	... Proceeded from Springfontein to garrison Colesberg Drift, Waggon Drift, and Dalton's Pont.
	No. 3 Co. ...	... Proceeded from Norvals Pont to garrison Clement's, Alleman's, and Kransfontein Drifts.
	No. 5 Co. ...	... Proceeded from Norvals Pont to garrison Doornhoek Drift and Sand Drift.
	No. 6 Co. ...	... Proceeded from Springfontein to garrison Glad Drift and Vesser's Drift.
	No. 7 Co. ...	... Proceeded from Springfontein to garrison Zoutpan's and Bosjesman's Dritts.
" 23	H.-Qrs. ...	... Proceeded from Norvals Pont to Colesberg Bridge.
" 24	Party ...	... Corporal Mainwaring and 8 men left Norvals Pont for Hamelfontein.
" 26	"	... Corporal Mainwaring and 8 men arrived at Hamelfontein.
Dec. 9	½ Co. No. 8 Co.	... Left Norvals Pont for Dornhoek Drift.
" 11	"	Arrived at Dornhoek Drift.

Diary – *continued.*

Date.	If Battn. or what Companies.	MOVE, &c.
1900		
Dec. 12	Detmt. No. 5 Co. ..	Left Dornhoek Drift for Sand Drift.
,, 18	No. 3 Co.	Left Drifts and arrived at Norvals Pont.
,,	,, ...	Left Norvals Pont for Oorlogspruit.
,, 19	Nos. 6, 7, & ½ Co. No. 1	Left Drifts for Petrusville.
,,	½ Co. No. 8 Co. ...	Left Doornhoek Drift for Norvals Pont.
,, 20	H.-Qrs.& Rt.½ Co.No.1	Left Drifts for Norvals Pont.
,,	½ Co. No. 5 Co. ...	Left Drift for Petrusville.
,,	No.6 Co.,½ Co.1&5Cos.	Arrived at Petrusville.
,, 21	½ Co. No. 7 Co. ...	Arrived at Petrusville.
,,	H.-Qrs.,½ Co.1 & 8 Cos.	Arrived at Norvals Pont.
,,	½ Cos. No. 1 & 8 Cos.	Left Norvals Pont for Rensburg.
,, 22	Party	Corporal Mainwaring and party left Hamelfontein for Petrusville.
,,	½ Co. No. 7 Co. ...	Arrived at Petrusville.
,, 23	½ Co. No. 8 Co. ...	Left Rensburg for Pleuman's Siding.
,,	Rt. ½ Co. No. 3 Co. ...	Left Oorlogspruit for Achtertang.
,, 24	½ Co. No. 5 Co. ...	Left Drift and arrived at Petrusville.
,,	Party...	Corporal Mainwaring's party arrived at Petrusville.
,, 28	½ Co. No. 8 Co. ...	Left Pleuman's Siding for Norvals Pont.
1901		
Jan. 1	Rt. ½ Co. No. 1 Co. ...	Left Rensburg for Norvals Pont.
,,	H.-Qrs.	Left Norvals Pont for Potfontein to join Col. Crabbe's column.
,, 2	,, ...	Arrived at Potfontein.
,, 11	3 Sec. No. 6 Co. ...	Left Col. Crabbe's column at Houtkraal and proceeded to Norvals Pont.
,, 12	,,	Arrived at Norvals Pont.
Feb. 11	No. 7 Co. ...	Left Col. Crabbe's column at Houtkraal and arrived at Krankuil.
,, 15	No. 5 Co. ...	Left by Col. Crabbe's column at Houtkraal.
,, 26	1 Sec. No. 6 Co. ...	Left at Krankuil by Col. Crabbe's column.
,, 28	No. 2 Co. ...	Left at Houtkraal by Col. Pilcher's column (arrived from Orange River Station).
Mar. 13	H.-Qrs.&½Co.No.1Co.	Left Col. Crabbe's column at Orange River Station and arrived at De Aar.
	1 Sec. No. 6 Co. ..	Left Krankuil and arrived at De Aar.
	No. 2 Co. ...	Left Houtkraal and arrived at De Aar.
Apr. 9	No. 4 Co. ...	Arrived at Norvals Pont from trek.
,, 11	,, ...	Left Norvals Pont for Hanover Road.
,, 12	Sec. No. 4 Co.	Left Hanover Road for Redfold Bridge.
,,	,, ...	Left Redfold Bridge for Hanover Road, having been relieved by Sec. No. 3 Co. from Achtertang.
May 26	½ Co. No. 7 Co. ...	Proceeded from Krankuil to De Aar.
,, 28	½ Co. No. 7 Co. ...	Proceeded from Krankuil to De Aar.
,,	Sec. No. 5 Co. ...	Proceeded from Houtkraal to Krankuil and Potfontein.
June 23	No. 7 Co. ...	Left De Aar for Philipstown.
,, 25	,, ...	Arrived at Philipstown.
July 18	½ Co. No. 1 Co., 3 Sec. of Nos. 6 & 8 Cos. ...	Left Norvals Pont for Hanover Road.
,,	No. 3 Co.	Left Oorlogspruit and Colesberg Junction for Hanover Road.
,, 19	½ Co. No. 1 Co., 3 Sec. of 6 & Nos. 3 & 8 Cos.	Arrived at Hanover Road. (*See* map at end.)

Diary—*continued.*

Date.	If Battn. or what Companies.	MOVE, &c.
1901		
July 19	No. 2 Co, ...	Left De Aar and arrived at Taaibosch, to garrison blockhouses. (*See* map at end.)
,, 20	No. 3 Co.& ½ Co. No.1	Left Hanover Road and arrived at Wildfontein to garrison blockhouses. (*See* map at end.)
,,	No. 8 Co.	Left Hanover Road and arrived at Dwaal to garrison blockhouses. (*See* map at end.)
,,	No. 5 Co.	Left Houtkraal, Potfontein, and Krankuil, and arrived at Riet Siding, to garrison blockhouses. (*See* map at end.)
,, 22	H-Qrs., ½ Co. No. 1, & 1 Sec. of No. 6 Co.	Left De Aar and arrived at Hanover Road.
,,	½ Co. No, 1 Co. ...	Left Hanover Road and arrived at Colesberg Junction.
,, 23	1 Sec. No. 3 Co. ...	Left Redfold Bridge and arrived at Wildfontein.
,, 24	½ Co. No. 1 Co. ...	Left Wildfontein for Colesberg Junction.
,, 25	,,	Arrived at Colesberg Junction.
,, 30	No. 1 Co.	Left Colesberg Junction and arrived at Rensburg, to garrison blockhouses.
Dec. 28	H.-Qrs., No. 1 Co. ...	Left Rensburg and arrived at Colesberg Junction.
1902		
Jan. 13	No. 7 Co.	Left Philipstown for Hanover Road.
,, 15	,, ...	Arrived at Hanover Road.
,, 29	Det.of Nos. 3 & 8 Cos.	Left Wildfontein and Dwall for Rosmead, under Lieut. J. H. Powell.
,,	Det. from all Cos. ...	Left for Schoombie, under Major L. R. Fisher-Rowe.
Feb. 8	,, ,, ,,	Left Schoombie for Victoria Road.
,, 10	Nos. 6 & 8 Cos. ...	Left Hanover Road, Taaibosch, and Dwaal, for section Achtertang to Naauwpoort.
,,	Draft No. 7 Co. ..	Left Hanover Road, Taaibosch, and Dwaal, for section Achtertang to Naauwpoort.
,,	Draft No. 1 Co. ...	Left Hanover Road, Taaibosch, and Dwaal, for section Achtertang to Naauwpoort.
Jan. 31	No. 7 Co. (50 men)...	Left Hanover Road and arrived at Naauwpoort.
Feb. 8	,, ...	Left Naauwpoort for Victoria Road.
Mar. 18	No. 2 Co. (100 men)	Left Taaibosch for Steynsburg Line.
,,	No. 1 Co. (100 men)	Left Colesberg Junction for Steynsburg Line.
,,	Dets. from all Cos. ...	Left Victoria Road to rejoin companies.
,,	Draft No. 7 Co. ...	Left Naauwpoort section and arrived at Riet.
,,	No. 5 Co.	Left Riet and arrived at De Aar.
,,	Drafts Nos. 6 & 8 Cos.	*En route* for Colesberg Junction from Victoria Road ; turned off at Naauwpoort for Steynsburg Line.
Apr. 11	No. 1 Co. (100 men) ⎫ No. 2 Co. (100 men) ⎬ Draft Nos. 6 & 8 Cos. ⎭	Left Steynsburg Line to rejoin Company Head-quarters.
,, 20	No. 5 Co.	Left De Aar to garrison sangars at Deelfontein.
,, 26	No. 3 Co.	Left Wildfontein for Steynsburg Line.
,,	No. 8 Co.	Left Colesberg Junction for Steynsburg Line.
,,	½ Co. No. 6 Co. ...	Left Tweedale for Steynsburg Line.
May 7	No. 1 Co.	Left Colesberg Junction for Wildfontein and Head-quarters.
,,	Det. No. 6 Co. ...	Left Tweedale for Wildfontein and Head-quarters.
,, 9	No. 5 Co.	Left sangars at Deelfontein and returned to De Aar.
,, 15	Det Nos. 1, 6 & 8 Cos.	Left Colesberg section for Wildfontein, Hanover Road, and Riet.
,,	No. 3 Co.	Left Steynsburg Line for Taaibosch.

Diary—*continued.*

Date.	If Battn. or what Companies.	MOVE, &c.
1902		
May 15	No. 8 Co. ...	.. Left Steynsburg Line for Riet.
,,	½ Co. No. 6 Co.	... Left Steynsburg Line for Hanover Road.
,, 16	Det. Nos. 1, 6 & 8 Cos.	Arrived at Wildfontein, Hanover Road, and Riet.
,,	No. 3 Co. ...	... Arrived at Taaibosch.
,,	No. 8 Co. ...	... Arrived at Riet.
,,	½ Co. No. 6 Co.	... Arrived at Hanover Road.
,, 21	Battalion ...	... Left section De Aar-Carolius (leaving 1 man per B. Hse.) for section Henning to Weltevreden.
,, 22	,, ...	... Arrived section Henning to Weltevreden.
June 1	No. 5. Co. ...	... Left De Aar to escort convoy to Britstown.
,, 5	Nos. 4 & 6 Cos.	... Left Putterskraal and Sterkstroom for Hanover Road.
,, 6	Nos. 1, 2, 3, 7 & 8 Cos.	Left Stormberg Junction, Twistniet, Cyphergat, and Molteno for Hanover Road.
,,	No. 6 Company	... Arrived at Hanover Road.
,,	No. 5 Co. ...	... Returned to De Aar from Britstown.
,, 7	No. 1, 2, 3, 4, 7, & 8 Cos.	Arrived at Hanover Road.
,, 8	No. 5 Co. ...	... Left De Aar and arrived at Hanover Road.
,, 16	Blockhouse garrisons (single man in each)	Vacated blockhouses and returned to Hanover Road, except Redfold and Seacow Bridge garrisons.
,, 27	16 Officers and 654 N.C.O.'s and men (reservists and time-expired) embarked on S.S. "Vienna" for England.	
July 8	Battalion parade ...	Farewell of Lt.-Col. Crabbe to the battalion.

Roll of Officers who served with the Battalion during the Campaign.

Rank and Name.	Date joined.	How posted.	Date and cause left Battn.	
Lt.-Col. E. M. S. Crabbe, C.B.	Battn.	Comdg. Officer	9.7.02	Expir. of term of command
,, Hon. J. T. St. Aubyn	10.7.02	,,		
Major D. A. Kinloch	Battn.	2nd in Command	2.5.00	To England
,, R. J. Cooper	1st Draft	Compy. Officer	2.5.00	,,
,, Hon. G. Legh	2nd Draft	2nd in Command	27.6.02	,,
,, Count Gleichen, C.M.G.	Battn.	Compy. Officer	13.1.00	To Staff employ
,, H. R. Crompton-Roberts	,,	,,	29.7.02	Invalided Leave
,, W. A. L. Fox-Pitt	7th Draft	,,		
,, G. E. Pereira, D.S.O.	25.6.02	,,		Left in Country
Capt G. D. White	4th Draft	Compy. Officer	27.6.02	To England
,, G. P. Du Plat Taylor	Battn.	,,	27.6.02	,,
,, N. A. L. Corry, D.S.O.	,,	,,	31.7.01	,,
,, G. C. W. Heneage	,,	,,	14.3.00	Invalided
,, L. R. Fisher Rowe	,,	,,		
,, F. E. G. Ponsonby, C.V.O.	6th Draft	,,	25.4.02	To England
,, Hon. G. A. A. Hood	11.10.00	,,	23.7.02	,,
,, G. C. Tryon	Battn.	,,	25.4.00	Invalided

Roll of Officers—*continued.*

Rank and Name.	Date joined.	How posted.	Date and cause left Battn.	
Capt. A. St. Leger Glyn	8.12.99	Compy. Officer	23.7.00	To England
„ M. Earle	23.11.99	„	23.12.99	Invalided
„ Sir F. E. W. Hervey-Bathurst, Bart.	Battn.	„	16.2.00	To Staff employ
„ P. A. Clive	23.12.99	„	12.5 01	„
„ G. F. Trotter	Battn.	Compy. Offr. and Transport Offr.	25.4.00	Invalided
„ G. S. Clive	21.4.00	Compy. Officer	25.12.00	„
„ J. S. Reeve	6th Draft	„	27.6.02	To England
„ Hon. A. V. Russell	Battn.	Machine Gun and Adjutant		
„ W. R Smith	7th Draft	Compy. Officer	27.6.02	To England
„ G. F. Trotter, D.S.O.	25.6.02	„		
Lieut. J. A. Morrison	8.12.99	Compy. Officer	19.1.00	Invalided
„ F. L. Fryer	Battn.	Adjutant	23.11.99	Killed
„ W. B. H. Blundell	„	Transport Offr.	23.11.99	Died wounds
„ Hon. E. H. Lygon	„	Compy. Offr. and Adjutant	23.3.00	Killed
„ Earl of Kerry	„	Compy. Officer	8.1.00	To Staff employ
„ D. W. Cameron	„	„	6.12.99	Invalided
„ G. W. Duberly	„	Compy. Offr. and Transport Offr.	27.6.02	To England
„ M. Gurdon-Rebow	„	Compy. Officer	16.9.01	Killed
„ A. E. Maxwell	„	„	17.1.00	Invalided
„ G. B. Russell	„	„	27.6.02	To England
„ B. Gordon-Lennox	10.1.00	„	6.7.00	Invalided
„ Lord T. T. O'Hagan	1st Draft	„	13.12.00	Died Enteric
„ Sir R. Filmer, Bart.	10.1.00	„	27.6.02	To England
„ A. H. Travers	Battn.	„	7.6.02	„
„ G. C. Hamilton	„	Compy. Offr.— Machine Gun	27.6.02	„
„ E. N. Vaughan	„	Compy. Officer	17.1.00	Invalided
„ Hon. R. Lygon	„	„	11.10.00	To England
„ E. G. Spencer-Churchill	1st Draft	„	23.7.02	„
„ J. H Powell	Battn.	„	27.6.02	„
„ E. H. Weller-Poley	„	„	27.6.02	„
„ C. Le d. Leslie-Melville	4th Draft	„		
„ V. Vivian	„	„		
„ B. N. Brooke	„	„		
„ R H. Hermon-Hodge	3rd Draft	„		
„ G. D. Jeffreys	25.6.02	„		
„ J. May	Battn.	Quartermaster	4.2.01	Died Apoplexy
„ W. J. Cook	„	Sgt.-Maj. & Qr.-Mr.	30.4.01	To England*
2nd Lieut. T. B. Leslie	Battn.	Compy. Officer	4.12.99	Died wounds
„ Marquis of Douro	5th Draft	„	27.6.02	To England
„ A. W. Cecil	6th Draft	„	2.7.02	„
„ I. O. Dennistoun, M.V.O.	„	„	27.6.02	„
„ W. D. Drury-Lowe	„	„	27.6.02	„
„ Lord R. Wellesley	11.6.00	„	27.6.02	„
„ C. V. Fisher-Rowe	6th Draft	„		
„ C. L. B. H. Blundell	31.1.01	„	27.6.02	To England
„ H. C. Woods	7th Draft	„		
„ E. F. Sartorius	„	„		

*Rejoined 7th Draft,

Roll of Officers—*continued.*

Rank and Name.	Date joined.	How posted.	Date and cause left Battn.
2nd Lieut. W. E. Nicol	7th Draft	Compy. Officer	
„ Lord J. R. Mahon	„	„	
„ W. T. Payne-Gall-wey	16.2.02	„	
„ J. F. Hubbard	25.6.02	„	21.8.02 To England
„ C. T. Clayton	„	„	
„ A. L. Napier	5.5.02	„	
„ M. E. M.-C.-Maitland	25.6.02	„	

Officers of other Corps attached.

Lt.-Col. Rev. T. F. Falkner, D.S.O.	On arrival of Battn. in S.A.	Senior C. of E. Chaplain	7.7.00 Invalided
Major E. P. Lowry	„	Senior Wesleyan Chaplain	—.11.00 To A.H.Q.
Capt. C. W. Profeit, M.B.	Battn.	Medical Officer	
„ Brouche		Compy. Officer	

Roll of Officers who served with the Battalion throughout the South African Campaign.

Rank and Name.	Remarks.
Capt. G. P. Du Plat Taylor	Went home with reservists in June, 1902, after the declaration of peace.
Capt. & Bt. Major L. R. Fisher-Rowe	—
Capt. & Bt. Major Hon. A. V. Russell	—
Capt. G. Duberly	Went home with reservists in June, 1902, after the declaration of peace.
Capt. G. B. Russell ...:	Ditto ditto
Lieut. G. C. Hamilton	Ditto ditto
Lieut. J. H. Powell	Ditto ditto
Capt. C. W. Profeit	Ditto ditto. Attached from R.A.M.C.

Roll of N.C. Officers and Men who served with the Battalion throughout the South African Campaign (including N.C. Officers and Men who went home in June with Reservists).

No. 1 Company.

Reg. No.	Rank and Name.	Reg. No.	Rank and Name.
7051	Pte. J. Arrowsmith	7665	Pte. J. Budge
7182	L.-C. G. Ayres	7321	Pte. R. Clyde
5349	L.-S. J. Ball	5643	Pte. J. Cowen
5884	Pte. J. Baker	5047	Pte. H. Davis
2925	Pte. S. Bartlett	5055	L.-S. G. Day
5188	Pte. J. Barnes	5708	Pte. J. Evans
7663	L.-C. J. Beirne	6974	Pte. G. Faulkner
3859	Pte. J. Bennett	4124	Pte. J. Fitzmaurice
7298	Pte. W. Bishop	7553	Pte. J. Friedman
5954	Pte. W. Blaythwait	4322	Pte. E. Freed
5179	Pte. T. Bowers	7659	Pte. T. Friend
6886	Pte. J. Brandreth	7374	Pte. F. Fudge
5702	Pte. J. Bryan	4654	L.-S. A. Goldsmith

Roll of N.C. Officers and Men—*continued*.

Reg. No.	Rank and Name.	Reg. No.	Rank and Name.
7349	Pte. H. Gordge	7107	Pte. C. Richardson
5485	Pte. T. Harris	7640	Pte. T. Roberts
7353	Pte. F. Hassett	5020	Pte. D. Robertson
6760	Pte. P. Hourigan	3630	Pte. A. Salter
5243	Pte. J. Jones	7488	Pte. J. Sayers
5551	Cpl. J. Kelly	7433	L.-C. C. Seeley
7378	Pte. W. Lewis	3209	I.-C. G. Skelton
7748	Pte. T. Madden	2514	Dr.-S. J. Skidmore
7633	Pte. A. Mason	3414	Pte. T. Smith
5814	Pte. H. McPherson	6769	Pte. T. Stevenson
5851	Pte. G. Mouger	6952	Pte. J. Sullivan
7258	Pte. J. Morrell	7500	Pte. R. Thompson
7050	Pte. P. Navin	195	Sgt. R. Trotter
7570	Pte. D. O'Shea	3693	Pte. G. Watts
6505	Dr. A. Peake	7398	Pte. W. Whyte
4396	I.-C. T. Peet	6688	Pte. G. Wood
5784	Pte. W. Phillips	9313	C.-S. A. Yorke
7443	L.-C. R. Rea	5728	Pte. W. Gurney

No. 2 Company.

Reg. No.	Rank and Name.	Reg. No.	Rank and Name.
5777	Pte. A. Argent	5657	Pte. G. Morgan
7386	Pte. H. Barker	3139	Pte. J. Morton
5142	Pte. T. Barrett	5537	Pte. T. Nelines
5841	Pte. W. H. Bates	6966	L.-C. G. Newcombe
3467	Pte. S. Berry	5546	Pte. A. Palfrey
7545	Pte. W. Blackman	6030	Pte. G. Paragreen
5967	L.-S. J. Bradfield	5538	L.-C. H. Perkins
5373	Pte. W. Bridle	6772	Pte. F. Pitkin
4147	Pte. J. Bryant	7516	Pte. J. Pitts
7074	Pte. W. Bull	7554	L.-C. A. Plummer
6972	Pte. W. Butler	3989	L.-C. J. Pollard
5736	Pte. T. Carson	5413	Pte. J. Roberts
7354	Pte. E. Cook	5301	Pte. W. Robins
6918	Pte. C. Cosson	5366	Pte. T. Robinson
3756	Pte. A. Cottrell	5856	Pte. H. Rogers
3988	Pte. C. Curran	3508	L.-S. J. Shaw
5818	Pte. E. Day	5357	L.-C. J. Shelley
6726	L.-C. E. Dobbs	5822	Pte. H. Slater
5984	L.-S. J. Freeman	3350	Pte. F. Smith
7377	Pte E. Fricker	5945	Pte. E. Smith
5569	L.-S. C. Godson	3096	L.-C. E. Spencer
7384	Pte. F. Goodwin	6856	Pte. G. Stafford
5722	Pte. F. Granger	5645	Pte. G. Taylor
4161	Dr. G. Grav	5334	Pte. W. Tomkinson
7598	Pte. A. Guthrie	3739	Pte. P. Trow
5608	Pte. C. Harrison	5700	Pte. E. Waite
6117	Pte. J. Hipple	2705	C.-S. G. Wall
4212	Pte. E. Hodgkins	6882	Pte. G. Walton
5569	Pte. P. Humphreys	7488	Pte. W. Watts
6108	Pte. G. Husband	5101	Pte. J. Webster
5232	Pte. F. Jervis	5594	Pte. T. West
5618	Pte. J. Kent	5406	Pte. J. Whalley
6832	Pte. W. Lawson	7848	S.-M.-Cook T. Willson
7355	Pte. J. Lewenden	5885	Pte. H. Wood
3137	Pte. D. Lewis	5186	Pte. H. Woolley
5598	Pte. T. Martin		

H

Roll of N.C. Officers and Men—*continued.*

No. 3 Company.

Reg.No.	Rank and Name.	Reg.No.	Rank and Name.
836	Armr.-S. C. Warren (*attached*)	7130	Pte. W. D. Jones
5792	L.-S. E. Arthur	5166	Pte. H. G. Knight
7647	Pte. F. Baker	4911	Sgt. C. Lees
7302	Pte. B. Baron	6748	Pte. S. Lind
7566	L.-C. P. Bishop	6969	Pte. W. Mallet
6949	Pte. A. Bolton	6646	Pte. J. Marshall
5763	Pte. G. Brant	3164	Pte. G. Morgan
6682	Pte. W. Brentnall	6788	Pte. G. Newns
5369	Pte. A. Briggs	3916	Pte. S. Nicholls
3872	Pte. W. Brindley	5362	Pte. W. Nicholls
3873	Pte. W. Brown	3775	Pte. S. Payne
7593	L.-C. A. Clewes	3971	Sgt. F. Peprell
3012	L.-C. G. Courtney	1921	Pte. C. Pope
3466	Pte. F. Daniells	5775	Pte. F. Prior
6008	Pte. J. Dixon	994	Sgt. J. Radford
5476	Pte. R. Dodd	7350	Pte. R. Richmond
7486	Pte. S. Ellwood	4837	Pte. R. Riddick
6675	Pte. W. Frost	5923	Pte. S. Roberts
3796	Pte. F. Frowd	6063	Pte. K. Roberts
6541	Pte. H. Fryer	7351	Pte. J. Rowe
7120	Pte. F. Glover	6202	L. C. C. Sharpe
3443	Spt. W. Gray	5359	Pte. J. Slatter
3852	Pte. S. Groves	5752	Pte. C. Sly
3014	Pte. W. Haggar	3893	Pte. S. Soar
7364	Pte. W. Harrison	5773	Pte. F. Spackman
7635	Pte. J. Harris	3703	Dr. J. Stacey
9099	Pte. E. Harbourne	7447	Pte. C. Stephens
6001	L.-S. H. Hickenbottom	7446	Pte. W. D. Thomas
6320	Pte. H. Higgins	7586	Pte. E. Thomas
7347	Pte. F. Higham	2207	Sgt. W. Tomlinson
5606	Pte. H. Hill	5193	Pte. C. Turner
7236	Pte. H. Houslander	3637	Pte. A. Whiteham
7515	Pte. E. Hughes	6081	Pte. T. Williams
3860	L.-C. A. Jervis	7637	Pte. E. Williams
2174	C.-S. C. F. Jones	7529	L.-C. G. Wilson
2124	Pte. H. M. Jones	6422	L.-C. M. Young
4000	Sgt. S. Jones		

No. 4 Company.

Reg.No.	Rank and Name.	Reg.No.	Rank and Name.
5557	Pte. H. Abbott	7376	Pte. J. Davies
8059	Sgt. J. Aitkin	3917	L.-S. J. Dolder
3141	Pte. T. Allen	5575	Pte. J. O. Eade
7531	Pte. C. Ambridge	6656	L.-C. W. Eades
5951	Pte. A. Atkinson	3861	Pte. E. French
3238	Pte. F. Baker	5859	Pte. W. Godfrey
6520	Pte. E. Bates	3614	Pte. G. Griffin
5647	Pte. F. Biggs	6897	Pte. R. Hanna
5583	Pte. J. Bligh	7370	Pte. J. Harrison
7478	Pte. H. Brown	7494	L.-C. A. Harvey
8555	Cpl. E. Bryant	7477	Pte. F. Hicks
5457	Pte. H. Bull	7657	Pte. A. Hoskin
6787	Pte. J. Cahill	4294	Sgt. R. Hughes
7175	Cpl. J. Cassels	6507	Pte. F. Jefferies
5450	Pte. A. Charles	5725	L.-C. C. Kenward
6037	Pte. F. Chadleigh	5694	Pte. E. Kerton

Roll of N.C. Officers and Men—*continued*.

Reg. No.	Rank and Name.	Reg. No.	Rank and Name.
5709	Pte. G. Lawman	6965	Pte. R. Russell
5693	Pte. J. Lewis	3251	Pte. J. Saunders
3502	Sgt. W. Lucas	3413	Pte. P. Sharp
150	C.-S. J. McKelvey	7181	Pte. L. Short
4335	L.-C. F. Marriott	7805	Pr.-Sgt. W. Smith
7623	Pte. J. Middleditch	5640	Pte. J. Smith
3496	L.-C. J. Miles	7275	Pte. E. Smith
5386	Pte. A. Mills	5523	Pte. J. Snelling
5724	Pte. G. Mortimer	5347	L.-C. G. Spilsbury
3728	L.-C. C. Neville	3762	L.-C. W. Stephens
5862	Pte. C. Newman	6669	Pte. J. Sugrue
5902	Pte. E. Parker	7305	Dr. T. Swingler
6867	Pte. A. Pickford	5609	Pte. C. Veal
5857	Pte. W. Pullinger	836	A.-S. C. Warren
3416	Pte. T Quick	2415	Dr. M. West
3254	Pte. J. Raine	6014	Pte. J. Wheeler
2957	Pte. T. Reeks	5372	L.-C. T. Whitbread
7363	Pte. R. Rees	5312	Pte. D. Williams
3826	Pte. E. Rowbottom	5827	Pte. W. Williams
7220	Pte. A. Rosson	6132	L.-S. J. Wilson
6659	Pte. G. Rushton	6892	Pte. W. Wright

No. 5 Company.

Reg. No.	Rank and Name.	Reg. No.	Rank and Name.
3740	L.-C. E. Abbott	3344	Pte. F. Hollis
6185	Pte. W. Attwood	3755	Pte. C. Holder
3883	Pte. J. Baggaley	7034	L.-C. J. Hopkins
5464	Pte. J. Beaucall	6875	Pte. J. Houghton
7581	Pte. J. Bennett	7490	Pte C. Howarth
7632	Pte. R. Benson	7589	L.-C. W. Hutchings
6568	Pte. J. Benstead	3562	Pte. G. Johnson
5858	Pte. C. Blackford	3428	Pte. J. Julian
5499	Pte. H. Blaker	7561	Pte. W. Langley
5916	Pte. P. Bloor	6212	Pte. J. Lewis
5481	Pte. W. Brice	7421	Pte. F. Lingard
6664	Pte. G. Campbell	3356	Pte. W. Lovatt
5488	Pte. H. Charlton	5819	Pte. T. Marklew
5631	Pte. C. Chamberlain	6955	Pte. J. McLean
3918	L.-S. W. Clapp	3518	Pte. D. McCarthy
3524	L.-C. A. Clifford	4680	Pte. F. Meakin
3136	Pte. J. Cobb	5718	Pte. O. Millwater
7148	Pte. H. Colston	6058	Pte. J. Molyneux
7225	Pte. T. Coulon	3243	Pte. E. Myers
5914	Pte. W. Cordwell	6747	Pte. R. Noyes
1543	Cpl. J. Cox	5824	Pte. A. Nunn
5448	Pte. W. Curley	3395	Pte. T. Polkey
5931	Pte. F. Desmond	5277	Pte. J. Posting
5428	Pte. T. Dickens	7482	Pte. W. Sage
3838	Pte. E. Dunn	3748	Pte. H. Simpson
6106	Pte. J. Dunn	5533	L.-C. T. Skinner
3929	Pte. F. Fisher	3338	Pte. H. Smith
3784	Pte. G. Fookes	5703	Pte. W. Smith
7497	Pte. R. Greenwood	420	Q.-M.-S. F. Spearing
5431	Pte. F. Harding	3319	Pte. A. Tothill
7498	Pte. J. Harper	4004	Pte. S. Ward
5936	Pte. E. Hicklin	7559	Pte. A. Wheadon
6749	L.-S. O. V. I. Hill	7331	Pte. T. Whitlock

H 2

Roll of N.C. Officers and Men—*continued*

No. 6 Company.

Reg. No.	Rank and Name.	Reg. No.	Rank and Name.
3998	O.-R.-S. F. Acock	6786	Pte. M. Leigh
6763	Pte. W. Baker	7285	Pte. J. Loughlin
6710	Pte. G. Ball	3242	Pte. W. Lovell
6976	Pte. C. Bateman	6430	Pte. A. McDowell
6349	Pte. H. Berry	7596	Pte. C. Maguire
3798	Pte. W. Berkeley	7431	Pte. H. Mason
6044	Pte. H. Bridgeman	5626	Pte. G. Massey
6588	Pte. C. Burton	6129	Pte. A. Mellor
3480	Pte. R. Butler	3939	Pte. R. Messeter
6812	Pte. E. Butter	1064	Pte. H. Morton
3647	L.-S. C. Carter	6204	L.-C. W. O'Connell
4558	Pte. E. Chandler	3103	Pte. J. Owen
7627	Pte. J. Chapman	5103	Pte. T. Pallant
5463	Pte. J. Collins	6234	Pte. H. Palmer
8124	Sgt. A. Cumner	3099	Pte. G. Peach
5471	Pte. S. Day	7465	L.-C. C. Powell
4778	Pte. T. Dennis	5721	Pte. C. Reeves
3127	Sgt. J. Dudley	5795	Pte. W. Reader
7164	Pte. C. Dunn	6898	Pte. W. Reilly
6002	Pte. F. East	6564	Pte. J. Richards
4781	Pte. A. Elder	3352	Pte. J. Sampson
6813	Pte. G. Elliott	6708	Pte. J. Sayers
3033	Pte. T. Ellis	6015	Pte. H. Scarsbrook
3832	Pte. J. Everest	6607	Pte. A. Sherwood
7588	Pte. W. Flooks	3411	Pte. P. Shevlin
6338	L.-S. O. Francombe	3286	L.-C. J. Smith
5973	Pte. F. Gardener	7452	Pte. W. Smith
7584	Pte. G. Gardener	7435	L.-C. W. Tedder
7203	Pte. R. Gordon	6333	L.-C. J. Tighe
3268	Pte. W. Grainger	5573	L.-C. H. Tavenor
3794	L.-C. E. Haddon	777	Sgt. F. Watkinson
3321	Pte. A. Hill	4624	Pte. W. Watson
5880	Pte. A. Hollis	6227	L. S. F. Watts
3473	Pte. N. Hooton	5744	Pte. A. Welberry
7059	Pte. J. Hubbard	1237	Pte. J. Whale
5780	Pte. J. Jones	6950	Pte. E. White
7415	Pte. J. Jones	6703	Pte. J. Wicks
5028	Dr. H. Joyce	5635	Pte. H. Wilkins
3355	Pte. J. Kendall	6989	Pte. H. Wilkinson
7755	Pte. F. Ladbrook	6702	L.-C. H. Young
7573	Pte. D. Lane		

No. 7 Company.

Reg. No.	Rank and Name.	Reg. No.	Rank and Name.
7642	Pte. F. Ager	6075	Pte. C. Bruton
7666	Pte. J. Allen	3498	L.-S. H. Buswell
6810	Pte. C. Arch	5192	L.-C. F. Caunt
7547	Pte. W. Armstrong	6097	Pte. C. Chadwick
5162	L.-S. W. Atkins	6947	Pte. W. Clipson
7474	Pte. J. Atkins	6958	Pte. H. Cole
5362	L.-S. J. Ball	5638	Pte. F. Colton
5469	Pte. J. Ball	5555	L.-C. H. Crook
3210	Pte. J. Barton	5887	Pte. T. Davies
6003	Pte. T. Barker	7296	Pte. C. Dawes
3468	Pte. H. Bowler	6029	Pte. W. Dickinson
4597	Pte. R. Brown	6797	Pte. A. Dickinson

Roll of N.C. Officers and Men—*continued.*

Reg. No.	Rank and Name.	Reg. No.	Rank and Name.
7610	Pte. F. Drabbe	7672	L.-C. T. Maloney
7604	L.-C. J. Dryden	5925	Pte. B. Murray
3153	Pte. J. Dunne	5370	Pte. C. O'Connor
7563	Pte. E. Emanuel	3283	Pte. F. Page
6887	L.-C. F Enright	6876	Pte. H. Pallant
4526	Pte. E. Ford	3207	Pte. W. Poole
6086	Pte. A. Gaskell	5937	Pte. A. Preston
1124	C.-S. H. Goodman	4684	Sgt. C. Riches
6862	L.-C. F. Gray	7555	Pte. J. Rodgers
3736	Pte. J. Harrison	7295	Pte. A. Rowe
4893	Pte. J. Harrison	6859	Dr. W. Scott
3732	Pte. S. Hathaway	5109	Pte. J. Stanley
5717	Pte. T. Hickey	3699	Pte. R. Stevenson
7161	Pte. E. Hill	6095	Pte. T. Stewardson
2582	Sgt. W. Hiscocks	3257	L.-S. G. Swanwick
5306	Pte. T. Horgan	7448	Pte. D. Thomas
3656	Pte. C. Horner	5873	Pte. G. Tillier
3276	Pte. H. Hugger	6196	Pte. J. Tuck
4013	Pte. J. W. Jones	3651	Pte. G. Wakelim
7613	Pte. G. Joyce	3203	Pte. H Walkeden
7030	Pte. W. Kelly	5559	Pte. J. Walker
5637	Pte. J. Kitchen	4645	Pte. J. Watson
6899	Pte. J. McClusky	5834	Pte. G. Webb
5849	Pte. D. McGowan	3376	Pte. F. Williams
3978	Pte. J. McHugh	3393	Pte. W. Wisher
5596	Pte. J. McKenna	6781	Pte. E. Woodward
5512	Pte. J. Maguire	2465	Cpl. R. Wragg
5509	Pte. O. Mahon	7636	L.-C. E. Brown

No. 8 Company.

Reg. No.	Rank and Name.	Reg. No.	Rank and Name.
3871	L.-C. W. Aldington	5364	Pte. F. Hearne
3903	Pte. W. Bennett	3469	Pte. W. Holden
3165	L.-S. R. Best	5860	Pte. W. Hurren
6864	Pte. A. Best	5164	L.-S. G. James
7653	Pte. H. Boydon	4073	L.-S. A. E. James
7432	L.-C. H. Bradshaw	3497	L.-C. G. James
4543	Sgt. A. E. Bright	7031	Pte. A. Jefferson
5842	Pte. F. Brown.	7630	Pte. J. Kerton
3428	Pte. R. Carmichael	3765	Sgt. J. Langley
7121	Pte. J. Carnell	7064	Pte. S. McKee
6805	Pte. T. Chandler	7063	Pte. J. Mackay
6883	Pte. T. Collett	6806	Pte. J. Martin
7043	Pte. W. Cousins	5169	Pte. C. Marsh
7085	Pte. S. Cousins	4496	Dr. J. Maslin
5339	Pte. C. Damm	5478	Pte. W. Medlin
4909	L.-C. W. Delooze	7128	Pte. J. Midgeley
5508	Pte. H. Dodd	4432	Pte. H. Moore
6009	Pte. W. Fergussoe	7307	Pte. E. Morley
4374	Pte. A. Field	6973	Pte. G. Palmer
5934	Pte. J. Foster	5304	Dr. H. Parfitt
1607	C.-S. E. Garraway	7658	Pte. F. Parker
5622	Pte. J. Girling	4552	Pte. E. Payne
6072	Pte. R. Hall	7106	Pte. C. Phillips
5684	Pte. W. Hart	7504	Pte. J. Phillips
6197	Pte. F. Harding	7462	Pte. F. Pike
5843	Pte. J. Hawley	7184	Pte. A. Ray

Roll of N.C. Officers and Men—*continued*.

Reg. No.	Rank and Name.	Reg. No.	Rank and Name.
6752	Pte. F. Rees	6916	Pte. R. Smith
6165	Pte. D. Robertson	7495	L.-C. J. Templeton
3346	Sgt. T. Rogers	5940	Pte. H. Tyson
4555	Pte. C. Reyman	3210	Pte. F. Walters
4870	Pte. T. Sargent	7429	Pte. E. Ward
6650	L.-C. A. Sawyer	6997	Pte. A. Wheatland
4910	Pte. J. Sharpe	6649	Pte. A. White.
6084	Pte. J. Sheppard	5458	Pte. F. Wilson.
7341	Pte. R. Smalldridge		

Officers, N.C. Officers and Men, who returned to England from various Causes, other than as Invalids and before embarkation of Battalion.

Officers.

Co.	Rank and Name.	Date of Embark.	CAUSE.
1	Lt.-Col. E. M. S. Crabbe ...	17.7.02	Expiration of Command.
4	Major R. J. Cooper	2.5.00	Appointed to command 1st Bn. Irish Gds.
4	Lt.-Col. D. A. Kinloch ...	2.5.00	,, ,, 1st Bn. Gren. Gds.
2	Capt. A. St. L. Glyn ...	23.7.00	Appointed Adjutant 1st Bn. Gren. Gds.
3	,, N. A. L. Corry ...	31.7.01	,, ,, ,, ,,
7	Lieut. Hon. R. Lygon ...	17.10.00	Appointed A.D.C. to Governor, Madras.
1	Lt. & Qr.-Mr. W. J. Cook ...	30.4.01	Sick Leave.
1	Lieut. A. H. Travers ...	7.6.02	Coronation Representative.
2	Capt. F. E. G. Ponsonby ...	25.4.02	Sick Leave.

N.C. Officers and Men.

			Date	Cause
4	3121	Pte. H. Abbott ...	31.7.02	Time expired.
1	5345	,, H. Brannigan ...	—.6.02	,,
3	1919	,, A. Best ...	21.6.02	,,
6	1858	,, E. Bridle ...	3.5.02	,,
5	1802	,, G. Betts ...	8.3.02	,,
1	1801	,, F. Biggs ..	14.3.02	,,
7	1912	,, F. Blaxill ...	21.6.02	,,
3	7590	,, A. Batts ...	2.5.00	Servant to Capt. Trotter.
6	7113	,, W. Brown	8.2.01	
2	6180	,, J. Coady...	31.7.02	Time expired.
7	1946	,, J. Cooper	24.7.02	,,
7	6891	,, T. Clegg ...	8.7.02	,,
3	8485	,, B. Charman	2.7.02	Servant to Lieut. Cecil.
2	3074	,, W. J. Clapp ...	2.5.00	,, Lt.-Col. Kinloch.
4	3436	,, J. Chapman ...	10.12.00	
6	7614	,, B. Clarke ...	18.6.00	Servant to Capt. H. Bathurst.
8	7141	,, B. Custerson ...	19.7.00	,, Major Nugent.
1	6778	,, P. Casey...	8.2.01	
3	3908	,, W. Caunt ...	4.10.01	
2	9477	C.-Sgt. A. Copeland...	7.6.02	Coronation Representative.
5	3638	Pte. A. Curtis	7.6.02	,, ,,
5	4398	Sergt. G. Dixon ...	12.8.02	Time expired.
4	1846	Pte. J. Davies ...	21.4.02	,,
5	1854	,, H. Davis ...	21.4.02	,,
9	5739	,, M. Doyle ...	2.7.02	,,
7	3426	,, L. Davis...	23.7.02	,,

N.C. Officers and Men—*continued*.

Co.	Reg. No.	Rank and Name.	Date of Embark.	CAUSE.
7	7242	Pte. G. Davies ...	... 12.8.02	Time expired.
4	7503	„ A. Davis ...	... 11.7.01	
5	5421	„ J. Davies ...	... 11.7.01	
7	7242	„ G. Davies ...	... 24.5.01	
3	5649	„ T. Dunn ...	... 31.7.01	Servant to Capt. Corry.
1	6005	„ R. Evans ...	... 23.7.02	Time expired.
7	5045	„ E. Eeles ...	... 10.12.00	Servant to Lieut. Lord Kerry.
8	5441	„ E. Etheridge	... 10.12.00	Lord Roberts's Staff.
4	3659	„ C. Eliott ...	... 11.7.01	
3	2775	„ F. Edwards	... 7.6.02	Coronation Representative.
4	4123	„ D. Fulcher	... 26.6.02	Time expired.
1	4124	„ J. Fitzmaurice	... 27.6.02	„
1	4644	„ H. Gowing...	... 31.7.02	„
5	6793	„ W. Greenslade	... 8.3.02	„
7	1914	L.-C. J. Gibbs ...	... 29.5.02	„
8	5616	J. Grigg ...	... 7.6.02	Coronation Representative.
7	5567	Pte. C. Gardner	... 7.6.02	„ „
3	7248	„ R. Gache ...	... 6.7.00	Servant to Lt.-Gen. Lennox.
6	6000	„ T. Gray ...	... 13.2.01	
8	1913	„ H. Hayward	... 29.5.02	Time expired.
6	2253	„ W. Hewlett	... 24.7.02	„
3	1519	„ E. Hayman	... 16.8.01	„
3	1845	„ M. Hudson	... 21.4.02	„
8	1842	„ A. Hipkiss...	... 21.4.02	„
8	1934	„ A. Hyatt ...	... 21.6.02	
4	4981	„ H. Hubbard	... 7.5.01	
3	6973	„ T. Hend-rson	... 8.1.01	
1	4006	„ G. Hodgkins	... 8.2.01	
3	7387	„ J. Hughes ...	... 5.10.01	
4	7765	„ W. Herbert	... —	Servant to Major Count Gleichen.
8	5963	„ W. Hack ...	... 7.7.00	Servant to Lt.-Col. Rev. Faulkner.
2	4634	„ F. Holmes...	... — 9.00	Servant to Capt. Ruggles-Brise.
7	3815	L.-C. T. Hall ...	... 10.12.00	Lord Roberts's Staff.
2	5395	Pte. T. Hawkes ...	... 7.6.02	Coronation Representative.
2	1927	Sergt. J. Ingleden ...	... 21.6.02	Time expired.
5	1945	Pte. T. Jackson ...	... 28.6.02	„
8	3525	„ W. Jervis ...	... 16.12.00	Servant to Lieut. Cameron.
7	1855	„ C. Keech ...	... 21.4.02	Time expired.
1	2915	„ A. Kincaid...	... 14.3.00	Servant to Capt. Heneage.
4	5543	„ C. Kenway	... 2.5.00	„ Lt.-Col. Cooper.
7	5235	„ A. King ...	... 29.7.02	„ Maj. C. Roberts.
6	6925	„ W. King ...	... 14.9.00	
4	6975	„ G. Loosley ...	... 17.10.00	Servant to Lieut. Hon. R. Lygon.
2	7722	„ H. Lamb ...	... 25.4.02	„ Capt. Ponsonby.
5	4761	„ G. Mayo ...	... 2.7.02	Time expired.
7	3396	„ J. Murphy ...	... 30.6.02	„
6	3905	„ G. Morris ..	... 7.6.02	Coronation Representative.
8	7231	L.-C. J. Mainwaring ...	... 7.6.02	„ „
7	6031	Pte. T. J. McEvoy	... 7.5.01	
1	6031	„ T. McEvoy	... — 6.02	Time expired.
5	8085	„ T. Martin ...	... 12.11.01	
1	3122	„ D. McNamara	... 28.11.01	
2	5361	„ W. Matthews	... 10.12.00	Lord Roberts's Staff.
1	1784	„ J. Olley ...	... 8.3.02	Time expired.
1	1434	„ H. Peet ...	... 21.6.01	„

N.C. Officers and Men—*continued*

Co.	Reg. No.	Rank and Name.	Date of Embark.	CAUSE.
3	2105	L.-C. E. Pearson	... 28.6.02	Time expired.
7	3277	Pte. W. Parish ...	... 10.12.00	Lord Roberts's Staff.
5	3406	„ A. Rendall...	... 23.7.02	Time expired.
6	5296	„ T. Ryan ...	... 21.10.00	Groom to Capt. Ruggles-Brise.
5	7481	„ H. Rix ...	... 8.2.01	
1	1356	„ H. Richens	... 28.11.01	
5	2104	„ A. Smy ...	... 24.7.02	Time expired.
3	5104	„ H. Stock ...	... 30.6.02	„
4	1822	„ A. Shaw ...	... 14.3.02	„
8	1835	„ F. Smith ...	... 10.4.02	„
1	2514	D. Sgt. J. Skidmore	.. 21.8.00	Promoted Sgt.-Major.
2	2889	L.-C. J. Sanderson	... 10.12.00	Lord Roberts's Staff.
1	5031	Sergt. F. Stevens	... 7.6.02	Coronation Representative.
5	1815	Pte. W. Thomas	... 14.3.02	Time expired.
7	1787	„ F. Thomas...	... 13.11.01	„
2	2756	„ J. Thompson	... 23.7.02	„
1	4599	„ A. Tiney ..	... 12.8.02	„
4	3182	„ G. Thatcher	... 11.7.01	
8	6798	„ A. Tanner ...	... 22.4.01	
8	5287	„ J. Turrill ...	... 22.4.01	
6	5672	„ W. Tindall...	... 28.11.01	
8	7046	„ C. Whates ...	... 29.3.01	
8	7601	„ J. Webb ...	... 22.4.01	
1	4549	„ F. Witts ...	.. 7.6.02	Coronation Representative.
3	1789	„ A. Wynn ...	... 8.3.02	Time expired.
1	1829	„ T. Winter ...	... 10.4.02	„
6	1832	L.-C. H. Watts...	... 21.4.02	„
6	1812	Pte. A. Watts ..	... 3.5.02	„
8	1933	„ A. Webster	... 21.6.02	„
6	7471	„ E. Whyte ...	... 28.11.01	Servant to Capt. P. Clive.

The above List does not include 654 N.C.O.'s and Men (Reservists) who embarked on 27.6.02, nor does it include 16 Officers who conducted them home.

Recapitulation Table of Officers, N.C. Officers, and Men invalided to England.

Co.	Officers.	Sergts. & Lance-Sergts.	Corporals & Lance-Corporals	Drum-Majors.	Privates.	TOTALS.		REMARKS.
						Officers.	N.-Com. Officers and Men.	
1	2	7	4	—	62	2	73	
2	3	3	6	—	49	3	58	
3	1	4	4	1	63	1	72	
4	2	4	2	—	58	2	64	
5	1	3	6	1	44	1	54	
6	1	3	5	1	39	1	48	
7	2	2	1	—	41	2	44	
8	1	4	5	—	47	1	56	
Totals	13	30	33	3	403	13	469	

Recapitulation Table of Officers, N.C. Officers and Men sent to England other than as Invalids.

(Not including Reservists who embarked on 27.6.02.)

Co.	Officers.	Sergts. & Lance-Sergts.	Corporals & Lance-Corporals.	Drum-Majors.	Privates.	TOTALS.		REMARKS.
						Officers.	N.C. Officers & Men.	
1	3	1	—	—	16	3	17	
2	2	2	1	—	7	2	10	
3	1	—	1	—	13	1	14	
4	3	—	—	—	12	3	12	
5	—	1	—	—	12	—	13	
6	1	—	1	—	11	1	12	
7	1	—	2	—	14	1	16	
8	—	1	2	—	14	—	17	
Totals	11	5	7	—	99	11	111*	

Prisoners.	Servants.	Time Expired.	Coronation Representatives.	Other Causes.	Total.
24	20	51	6	10	111*

Names of Officers, N.C. Officers and Men who have been awarded Honours and Promotion for Services rendered whilst with the Battalion during the Campaign.

Co.	Reg. No.	Rank and Name.	Honour or Promotion Awarded.
1		Lt.-Col. E. M. S. Crabbe	Companion of the Bath and mentioned in Despatches.
4		,, D. A. Kinloch	Companion of the Bath.
Attd.		,, Rev. T. F. Falkner	Companion of the D.S.O.
4		Maj. Count A. Gleichen, C.M.G.	Companion of the D.S.O. and mentioned in Despatches.
.8		Capt. G. P. Du Plat-Taylor	Brevet Major.
3		,, N. A. L. Corry	Companion of the D.S.O.
2		,, M. Earle	,, ,,
1		,, G. F. Trotter	,, ,,
5		,, L. R. Fisher-Rowe	Brevet Major and mentioned in Despatches.
5		,, Hon. A. V. F. Russell	,, ,, ,,
1		Lt. & Qr.-Mr. J. May	Hon. Captain and mentioned in Despatches.
1		Sgt.-Maj. W. J. Cook	D.C. Medal.
1		,, J. Rolinson	,, ,,
1		,, A. Thomas	,, ,,

Honours and Promotion for Services—*continued.*

Co.	Reg. No.	Rank and Name.	Honour and Promotion Awarded.
8	3448	Pte. E. Mahoney	D.C. Medal.
7	5235	„ A. J. King	„ „
8	4909	„ W. Delooze	„ „
7	5370	„ C. O'Connor	„ „
3	3872	„ W. Brindley	„ „
2	5395	„ T. Hawkes	„ „
5	6793	„ W. J. Greenslade	„ „
4		Maj. Hon G. Legh	Mentioned in Despatches.
7		„ H. R. Crompton-Roberts	Companion of the D.S.O. and mentioned in Despatches.
6		Capt. Sir F. Hervey-Bathurst, Bart.	Mentioned in Despatches.
4		„ G. D. White	„ „
1		Lieut. G. Duberley	„ „
8		„ J. H. Powell	„ „
5	420	Qr.-Mr.-Sgt. F. Spearing	D. C. Medal and mentioned in Despatches.
5	3070	Col.-Sgt. W. Acraman	„ „ „
3	9477	„ A. Copeland	Mentioned in Despatches.
8	1607	„ E. Garraway	„ „
3	994	Sgt. J. Radford	„ „
5	3566	L.-Sgt. F. Priest	„ „
3	3433	Sgt. W. Gray	„ „
4	7405	P.-Sgt. W. Smith	„ „
7	7292	L.-Sgt. F. Ireson	„ „
8	7231	L.-Cpl. T. Mainwaring	„ „
7	3815	„ F. Hall	„ „

Miscellaneous Movements of Officers.

Rank and Name.	Particulars.
Lt.-Col. E. M. S. Crabbe, C.B....	H.P. 23.11.99—Rejd. 6.12.92—H.P. 23.3.00—Rejd. 29.4.00—Left Bn. (to command column) 12.3.01—Rejd. 12.3.02
„ D. A. Kinloch, M.V.O.	H.P. 12.2.00—Rejd. 16.2.00—Left Bn. 30.4.00 to take command of 1st Bn. and left on duty 16.6.02—Rejd. 22.6.02—Left Bn. 9.7.02 for Eng.
„ Hon. J. T. St. Aubyn...	Joined Bn. 10.7.02
Major R. J. Cooper	Left Bn. 30.4.00 to take command of 1st Bn. Irish Gds.
„ Hon. G. Legh	Joined Bn. 29.3.00—To Eng. 27.6.02
„ Count Gleichen, C.M.G.	H.P. 28.11.99—Rejd. 30.12.99—Left. Bn. 13.1.00
„ W. A. Fox-Pitt ...	Left Bn. 5.5.02 to join draft at Vryburg—Rejd. 28.6.02
„ H.R. Crompton-Roberts	H.P. 26.5.02—Eng. 29.7.02
„ G. E. Pereira, D.S.O....	Joined Bn. 25.6.02
Capt. G. D. White	H.P. 21.2.02—Rejd. 28.2.02 —Eng. 27.6.02
„ G. P. Du Plat Taylor...	H.P. 16.1.00—Rejd. 9.2.00—Eng. 27.6.02
„ N. A. L. Corry ...	Leave to Eng., embarked 31.7.01
„ G. C. W. Heneage ...	H.P. 11.1.00—To Eng., embarked 14.3.00
„ F. Ponsonby, C.V.O. ...	H.P. 17.2.02—To Eng., embarked 25.4.02
„ Hon. G. A. Hood ...	Joined Bn. 11.10.00—Left. Bn. 13.1.02—Leave 23.7.02 to Eng.
„ W. R. A. Smith ...	Eng. 27.6.02
„ G. C. Tryon	Left at Base—Joined Bn. 5.2.00—H.P. 21.3.00—Embarked Eng. 25.4.00

Miscellaneous Movements of Officers—*continued.*

Rank and Name.		Particulars.
Capt.	A. St. L. Glyn... ...	Joined Bn. 8.12.99—Left Bn. 7.7:00—Embarked Eng. 23.7.00
„	M. Earle	Joined Bn. 23.11.99—Left Bn. 28.11.99—Embarked Eng. 23.12.00
„	Sir F. Hervey-Bathurst, Bart.	Left Bn. 16.2.00—Eng. 18.6.00
„	P. A. Clive ... · ...	Joined Bn. 23.12.99—H.P. 4.2.00—Rejd. 9.2.00—H.P. 23.8.00 — Rejd. 9.9.00 — H.P. — Rejd. 15.11.00—Left Bn. 12.5.01
„	G. F. Trotter	H.P. 23.3.00 — To Eng.. embarked 25.4.00 — Rejd. 25.6.02
„	G. S. Clive	Joined 21.4.00—H.P. 30.10.00—To Eng., embarked 25.12.00
Capt. &Adj.}	Hon. A. V. Russell ...{	H.P. 23.11.99—Rejd. 27.11.99—H.P. 16.2.00—Rejd. 2.3.00—H.P. 23.3.00—Rejd. 31.3.00—Left Bn. 16.3.01—Rejd. 11.3.02
Capt.	J. S. Reeve ,.. ...	To Eng. 27.6.02
Capt. & Bt. Maj.}	L. R. Fisher-Rowe ...{	H.P. 16.12.92—Rejd. 8.1.00—H.P. 15.11.30—Rejd. 23.11.00
Lieut.	J. A. Morrison	Joined 8.12.99—H.P. 19.1.00
Lt. & Adj.}	F. L. Fryer	
Lieut.	W. B.-H.-Blundell ...	
Lt. & Adj.}	Hon. E. Lygon ...	H.P. 28.11.99—Rejd. 30.11.99
Lieut.	Earl of Kerry	Leave 2.1.00—A.D.C. 8.1.00
„	D. W. Cameron ...	H.P. 23.11.99—To Eng. embarked 16.12.99
„	G. W. Duberly... ...	H.P. 17.3.01—Rejd. 13.6.01—H.P. 11.1.02—Rejd. 15.1.02—H.P. 26.5.02—To Eng. 27.6.02
„	M. Gurdon-Rebow ...	H.P. 23.11.99 — Rejd. 27.11.99 — H.P. 5.11.00 — Re.d. 3.12.00
„	A. E. Maxwell... ...	H.P. 27.11.99—To Eng. embarked 17.1.00
„	G. B. Russell	Left at Base—Rejd. 30.11.99—H.P. 17.1.00—Reid. 9.2.00—To Eng. 27.6.02
„	Hon. B. Gordon-Lennox	Joined Bn. 10.1.00—H.P. 19.4.00
„	Lord T. T. O'Hagan ...	H.P. 1.12.00
„	Sir R. Filmer, Bt.	Joined Bn. 10.1.00—To Eng. 27.6.02
„	A. H. Travers	H.P. 28.11.99—Rejd. 12.12.99—To Eng. 7.6.02
„	G. C. Hamilton ...	H.P. 29.11.99—Rejd. 26.12.99—H.P. 16.2.00—Rejd. 26.3.00 — Left Bn. 28.10.00 — Rejd. 27.9.01 — Left Bn. 10.2.02 — Rejd. 24.6.02 — To Eng. 27.6.02
„	E. N. Vaughan ...	H.P. 23.11.99—To Eng., embarked 17.1.00
„	Hon. R. Lygon ...	H.P. 23.11.99—Rejd. 13.12.99—H.P. 25.1.00—Rejd. 3.3.00—Left Bn. 11.10.00—Eng. 17.10.00
„	E. G. Spencer-Churchill	Eng. 23.7.02
„	J. H. Powell	H.P. 16.12.99—Cape Town—Rejd. 16.2.00—To Eng. 27.6.02
„	E. H. Weller-Poley ...	H.P. 30.11.99—Rejd. 12.12.99—H.P. 28.1. —Rejd. 10.2—Eng. 27.6.02
„	C. Le d. Leslie-Melville	Leave 14.8.02
Lt. & Q.-M.}	J. May	H.P. 13.9.00—Rejd. 28.9.00
Lt. & Q.-M.}	W. J. Cook ... ...{	H.P. 20.11.00—To Eng., embarked 30.4.01—Rejd. 7th Draft · · H.P. 21.5.02—Rejd. 27.5.02

Miscellaneous Movements of Officers—*continued.*

Rank and Name.	Particulars,
Lieut. G. D. Jeffreys...	Joined 25.6.02
2nd Lt. V. Vivian	H.P. 25.3.01—Rejd. 6.4.01—H.P. 30.4.02—Rejd. 26.5.02
„ B. N. Brooke ...	
„ R. Hermon-Hodge	Left Bn. 12.3.01—Rejd. 13.3.02
„ T. B. Leslie ...	H.P. 23.11.99
„ Marquis of Douro	H.P. 30.5.01—Rejd. 11.6.01—To Eng. 27.6.02
„ Lord R. Wellesley	H.P. 12.11.00—Rejd. 17.12.00—Sick 23.1.01—H.P. 11.2.01—Rejd. 6.3.01—To Eng. 27.6.02
„ C. L. B.-H.-Blundell ...	Joined Bn. 31.1.01—To Eng. 27.6.02
„ A. W. J. Cecil	H.P. 13.5.02—To Eng. 2.7.03
„ I. O. Dennistoun, M.V.O.	To Eng. 27.6.02
„ W. D. Drury-Lowe ...	H.P. 11.3.02—To Eng. 27.6.02
„ C. V. Fisher-Rowe ...	H.P. —2.02—Rejd. 3.3.02—Left Bn. 5.5.02—Rejd. 25.6.02
„ H. C. Woods ...	
„ E. F. Sartorius	
„ W. E. Nicol ...	
„ Lord Mahon ...	H.P. 20.2.02—Rejd. 22.3.02
„ W. T. Payne-Gallwey...	H.P. 30.3.02 - Rejd. 4.5.02—Leave 18.8.02
„ A. L. Napier ...	Joined 5.5.02
„ J. F. Hubbard	Joined 25.6.02—Hosp. 1.7.02—Rejd. 19.7.02—Hosp. 23.7.02 - Eng. 21.8.02
„ C. T. Clayton ...	Joined 25.6.02
„ M. E. M.-C.-Maitland...	Joined 25.6.02
Capt. C. W. Profeit, M.B. ...	
Lt.-Col. Rev. Falkner, D.S.O.	H.P. 5.6.00—Embarked for Eng. 7.7.00
Capt. Brouche ...	Left Bn. 31.1.00
Rev. E. P. Lowry ...	Left Bn. —.11.00

Roll of Officers, N.C. Officers and Men who having been invalided or otherwise to England, rejoined the Battalion in S. Africa.

Present Co.	No.	Rank and Name.	Former Co.	Rejoined.	2nd Casualty.
8		Capt. G. F. Trotter, D.S.O.	1	25.6.02	
1	2514	Sgt.-Maj. J. Skidmore	1	4.4.01	
5	4981	Pte. H. Hubbard	4	29.8.01	
3	2174	Col.-Sgt. C. Jones	3	5th Draft	
1	195	Sgt. R. Trotter	1	5th Draft	
5	7592	Pte. A. E. Clarke	5	7th Draft	
1	6778	„ P. Casey	1	„	Eng., Reservists
2	5421	„ J. Davies	5	„	„
2	5649	„ J. Dunn	3	„	„
1	6031	„ J. McEvoy	7	„	Eng., Reservists
5	7481	„ H. Rix	5	„	To Eng. 27.6.02
8	6798	„ A. Tanner	8	„	
8	5287	„ J. Turrell	8	„	
8	7601	„ J. Webb	8	„	
4	5963	„ W. Hack	8	„	
1	6022	Sgt. H. Porter	1	25.6.02	
2	7793	Pte. J. Truebody	2	„	

Roll of Officers, N.C. Officers and Men, rejoined—*continued.*

Present Co.	No.	Rank and Name.	Former Co.	Rejoined.	2nd Casualty.
2	3526	Sgt. T. Wyatt	4	25.6.02	
3	5049	L.-Cpl. J. Richards	3	,,	
3	3675	Pte. T. Cridge	3	,,	
3	6963	,, T. Henderson	3	.,	
5	5017	L.-Cpl. J. King	5	.,	
5	4761	Pte. G. Mayo	3	,,	To Eng. 2.7.02
5	7954	,, J. Quirke	1	,.	
6	7113	,, W. Brown	6	,,	
6	5459	,, A. Chandler	6	,,	
6	6925	,, W. King	6	,.	
6	7776	,. D. Thomas	6	..	
6	7174	,, C. Ryde	6	,.	To Eng. 8.7.02
7	7242	,, G. Davies	7	,,	To Eng. 12.8.02
8	7590	,. A. Batts	3	,,	
8	7758	,. A. Bloomfield	8	,,	
8	7103	,, R. Courtney	1	.,	
8	6822	,, J. Duffy	8	,,	
8	7246	,, J. Gayton	7	,,	
8	7629	,. J. Peake	8	,,	
8	7881	,. G. Sweetland	1	..	
3	7294	,, J. Lingard	3	27.5.01	To Eng. 27.6.02
1	5298	,, J. Morgan	1	25.6.02	To Eng. 8.7.02
6	4286	,, M. Allen	5	6th Draft	

Itinerary of No. 2 Company, 3rd Battalion Grenadier Guards, from 15th November, 1900 (the date of leaving the Battalion at Springfontein, O.R.C.)

Date. 1900	From.	To.	No. of miles.
Nov. 15	Springfontein	Jagersfontein Road	17
,, 16	Jagersfontein Road	Kruger's Siding	9
,, 17	Kruger s Siding	Edenburg	17
,, 18 ⎱ ,, 21 ⎰	Edenburg	Joined Col. Herbert's column.	
,, 22	Edenburg	E. of Reddersburg	16
,, 23	E. of Reddersburg	Kleinfontein	21
,, 24	Kelly's Farm	Near Dewetsdorp	4
,, 25	Near Dewetsdorp		
,, 26	Near Dewetsdorp	Dewetsdorp	3
,, 27	Dewetsdorp	Helvetia	22½

No. 2 Co. now joined Col. Pilcher's column, formed its Baggage Guard, and, when possible, rode on waggons.

,, 28	Helvetia	Smithfield	26
,, 29	Smithfield	Roosinpoort	18
,, 30	Roosinpoort	Slikspruit	12
Dec. 1	Slikspruit	Bethulie	10
,, 2	Bethulie	Kirkham Halt	17
,, 3	Kirkham Halt	Klein Bloemfontein	22
,, 4	Klein Bloemfontein	Kinderfontein	8
,, 5	Kinderfontein	Grysdam	9
,, 6	Grysdam	Bethulie	19

Itinerary of No. 2 Company—*continued.*

Date. 1900	From.	To.	No. of miles.
Dec. 7 to 8	Bethulie	Hughes' Farm	40
„ 8	Hughes' Farm	Myburg Station	10
„ 9 to 10	Myburg Station	Aliwal North	18
	Aliwal North	Rooxville	22
„ 11	Rooxville	Smithfield	23
„ 12	Smithfield	Rietput	19
„ 13	Rietput	Helvetia	20
„ 14	Helvetia	Geluk	30
„ 15	Geluk	Thapatchu	28
„ 16	Thapatchu		
„ 17	Thapatchu	Brakfontein	9
„ 18 „ 19	Brakfontein		
„ 20	Brakfontein	Modderpoort	25
„ 21	Modderpoort	Clocolan	17
„ 22	Clocolan		
„ 23	Clocolan	Peru	9
„ 24	**Reconnaissance in force ; action**		10
„ 25	Peru		
„ 26	Peru	Lager's Drift	17
„ 27	Lager's Drift	Hammonia (*riâ* Ficksburg)	25
„ 28	Hammonia	Roi-krantz	14
„ 29	Roi-krantz	Rexford	16
„ 30	Rexford	Luipardsfontein	9
„ 31	Luipardsfontein	Tweepoort	10
1901 Jan. 1	Tweepoort	Lindley	18
„ 2 „ 3	Lindley		
„ 4	Lindley	Pleasier	12
„ 5	Pleasier	Nox (near Reitz)	13
„ 6	Nox	Windbult	15
„ 7	Windbult	Honing Kop	28
„ 8	Honing Kop	Zuring Krans	18
„ 9	Zuring Krans	Senekal	13
„ 10	Senekal	Rietspruit	20
„ 11	Rietspruit	Winburg	21
„ 12 to 16	Winburg		
„ 17	Winburg	Brakenfontein	10
„ 18	Brakenfontein	Allandale	7
„ 19	Allandale		
„ 20	Allandale	Eukula	13
„ 21	Eukula	Leeuwkop	6
„ 22	Leeuwkop	Kopje's Kraal	16
„ 23 „ 24	Kopje's Kraal		
„ 25	Kopje's Kraal	Wildebeestekop	9
„ 26 „ 27	Wildebeestekop		
„ 28 „ 29	Wildebeestekop	Near Welkom	28
„ 29	Near Welkom	Tabacksburg (Action)	6

Itinerary of No. 2 Company—*continued.*

Date. 1901	From	To	No. of miles.
Jan. 30	Tabacksburg	Steynrust	26
,, 31	Steynrust	Vlakkraal	19
Feb. 1	Vlakkraal	Bloemfontein (*viâ* Sanna's Post)	31
,, 2	Bloemfontein	Springfontein	} By rail
,, 3	Springfontein	Bethulie	
,, 4 to ,, 7		Bethulie	
,, 8	Bethulie	Steerfontein	16
,, 9	Steerfontein	Fisher's Farm	13
,, 10	Fisher's Farm	Zonderhout	14
,, 11	Zonderhout	Kaaliesfontein (W. of Phillipolis)	30
,, 12	Kaaliesfontein	Sand Drift	7
,, 13	Sand Drift	Kattegat	7
,, 14	Kattegat	Venterspoort	21
,, 15	Venterspoort	Strydam Farm (*viâ* Philipstown)	32
,, 16	Strydam Farm	Rhenoster Vlakte	14
,, 17	Rhenoster Vlakte	Quagga Pan	18
,, 18	Quagga Pan	Steenbok Vlakte	25
,, 19	Steenbok Vlakte	Slingers Pan	27
,, 20	Slingers Pan	Klip Drift (Brak River)	32
,, 21	Klip Drift	Kara Bee	13
,, 22	Kara Bee	Driehoeks Pan	28
,, 23	Driehoeks Pan	Slingers Pan	19
,, 24	Slingers Pan	Joostenberg	38
,, 25	Joostenberg	Hope Town	12
,, 26	Hope Town		
,, 27	Hope Town	Orange River Station	12
,, 28	Orange River Station	Houtkraal, C.C.	By rail

No. 2 Company here rejoined Head-Quarters of the Battalion.

Itinerary of No. 4 Company, 3rd Bn. Grenadier Guards, from 15th November, 1900 (the date of leaving the Battalion at Springfontein, O.R.C.).

1900			
Nov. 15	Springfontein	Jagersfontein Road	17
,, 16	Jagersfontein Road	Sapfontein	14
,, 17	Sapfontein	Edenburg	12
,, 18 to ,, 21		Edenburg	Joined Col. Herbert's Column.
,, 22	Edenburg	Boezakfontein	15
,, 23	Boezakfontein (nr. Reddersburg)	Kleinfontein	22
,, 24	Kleinfontein*	W. of Dewetsdorp	10
,, 25	W. of Dewetsdorp*		
,, 26	W. of Dewetsdorp*	Dewetsdorp	3

*Action with De Wet.

| ,, 27 | Dewetsdorp | Helvetia | 24 |

From here, when possible, the Company rode on waggons.

,, 28	Helvetia	Smithfield	29
,, 29	Smithfield	Grootvlei	18
,, 30	Grootvlei	Rosynpoort	20
Dec. 1	Rosynpoort	Slikspruit Drift	11
,, 2	Slikspruit Drift	Strydfontein	7

Action with De Wet.

Itinerary—*continued.*

Date. 1900		From	To	No. of miles.
Dec.	3	Action continued		
,,	4	Strydfontein	Pampasfontein	9
,,	5	Pampasfontein		
,,	6	Pampasfontein	Slikspruit Drift	26
,,	6	Slikspruit Drift	Bethulie	14
,,	7 8	Bethulie		
,,	9	Bethulie	—	} By rail
,,	10	—	Aliwal North	
,,	10	Aliwal North	Kruidfontein	10
,,	11	Kruidfontein	Eldorado	36
,,	12	Eldorado		
,,	13	Eldorado	Reedsdale	14
,,	14	Marched out to attack Damers Nek.		5
,,	15	Reesdale (*via* Rouxville)	Smithsdal	35
,,	16	Smithsdal	Odendal Drift	20
,,	17	Odendal Drift		
,,	18	Odendal Drift	Sjaartsfontein	17
,,	19	Sjaartsfontein	Aliwal North	12
,,	20	Aliwal North		

*Right-half Company, No. 4 Company, under command of Capt. G. D. White, remained here.

,,	21	Aliwal North	—	} By rail
,,	22	—	Steynsburg	
,,	23	Steynsburg	Roiterskraal	24
,,	24	Roiterskraal	Roodepoort	24

Convoy attacked by enemy under Kreitzinger.

,,	25	Roodepoort	Outevreden	20
,,	26	Outevreden	Ezelshoek	25
,,	27	Ezelshoek	Steynsburg	24
,,	28	Steynsburg	Tweefontein	28
,,	29	Tweefontein	Pleister Hewel	15
,,	30	Pleister Hewel	Leeuwfontein	27
,,	31	Leeuwfontein	Norvals Pont	24
1901				
Jan.	1	Norvals Pont	—	} By rail
,,	2	—	Aliwal North	
,,	3	Aliwal North (joined by Capt. White and Right-half Company)		

1900				
Dec.	22	Aliwal North	Steynsburg	} By rail
,,	23	Steynsburg	Albert Junction	

(Outposts attacked—1 wounded.)

,, to 1901 Jan.	24 2	Albert Junction		
,,	3	Albert Junction	Aliwal North	By rail

Joined Left-half Company under Lieut. E. G. Spencer-Churchill.

1901				
Jan.	4	Aliwal North		
,,	5	Aliwal North	—	} By rail
,,	6	—	Dordrecht	

Itinerary of No. 4 Company—*continued.*

Date. 1901	From.	To.	No. of miles.
	Right half Company, under command of Capt. G. D. White, continues, and Lieut. Spencer-Churchill with Left-half Company remains.		
Jan. 6	Dordrecht	Toom Nek	20
,, 7	Toom Nek	Droogefontein	18
,, 8	Droogefontein	RoodaNek(*vid*Plaatfont'n)	30
,, 9			
,, 10	Rooda Nek	Windvögel Spruit ,,	22
,, 11	Windvogel Spruit	Jamestown	18
,,	Jamestown	Oorlogspoort	19
,, 12	Oorlogspoort	Dordrecht	13
	and rejoined Lieut. Spencer-Churchill and Left-half Company.		
,, 12	Dordrecht	Oorlogspoort	13
,, 13	Oorlogspoort	Jamestown	19
,, 14	Jamestown	Botenfontein	30
,, 15	Botenfontein	Burghersdorp	21
,, 16	Burghersdorp		
,, 17	Burghersdorp	Kraaifontein	26
,, 18	Kraaifontein	Aliwal North (*vid* Sand Drift)	20
,, 19	Aliwal North	Klipfontein	18
,, 20	Klipfontein	Dronkfontein	10
,, 21 } ,, 22 }	Dronkfontein		
,, 23	Dronkfontein	Kroomdrai	7
	Capt. G. D. White, 1 Section and Convoy continues alone.		
,, 24	Kroomdrai	Aliwal North	13
,, 25	Aliwal North	Kroomdrai	13
	and rejoins Lieut. Spencer-Churchill.		
,, 26	Kroomdrai		
,, 27	Kroomdrai	Slootkraal	10
,, 28	Slootkraal	Karreepoort Drift	18
,, 29	Karreepoort Drift	Badfontein	16
,, 30	Badfontein	Bethulie	11
,, 31	Bethulie	Bethulie Bridge	25
Feb. 1	Bethulie Bridge	Rhenoster Hoek	23
,, 2 } to ,, 5 }	Rhenoster Hoek		
,, 6	Rhenoster Hoek	*vid* Knapdaar and back with convoy }	24
,, 7 } to ,, 12 }	Rhenoster Hoek		
,, 13	Rhenoster Hoek	Knapdaar	12
,, 14	Knapdaar	Burghersdorp	25
,, 15	Burghersdorp	Rosmead	By rail
,, 16 } to ,, 19 }	Rosmead		
,, 20	Rosmead	Roodehoogte	{ By
,, 21	Roodehoogte	Bethesda Road	{ rail
,, 22	40 men were here despatched by rail to Middleburg, Cape Colony.		

1

Itinerary of No. 4 Company—*continued.*

Date. 1901	From.	To.	No. of miles.
Feb. 22	Bethesda Road	N. of Compass Berg	22
		Enemy attacked latter camp.	
„ 23	N. of Compass Berg	Roodehoogte	31
„ 24 „ to Mar. 1	Roodehoogte	Movement each day to surround Kreitzinger.	
„ 2	Roodehoogte *via* Bulhoek	Rooinek	17
„ 3	Rooinek	Roodehoogte	7
„ 4 „ 5	Roodehoogte		
„ 6	Roodehoogte	—	
„ 7	—	Graff Reinett	50
„ 8 „ to „ 16	Graff Reinett		
„ 17	Graff Reinett	Rosmead	By rail
„ 18 „ to „ 20	Rosmead		
„ 21	Rosmead	Kroomhooghte	By rail
„ 22	Kroomhooghte		
„ 23	Kroomhooghte	Schilderkrans	20
„ 24	Schilderkrans	Vlakfontein	15
„ 25	Vlakfontein	Olifantsfontein	18
„ 26	Olifantsfontein	Tweefontein	37
„ 27	Tweefontein	Steynsburg	22
„ 28	Steynsburg	Elandsfontein	28
„ 29	Elandsfontein	Damfontein	15
„ 30	Damfontein	Slingersfontein	20
„ 31	Slingersfontein	Vlakfontein	17
Apr. 1	Vlakfontein	Keerom	21
„ 2	Keerom	Karreefontein	15
„ 3	Karreefontein	Langfontein	25
„ 4	Langfontein		
„ 5	Langfontein	Knapdaar	7
„ 6	Knapdaar	Constantia	27
„ 7	Constantia		
„ 8	Constantia	Springfontein	{ By
„ 9	Springfontein	Norvals Pont	{ rail

and rejoined Battalion.

Total trek	...	Lt. Spencer-Churchill's Det.	... 211
„ „	...	Capt. G. D. White's „	... 166
„ „	...	Whole Company	... 1132
		Total ...	... 1509

At Norvals Pont the Company split up and proceeded by rail to garrison Hanover Road Station and Redfold Siding.

Roll of Officers, N.C. Officers and Men left in South Africa on the embarkation of the Battalion for England.

Co.	No.	Rank and Name.		Reason left in South Africa.
6	3633	L.-Sgt. A. Hickman	...	Serving with S.A.C. (obtaining discharge).
7	7636	L.-Cpl. E. Brown ...	...	Hospital.
8	7085	„ S. Cousins ...	...	„
3	3802	„ E. Witherstone	...	On furlough till re-transfer to A.R.
8	3930	Pte. A. Koster	...	„ „ „
1	2737	„ W. Hills	...	Hospital.
2	8945	„ W. Gibbons	..	„
5	9187	„ G. Final	...	„
7	4937	„ C. Cook	...	„
8	6397	„ J. Rowledge	...	„
7	7718	„ S. Wallis	...	„
1	5728	„ W. Gurney	...	„
3	7790	„ W. Slade	...	„ (prisoner)
4	7767	„ G. Twitty	...	For embarkation with Guards' Brigade Staff.
8	6458	„ W. Lafford	...	„ „ „ „
6	8607	„ J. Butler	...	„ „ „ „
3	8743	„ G. Hibbert	...	Absent.
7	9190	„· A. Perkins	...	Servant to Major G. Pereira, D.S.O. (attached to 2nd Battalion).
3	7893	„ G. Jones	...	For transfer to A. Reserve on 30.9.02.
3	8071	„ A. Buckley	...	„ „ „ „
4	7779	„ J. Kiernan	...	„ „ „ „
5	8082	„ D. Hughes	...	„ „ „ „
5	4977	L.-Sgt. A. Childs	...	„ „ „ „
6	7759	Pte. T. Vahey	...	„ „ „ „
6	7639	„ H. Wentworth	...	„ „ „ „
6	5436	„ E. Lind	...	„ „ „ „
6	7890	„ E. Boyland	...	„ „ „ „
6	7757	„ W. Booker	...	„ „ „ „
8	7649	„ F. Roadknight	...	„ „ „ „
		Major G. Pereira, D.S.O. ...		(Attd. to 2nd Battalion).

Officers in Command of the Battalion during the Campaign.

Rank and Name.	Dates		Reason.
	From.	To.	
Lt.-Col. E. M. S. Crabbe... ...	15.11.99	23.11.99	C.O.
Major D. A. Kinloch	24.11.99	6.12.99	Col. Crabbe wounded.
Lt.-Col. E. M. S. Crabbe... ...	7.12.99	23.3.00	
Major D. A. Kinloch	24.3.00	29.4.00	Col. Crabbe wounded.
Lt.-Col. E. M. S. Crabbe... ...	30.4.00	21.12.00	
Major H. R. Crompton-Roberts..	22.12.00	19.7.01	Col. Crabbe appointed to command a column.
„ Hon. G. Legh	20.7.01	11.1.02	„ „ „
„ H. R. Crompton-Roberts ...	12.1.02	30.1.02	„ „ „
„ Hon. G. Legh	31.1.02	12.3.02	„ „ „
Lt.-Col. E. M. S. Crabbe, C.B. ...	13.3.02	9.7.02	Expiration of period of Command.
„ Hon. J. T. St. Aubyn ...	10.7.02	end	C.O.

Roll of N.C. Officers and Men transferred to Army Reserve in South Africa whilst Battalion was in that Country.

No.	Rank and Name.	Date transferred to Army Reserve.	Remarks,
3029	Sgt. E. Palmer	1.2 01	Johannesburg Police.
2981	,, W. Deeks	7.1.01	,, ,,
2410	,, R. Metcalfe	28.3.01	,, ,,
3303	,, W. Petherick ...	21.4.01	I.M.R. Police.
2531	Cpl. J. Uzzell	8.1.01	Johannesburg Police.
3605	,, R. Rawlinson ...	10.7.01	,, ,,
3222	L.-C. C. Dawson	8.1.01	,, ,,
1795	,, C. P. Jones	8.1.01	,, ,,
3895	,, W. Heritage ...	1.3.01	,, ,,
3204	,, H. Mathers	10.7.01	,, ,,
2492	,, R. Smith	20.8.01	,, ,,
4849	Pte. G. Ashby	4.4.01	,, ,,
4548	,, F. Brewis	7.1.01	,, ,,
3446	,, J. Humphries ...	17.7.02	,, ,,
2040	,, J. Turner	17.7.02	,, ,,
3577	,, B. Liddiatt	17.7.02	,, ,,
2766	,, E. Liddiatt	17.7.02	,, ,,
3949	,, R. Tucker	17.7.02	,, ,,
2323	,, F. Gunn	17.7.02	,, ,,
2107	,, H. Hodges	17.7.02	,, ,,
4912	,, W. James	17.7.02	,, ,,
4079	,, E. Gibson	17.7.02	,, ,,
3097	,, C. Seabourne ..	17.7.02	,, ,,
7546	,, W. Smith	18.7.02	,, ,,
3267	L.-C. C. Taylor	13.8.02	S. African Constabulary.

Roll of Civilians who served with the Battalion in the Campaign.

Name.	From	To	How Employed.	Remarks.
E. Melandri	15.11.99	10.1.01	Officers' Mess Waiter	Dismissed.
A. Hopkins ...	15.11.99	12.2.01	,, ,,	To Kitchener's F. Scouts.
W. Daais ...	15.11.99	2.2.00	Chef	Dismissed.
W. Tyler ...	18.11.99	12.2.00	Transport Conductor	To A. S. C.
A. Hubbard...	14.2.00	25.8.00	,, ,,	,,
W. Rand ...	8.7.00	6.11.00	Servant to Capt. White	Died, Pretoria.
S. Offord ...	26.3.00	13.2.01	Servant to Maj. Hon. G. Legh	
W. Coffey ...	20.11.00	1.9.01	Transport Conductor	To A. S. C.

Extract from Guards' Brigade Orders issued at Silverton, near Pretoria, on the 9th June, 1900.

No. 2. Field-Marshal's Order.

"*a.* In congratulating the British Army on the occupation of Johannesburg and Pretoria, the one being the principal town, and the other the capital of the Transvaal ; and also on the relief of Mafeking, after an heroic defence of over 200 days, the Field-Marshal Commanding-in-Chief desires to place on record the high appreciation of the gallantry and endurance displayed by the Troops, both those who have taken part in the advance across the Vaal River, and tho-e employed in less arduous duties in protecting the line through the Orange River Colony.

"*b.* After the Force reached Bloemfontein on the 13th March, 1900, it was necessary to halt there for a certain period—through railway communication had to be restored before supplies and necessaries of any kind could be got up from the base.

"The rapid advance from the Modder River and the want of forage *en route* had told hardly on the horses of the Artillery, Mounted Infantry, Cavalry, and the transport mules and oxen, and to replace these casualties a considerable number of animals had to be provided.

"Throughout the six weeks the Army remained halted at Bloemfontein, the enemy showed considerable activity, especially in a S.E. portion of the Orange River Colony ; but by the beginning of May everything was ready for an advance into the enemy's country, and on the 2nd of May active operations were again commenced.

"*c.* On 12th May, Kroonstad, where Mr. Steyn had established the so-called Government of the Orange Free State, was entered.

"On 17th May, Mafeking was relieved.

"On 31st May, Johannesburg was occupied ; and on 5th June the British Flag waved over Pretoria.

"During these 35 days the main body marched a distance of 300 miles, including 15 days' halt, and engaged the enemy on six different occasions.

"*d.* During the recent operations the sudden variations in temperature between warm sun in the daytime and cold at night, have been particularly trying to the Troops, and owing to the necessity for rapid movements, the soldiers have had frequently to bivouac after hard and trying marches without firewood and with scanty rations.

"*e.* The cheerful spirit with which difficulties have been overcome and hardships disregarded is deserving of the highest praise, and in thanking all ranks for their successful efforts to attain the objects in view, Lord Roberts is proud to think that the soldiers under his command have worthily upheld the traditions of Her Majesty's Army in fighting and marching, and the admirable discipline which has been maintained throughout a period of no ordinary trial and difficulty."

Copy of Telegram received by the G.O.C. Guard's Brigade from the General Commanding-in-Chief, South Africa, and transmitted to O.C. 3rd Bn. Grenadier Guards.

"Belfast, 17th December, 1901.

"Please congratulate Guards' Blockhouse Line at Hanover Road on the efficiency of their work. 1 am very pleased at the way the line is held and results obtained.

"The General Officer Commanding is specially pleased at the rapidity in which No. 6430, Private McDowell and No. 7627, Private Chapman, 3rd Bn. Grenadier Guards, who were sentries on Nos. 40 and 41 Blockhouses, grasped the situation on the occasion of Kreitzinger's Commando crossing the line on the 16th inst."

LAST DRAFT.

APPENDIX.

OFFICERS.

Maj. G. Pereira
Capt. G. Trotter, D.S.O.
Lt. G. Jeffreys
2nd Lt. J. Hubbard
2nd Lt. Clayton
2nd Lt. Napier
2nd Lt. Maitland
Act. Sgt. Maj.—Sgt. Myles

O.C.—Maj. Fox-Pitt
2nd Maj. Pereira
Adjt.—2nd Lt. C. V. Rowe
Qr.-Mr.—2nd Lt. Clayton

No. 1 Company.

Lt. Jeffreys
2nd Lt. Maitland
P. Sgt.—Sgt. Wyatt

No. 2 Company.

Capt. G. Trotter, D.S.O.
2nd Lt. J. Hubbard
P. Sgt.—Sgt. Cooke

Act.-Sgt.-Maj.—Sgt. Myles
Act.-Pay. & Qr.-Mr.-Sgt.—Sgt. Rolfe

1902.

12th April The draft of 500 men left Southampton the afternoon of 12th April on the S.S. "Canada." Called at Queenstown and Las Palmas, and arrived at Cape Town **4th May** at 8 a.m. on Saturday, 4th May. We left Cape Town by train at 8 p.m., and journeyed straight up to Vryburg, **7th May** which we reached on the 7th May.

At De Aar, on the 6th, Gen. I. Jones and Col. E. Crabbe, O.C. 3rd Battalion, had met us; and here Fox-Pitt and Rowe joined us, and Napier went off to the 3rd Battalion.

At Vryburg the organization of the draft was as per margin. We detrained at Vryburg on the morning **8th May** of 8th May, and camped there for 24 hours. We then got an urgent Order from G.O.C. District to reinforce at once the blockhouse line from 2 miles north of Vryburg to a place 5 blockhouses north of Dornbult, which was then occupied by a Militia battalion of Green Howards and a few Colonials. In all, we were to take over about 40 blockhouses along the railway, as a big drive was coming in within a week.

We moved off, shortly after our arrival, and dropped the whole of No. 2 Company between Vryburg and Devondale, in about 20 blockhouses; Trotter taking up his quarters at Devondale, where also the Green Howards' **9th May** headquarters were. No. 1 Company stayed the night at Devondale, and next morning we went off by train, leaving the blockhouses from Devondale to Salt Pan (about 10) to the Green Howards, and took over the 20 blockhouses north of Salt Pan, which took us to 5 blockhouses past Dornbult, at which place Jeffreys took up his quarters.

The blockhouse line was in a very poor condition; very little wire and small trenches; the blockhouses were the only things that were complete. About 10 men in each blockhouse, and about half a mile apart. **10th May** Worked hard on the line the next day. The drive came in, and Von Donop's Column came in opposite us. **11th May** Had only caught 2 Boers, nearly all had escaped round the right flank. (Von Dunop's was the right hand column of all.) The drive extended as far south as Kimberley, and 450 Boers were taken by the columns south of Vryburg.

18th May We remained on the line till the 18th May, then we collected and went to Devondale, where we stayed one **19th May** night, then entrained for Maritzani and got there about **20th May** mid-day and took up a blockhouse line across country nearly as far as Polfontein. There was a message that **27th May** there were a party of Boers trying to cross the line 4 miles east of Rooidam, but nothing came of it. On the **28th May** 28th May we began to move eastwards again, and during the next three days were occupied in taking over the

31st May
1st June
blockhouse line across country up to Lichtenburg. On the night of the 31st May and 1st June about 100 Boers tried to break the line 5 miles out of Lichtenburg. They cut one strand, but retired leaving nothing behind them. One of our men was hit in the ear (very slight).

2nd June
News of Peace was brought us on 2nd June.

20th June
21st June
We remained on this line till the 20th June, when we collected at Polfontein, and on the 21st marched on Mafeking. Starting at 7 a.m. we got in at 7 p.m. with a two hours' halt at mid-day. We slept the night in

22nd June
the train, and also on the 22nd. About 350 reservists went off to Cape Town and the remaining 150 went to Hanover Road to join the 3rd Battalion. All the officers went to Hanover Road, the reservists joining the reservists of the 3rd Battalion at Cape Town.

Particulars of the Drafts sent from Englan

Particulars.	1st Draft.	2nd Draft.	3rd Draft.	4th Draft.	5th Draft.
Embarked at Date ... ... Name of Ship Dis. Capetown Joined Battn. Date	Southampton 3.1.00 "Kildonan Castle" .1.00 Modder River 25.1.00	Southampton 12.2.00 "Majestic" 3.3.00 Glen Bridge 26, 27 & 29.3.00	Tilbury Docks 17.3.00 "Braemar Castle " 8.4.00 Bloemfontein 30.4.00	Southampton 23.5.00 "Britannic" 11.6.00 Donkerhoek ...	Southampton 9.8.00 "Britannic" 28.8.00 Pretoria 7.10.00

No. of Sergts.
  ,, Corpls.
  ,, Ptes.
	1
	1
	98
		1
		2
		97
			1
			2
			97
				1
				2
				97
					3
					4
					193

Names of Offi- cers	Maj.R.Cooper Lt. Lord T. O'Hagan Lt. E. G. Spencer- Churchill	Maj. Hon. G. Legh	2nd Lt. R. H. Hermon- Hodge	Capt. G. D. White Lt. C. Le d. Leslie-Mel- ville 2nd Lt. N. Vivian 2nd Lt. B. N. Brooke	2nd Lt. Max quis o Douro
Casualties during voy- age	Nil	Nil	Nil	Nil	No. 2034 Pte H. Pywel died at se on 12.8.0 (epilepti fit)

to join the Battalion in South Africa.

—	—	6th Draft.	7th Draft.	—	Special Draft ; and for a time separate det'm't.
Southampton 12.3.01 "Canada"	— 1.8.01 "Auranic"	Southampton 7.11.01 "Bavarian"	Southampton 16.1.02 "Bavarian"	Southampton 17.6.02 "Staffordshire"	Southampton 12.4.02 "Canada"
30.3.01 De Aar 4.4.01;	23.8.01 Hanover Road 29.8.01	28.11.01 Hanover Road 30.11.01	5.2.02 Hanover Road 8.2.02	7.7.02 Hanover.Road 10.7.02	3.5.02 Hanover Road 25.6.02
Sgt.-Major	... ... Pte. Hubbard	 6	10 10 580	... ... Pte. J. Harrison	4 6 107
Nil	Nil	Capt. F. Ponsonby, C.V.O. Capt. J. S. Reeve 2nd Lt. A. W. Cecil 2nd Lt. J. Dennistoun 2nd Lt. W. D. Drury-Lowe 2nd Lt. C. V. Fisher-Rowe	Maj. W. A. L. Fox-Pitt Capt. W. R. Smith 2nd Lt. H. C. Woods 2nd Lt. E. F. Sartorius 2nd Lt. W. E. Nicol 2nd Lt. J. R. Mahon, Vct. Lt. & Qr.-Mr. W. J. Cook	Lt.-Col. Hon. J. T. St. Aubyn	Maj. G. Pereira, D.S.O. Capt. G. F. Trotter, D.S.O. Lt. G. D. Jeffreys 2nd Lt. J. F. Hubbard 2nd Lt. C. T. Clayton 2nd Lt. M. E. M.-C.-Maitland 2nd Lt. L. Napier
Nil	Nil	Nil	Nil	Nil	Nil

Table showing Increase and Decrease in Strength of the Battalion during the South African Campaign.

	Numbers		Killed in Action		Died of Wounds		Died of Disease		Died Accidental Causes	To England as Invalids		To England as Prisoners	To Staff Employ, to England, Other Causes	To Army Reserve in S.A.	Transferred to other Battalions	Deserted	To Staff Employ and left in Country		Total Casualties		Total who Returned to England with Reservists and Battalion	
	Officers	Men	Officers	Men	Officers	Men	Officers	Men		Officers	Men						Officers	Men	Officers	Men	Officers	Men
Original Battalion	30	1085	3	34	2	18	1	53	4	7	316	18	43	11	6	2	3	6	21	511	9	574
1st Draft	3	100	—	—	—	—	1	10	—	—	28	1	4	2	—	—	—	—	3	45	—	55
2nd „	1	100	—	—	—	—	—	5	—	—	24	2	1	1	—	—	—	6	—	39	1	61
3rd „	1	100	—	—	—	—	—	7	—	—	19	1	—	—	—	—	—	2	—	29	1	71
4th „	4	100	—	2	—	—	—	3	—	—	22	1	1	3	1	—	—	1	—	32	4	68
5th „	1	200	—	—	—	—	—	8	—	—	41	1	27	8	—	—	—	—	—	87	1	113
6th „	6	6	—	—	—	—	—	—	—	1	—	—	2	—	—	—	—	—	2	2	4	4
7th „	7	600	—	—	—	—	—	2	—	—	13	—	1	—	3	—	—	9	—	25	7	575
Major Pereira's Draft	7	117	—	—	—	—	—	—	—	1	5	—	7	—	1	—	1	5	2	20	5	97
Miscellaneous Increases	14	30	—	—	—	—	—	—	—	4	1	—	1	—	1	—	2	—	9	3	5	27
TOTALS	74	2438	3	36	2	18	2	88	4	13	469	24	87	25	11	2	6	29	37	793	37	1645

www.ingramcontent.com/pod-product-compliance
Lightning Source LLC
Chambersburg PA
CBHW030407100426
42812CB00028B/2865/J